Strictly Academic

Strictly Academic
A READING AND WRITING TEXT

Pat Currie / Ellen Cray
Carleton University

NEWBURY HOUSE PUBLISHERS
A division of Harper & Row, Publishers, Inc.
New York, Philadelphia, San Francisco, Washington,
London, Mexico City, São Paulo, Singapore, Sydney

Sponsoring Editor: Robert Miller
Project Editor: Donna DeBenedictis
Text Design: York Production Services
Cover Design: Nadja Furlan-Lorber
Text Art: York Production Services
Production Manager: Jeanie Berke
Production Assistant: Brenda DeMartini
Compositor: York Graphic Services, Inc.
Printer and Binder: R. R. Donnelley & Sons Company
Cover Printer: New England Book Components

STRICTLY ACADEMIC: A Reading and Writing Text

NEWBURY HOUSE PUBLISHERS
A division of Harper & Row, Publishers, Inc.

 Language Science
Language Teaching
Language Learning

Library of Congress Cataloging-in-Publication Data
Currie, Pat.
  Strictly academic.

  1. English language—Text-books for foreign
speakers.   2. English language—Rhetoric.   3. College
readers.   I. Cray, Ellen.   II. Title.
PE1128.C87   1987   808'.042   87-1621
ISBN 0-06-041411-1

87 88 89 90 9 8 7 6 5 4 3 2 1

ACKNOWLEDGMENTS

We gratefully acknowledge the following authors and publishers for allowing us to reprint their materials.

pp. 5–6: "Preparation Overcomes Fear of Conversation," by Peter Griffiths, the *Citizen,* Ottawa, August 22, 1983. Reprinted by permission.

pp. 8–11: "Case Study," from *The Good Language Learner* by N. Naiman, M. Frohlich, H. H. Stern, and A. Todesco (1978). Research in Education Series no. 7, Toronto, Ontario. Reprinted by permission of the publisher OISE Press.

pp. 18–19: "Migraine: The King of Pain," by Elaine Flaherty, the *Citizen,* Ottawa, December 7, 1984. Reprinted by permission.

p. 21: "Headaches May Be Triggered by the Food You Crave Most," in the *Citizen,* Ottawa, December 7, 1984. Reprinted by permission.

pp. 25–26: "The Skin Senses." Spec. material from p. 80 in *The Psychology of Being Human,* 3rd edition by Zick Rubin and Elton B. McNeil. Copyright © 1981 by Zick Rubin. Reprinted by permission of Harper & Row, Publishers, Inc.

pp. 29–30: "Frontiers of Pain Control." Spec. material from p. 82 in *The Psychology of Being Human,* 3rd edition by Zick Rubin and Elton B. McNeil. Copyright © 1981 by Zick Rubin. Reprinted by permission of Harper & Row, Publishers, Inc.

pp. 30–31: "Can Hypnosis Reduce Pain?" Spec. material from p. 126 in *The Psychology of Being Human,* 3rd edition by Zick Rubin and Elton B. McNeil. Copyright © 1981 by Zick Rubin. Reprinted by permission of Harper & Row, Publishers, Inc.

p. 34: "Biofeedback: The Mind Can Be Trained to Control Aches and Pains," in *The Canadian Press,* October 13, 1981. Reprinted by permission.

pp. 45–47: "The Interpretation of Dreams." Pages 114–117 from *The Psychology of Being Human,* 3rd edition by Zick Rubin and Elton B. McNeil. Copyright © 1981 by Zick Rubin. Reprinted by permission of Harper & Row, Publishers, Inc.

pp. 57–58: "Dreams: A Key to the Workings of Our Brains?" by Judy G. Campbell, from *This Week at Carleton,* Vol. 2, No. 3, 1981. Reprinted by permission.

pp. 59–60: "The History of Dreams," by Bonnie Kreps, in *Homemaker's Magazine,* June 1981. Reprinted by permission of the author.

pp. 62–63: "The Dream Environment," by Bonnie Kreps, in *Homemaker's Magazine,* June 1981. Reprinted by permission of the author.

pp. 70–79: "Animals That Try to Talk," from *The Articulate Mammal* by Jean Aitchison (1976, 1983). Reprinted by permission of Century Hutchinson Publishing Group Ltd., London.

pp. 81–82: "Translating Bird Song," from *The Articulate Mammal* by Jean Aitchison (1976, 1983). Reprinted by permission of Century Hutchinson Publishing Group, Ltd., London.

pp. 84–89: "Canine Communication," from *Eloquent Animals: A Study in Animal Communication* by Flora Davis. Copyright © 1978 by Flora Davis. Reprinted by permission of the Putnam Publishing Group.

pp. 89–91: "The Chemical Language of Olfactory Signals," from *Animal Languages* by Fernand Méry.

pp. 91–97: "Chimpanzees," "Small Mammals," and "Marine Mammals," from *Languages of the Animal World* by J. H. Prince (1975). Reprinted by permission of the publisher E. P. Dutton.

pp. 97–100: "Birds," from *Eloquent Animals: A Study in Animal Communication* by Flora Davis. Copyright © 1978 by Flora Davis. Reprinted by permission of the Putnam Publishing Group.

pp. 100–102: "Calls With and Without Song," from *Languages of the Animal World* by J. H. Prince (1975). Reprinted by permission of the publisher E. P. Dutton.

pp. 102–103: "Bird Displays and Signals," from *Eloquent Animals: A Study in Animal Communication* by Flora Davis. Copyright © 1978 by Flora Davis. Reprinted by permission of the Putnam Publishing Group.

pp. 114–115: "The Green House Effect," by Charles A. White, *Canada and the World* magazine, January 1984. Reprinted by permission.

p. 116: "'Greenhouse Effect' and Methane Rise," *The New York Times,* October 16, 1984. Copyright © 1984/85 by The New York Times Company. Reprinted by permission.

p. 118: "'Greenhouse Effect' May Cause Havoc in Canada," *The Canadian Press,* October 22, 1984. Reprinted by permission.

p. 119: "'Greenhouse Effect' Could Hit by 2000," The Associated Press, January 10, 1984. Reprinted by permission.

pp. 119–120: "Greenhouse Effect May Shrink Lakes, Cut Water Supply," by Christine Spencer, the *Citizen,* Ottawa, November 17, 1983. Reprinted by permission.

pp. 123–126: "Hothouse Earth," by Kevin McKean, © *Discover* magazine, December 1983, Time Inc. Reprinted by permission.

pp. 133–135: "Nobel Prizes." Reprinted with permission from *Encyclopaedia Britannica,* 14th edition, © 1972 by Encyclopaedia Britannica, Inc.

p. 136: "King Presents Prizes," The Associated Press, December 10, 1983. Reprinted by permission.

p. 138: "3 Americans Win Nobel Science Prizes," *The Canadian Press,* October 19, 1983. Reprinted by permission.

pp. 139–140: "Nobel Climaxes Solitary Quest," by Paul Raeburn, The Associated Press, October 11, 1983. Reprinted by permission.

pp. 140–143: "At Long Last—A Nobel for a Loner," by Gina Maranto, ©

ACKNOWLEDGMENTS

Discover magazine, December 1983, Time Inc. Reprinted by permission.

pp. 144−145: "From Heresy to Eternity," by Shannon Brownlee, © *Discover* magazine, December 1984, Time Inc. Reprinted by permission.

pp. 146−147: "Debreu Won Nobel Prize for Economic Equilibrium Theory," by Deborah Dowling, the *Citizen,* Ottawa, October 22, 1984. Reprinted by permission.

pp. 147−148: "At 80, Nobel Winner Still in Love with Science," by April Lindgren, the *Citizen,* Ottawa, November 8, 1984. Reprinted by permission.

pp. 148−149: "2 Americans Win Nobel Medicine Prize," by John N. Wilford, *The New York Times,* October 15, 1985. Copyright © 1984/85 by The New York Times Company. Reprinted by permission.

pp. 150−151: "Stuttgart Researcher Wins '85 Nobel Prize in Physics," by Walter Sullivan, *The New York Times,* October 17, 1985. Copyright © 1984/85 by The New York Times Company. Reprinted by permission.

pp. 151−152: "2 Americans Share Nobel in Chemistry," by Harold M. Schmeck, Jr., *The New York Times,* October 17, 1985. Copyright © 1984/85 by The New York Times Company. Reprinted by permission.

pp. 157−159: "History of Computers: The Problem Solver," by R. J. Taylor, *Canada and the World* magazine, February 1982. Reprinted by permission.

pp. 160−162: "Machines Built to Emulate Human Experts' Reasoning," by Robert Reinhold, *The New York Times,* March 29, 1984. Copyright © 1984/85 by The New York Times Company. Reprinted by permission.

pp. 165−179: "Artificial Intelligence: An Assessment of the State-of-the-Art and Recommendation for Future Directions," by David Waltz. Reprinted with permission by the American Association for Artificial Intelligence from the *AI Magazine* (Fall 1983) 55:67.

pp. 191−192: "Here's Lucy—Our Cousin," by Charles A. White, *Canada and the World* magazine, April 1979. Reprinted by permission.

pp. 193−197: "The Leakeys: A Towering Reputation," by John N. Wilford, *The New York Times,* October 31, 1984. Copyright © 1984/85 by The New York Times Company. Reprinted by permission.

pp. 202−205: "Facing Up to Man's Past," by Kevin McKean, © *Discover* magazine, July 1983, Time Inc. Reprinted by permission.

pp. 210−213: "Were Lucy's Feet Made for Walking?" by R. Lewin, SCIENCE magazine, Vol. 220, pp. 700−702, k3 May 1983. Copyright 1987 by the American Association for the Advancement of Science. Reprinted by permission.

CONTENTS

CONTENTS

TO THE INSTRUCTOR

Strictly Academic was written for a very specific audience—first and second language learners who plan to enter academic programs in North America. These students need language training as well as exposure to academic texts and tasks. Regardless of their field of study, students in academic courses face difficult and complex tasks: reading, understanding, and integrating text from a variety of sources, and then selecting, synthesizing, and shaping the necessary information into clear, well-organized text.

As instructors we were troubled that we weren't preparing students adequately for the complexity of academic courses. Often students can't handle the large amount of text required in regular courses. They cannot integrate the material they hear in lectures and read in textbooks in order to write exams and essays. Consequently, *Strictly Academic* has been designed (and class tested) to help students make this difficult transition as they develop their language skills and the strategies necessary for success. The basic approach is to have students perform academic tasks using authentic text. As they work through these reading and writing tasks, which have been broken down into manageable steps, they learn to do them more effectively and efficiently. The content provides the vehicle and motivation for the acquisition of language skills and strategies.

At the university level, students are frequently asked to demonstrate knowledge through writing. The writing activities in *Strictly Academic* are designed to help students develop an independent, productive approach to academic writing. Students should be told that as they write they will not only improve their language skills, but also clarify and consolidate the subject matter. Through writing they will learn much.

As an instructor you may find that some students are puzzled by *Strictly Academic* because it doesn't look like other textbooks they might have used. They may expect their language course to focus on grammar; they may want to write essays about some general topic and then have you correct their errors. Researchers are now telling us that professors care less about perfect language than they do about the content of student writing. We find it helpful to tell students this. We have found that students soon understand that the material here offers them practice in doing what they will be doing in academic courses.

The *Instructor's Manual* accompanying this textbook has a separate section for each thematic chapter. Each section in the manual begins with an overview of the chapter's contents and proceeds with an explanation of the chapter's activities. We have included the purpose of each activity as well as suggestions for conducting the activities. Answer keys are also provided. Finally, we discuss the rationale behind the pedagogical approach of the text. We feel that both instructors and students are more comfortable using a text if they know its underlying philosophy.

Acknowledgments

First we would like to thank the students in our ESL classes over the last several years who used this material while it was being developed and did so with relative good cheer, even when we asked the impossible.

We would also like to thank Stan Jones, who encouraged us, and Christina Thiele, who was heroic in her determination to make a messy collection of pages look like a book. Her hours at the word processor could not have been easy. The typing of the manuscript was made possible by a grant from Carleton University.

We would like to express our appreciation to the many reviewers of this book whose comments and suggestions were very helpful:

Marcellette G. Williams, *Michigan State University*

Barbara Hoekje, *University of Pennsylvania*

Elizabeth Soden, *University of Michigan*

Suzanne Flynn, *Massachusettes Institute of Technology*

Neil Naiman, *Glendon College, York University (Canada)*

Ellen Rosenfield, *University of California–Berkeley*

And finally we want to thank Raewen, Michael, Sebastian, Helena, and David, who did their best to maintain family life when we weren't around.

Pat Currie
Ellen Cray

TO THE STUDENT

If you're using *Strictly Academic,* you probably are planning to enter a college or university, where many new demands will be made on you. You're probably considered an advanced language learner; you now may be able to speak English without difficulty in everyday life. But when you begin a course of study, you'll discover that you need new language and academic skills. Your academic courses will require that you read large amounts of text in books and journals and that you understand what you have read. You'll have to take notes while listening to long lectures, and you may have to participate in seminars and discussion groups. You'll have to write a number of different types of texts, including exams and essays. And this writing won't be easy to do. It will require that you review what you have read and heard, select relevant information, and then arrange this information into clear and concise text. Complex tasks like these require a certain level of language and academic skills.

Strictly Academic is based on the theory that you can develop and practice these skills before you enter a college or university. In order to prepare you for further study, the book's activities match as closely as possible what you'll do in academic classes. All the readings are authentic text; that is, they were written for native speakers of English and have not been changed in any way. The writing tasks, both exam questions and essay topics, are like those you'll be given in academic classes. While using this book you'll be given the opportunity to learn about a wide range of strategies that will be very valuable when you begin course work. We will show you, for example, how to understand what a textbook is about and what the author thinks is important. We will also show you how to predict what information professors will ask for on exams.

We believe that the more you use language, the more language you learn. This book gives you lots of exposure to language; you have to read a lot and you have to discuss what you have read and what you have written with other students and with your teacher. So not only are you developing academic skills, you are also improving your general language ability.

There are eight chapters in this book. Each chapter is devoted to a particular topic, such as dreams or the Nobel Prize. You'll be given several different texts to read and then asked to answer exam questions or write an essay. In other words, each chapter is like a section of an academic course.

One of the most important things you'll learn while using this book is that any academic task can be broken down into a series of steps. You'll discover, for example, that writing an essay involves more than just sitting down and writing. You first must gather your information, plan what you want to say, and then write several drafts before you are finished. By approaching both reading and writing tasks as a series of steps to be completed, you'll stand a much better chance of completing the tasks successfully.

This book may look different from any other textbook you have used. We realize that at times you may find the material challenging, if not downright difficult. But we feel that if you're willing to spend the time and energy, *Strictly Academic* will help you develop skills that are essential for college and university courses.

Pat Currie
Ellen Cray

1

A SELF-IMPROVEMENT HANDBOOK FOR ENGLISH

CHAPTER CONTENTS:

You may find that although you're making progress in learning English, you're still experiencing difficulties in one or two specific areas; for example, you may find that you don't know enough vocabulary or that you're having trouble with pronunciation. Furthermore, your area of difficulty may well be an individual problem with the result that there is less class time spent on it than you might want or need.

In this chapter you will be reading about and talking to good language learners who have overcome problems with English. You'll then write a self-improvement handbook for students who need help with English. The purpose of this handbook is to provide descriptions of techniques that students might find helpful when improving their English.

When working on this handbook, you'll get to practice a number of important language skills. First you'll learn how to skim text in order to locate important information. You'll also discover where authors put focus statements; that is, statements which tell the reader what the text is about. Writing this handbook will introduce you to effective writing techniques. In this chapter you will focus on the steps to follow before you begin writing and on developing ways to write a text that are easy and interesting for your readers. These are important skills for anyone planning to study in English.

THINKING ABOUT THE TOPIC

As a class, discuss specific problems you are still having with English. Choose the 3 or 4 that are the most common in the class.

1.

2.

3.

4.

5.

Form equal groups. Each group will focus on a different problem. The problem your group selects will be your responsibility for the handbook.

Language Learning Techniques

How helpful would you consider these techniques for learning English? Individually rate each of the following techniques on a scale of 1 to 5. Read the key before you start. This is your personal opinion, so you don't need to consult other students in the class.

KEY
5 Extremely helpful
4 Very helpful
3 Quite helpful
2 Not very helpful
1 Virtually useless

1. Talking to someone on the bus every day.   1   2   3   4   5
2. Looking up every unfamiliar word in whatever you're reading.   1   2   3   4   5
3. Reading newspaper reports on subjects you're familiar with.   1   2   3   4   5
4. Taping newscasts or lectures and listening carefully to how people pronounce words.   1   2   3   4   5
5. Reading English comic books.   1   2   3   4   5
6. Finding an English-speaking girlfriend or boyfriend.   1   2   3   4   5
7. Looking for words in your language which are similar to English words.   1   2   3   4   5
8. Writing letters in English to someone.   1   2   3   4   5
9. Keeping a list of all the unfamiliar words you come across.   1   2   3   4   5
10. Joining a club that you're interested in.   1   2   3   4   5

Share and discuss your answers in groups. You might want to add items to the questionnaire.

"PREPARATION OVERCOMES FEAR OF CONVERSATION"

The article you are about to read was written by someone who is sensitive to the audience. Good writers know who their readers are. They take into account the readers' attitudes toward the topic, the extent of their knowledge about it, and the possible gaps that exist in their knowledge. The good writer has the ability not only to select information that will be both interesting and useful to the reader, but also to organize it in a way that the reader will be able to follow the text easily.

Often you do not have to read all of a text to get the information you need. In deciding whether or not to read the entire article, it is a good idea to read the first and last paragraphs. Turn to pages 5 and 6 and read these two paragraphs. Answer the following questions:

1. a. Who is the intended audience of this article?

  b. In these two paragraphs, what evidence is there that the writer has chosen information that will motivate the reader to read the entire text?

2. In good writing, there is usually one sentence or group of sentences which tell the reader what kind of information the text will focus on. Read paragraph 2. Underline or highlight this focus sentence.

3. What is the purpose of this article?

4. Quickly skim the rest of the article. How has the writer made it easy for the reader to know exactly which conversation skills she or he will learn about?

List the skills below:

1.

2.

3.

4.

5.

6.

7.

8.

9.

Now read the entire article to find out how to improve your conversational abilities.

Preparation overcomes fear of conversation

The biggest barrier to conversation is fear. Fear of how others will react to them, fear of making mistakes, or of making a fool of themselves, can paralyze people and prevent them from feeling at ease with others.

Fear of conversation is merely anxiety exaggerated. A good way to tackle such anxiety is to prepare yourself. This can be best done by learning and practicing the following skills of conversation making.

USING OPEN-ENDED QUESTIONS

Instead of wording your questions in ways that elicit "yes" or "no" answers, such as "Are you going to . . . ?", questions such as "How do you feel about . . . ?" will involve the other person in telling you more about him- or herself.

There are two types of open-ended questions, those which begin with "who, what, when or where," and provide direct answers, and those that begin with "how" or "why," and which encourage others to give more detailed responses.

ATTEND TO FREE INFORMATION

Free information is what a person gives without being questioned directly. It may occur when a person spontaneously goes beyond answering an open-ended question. Listen for those free bits of information, and use them.

People do not normally volunteer information they don't wish to talk about. Thus, if you get free information, it's usually a sign it is all right to discuss that topic. Follow up free information with open-ended questions or comments, and you're onto a good conversation.

GIVING SELF-DISCLOSURE

Self-disclosure is free information you give about yourself in a conver-sation. It helps others to respond to you with open-ended questions. Remember, people do not have to respond to your free information. You may share things they don't want to talk about at the time.

In conversation, you share ideas, experiences, desires or feelings without placing demands on others to respond. If they are interested they will respond. Sharing facts is the least threatening form of self-disclosure. It can be what you've read, heard or seen. Sharing ideas or experiences involves risking more, and sharing feelings is often more difficult and doesn't occur until a relationship has formed. Sharing is different from bragging. A bragger keeps on talking whether or not others are interested.

CHANGING TOPICS

If you want to change the current topic of conversation, ask an open-ended question on some earlier free information given, or make a self-disclosure statement about another topic. Be direct, if necessary, and state: "I am really more interested in hearing more about . . . " As part of a conversation you have the right to try to change the topic, although the new one must be agreeable to both.

BREAKING INTO ONGOING CONVERSATION

When a group is talking, walk up to them and stand by quietly. If they are willing to have you join, they will show this by giving you eye contact now and then, or shifting their body angle so you become part of their group. If they don't, then move on, but without shame. It is up to them to let you know if their conversation is private.

Once standing by, listen to the nature of the conversation, and then join in, when appropriate, with some self-disclosure, opinion, fact, or free information.

SILENCES

Don't worry when conversation lags. Periods of silence are normal in conversation. You don't need to fill every moment with words. Silences are relaxing. They provide thinking time for all involved. Finally someone, perhaps you, will bring up a new topic. If that topic dies, then someone else will bring up another.

TELLING STORIES

Stories, experiences and jokes can add to a converstaion. However, don't start a story or joke you can't end. It needs a beginning, a middle and an end. Stories about your experiences with a topic being discussed can add much to a conversation.

NON-VERBAL CUES

A good conversationalist is also a good listener. Good listening involves good body posture, standing erect, not stooped, smiling when appropriate, nodding slightly when you agree with what is said, and appropriate eye contact. Nobody likes being stared at. Equally, people don't like being ignored. Keep your head up, and "touch eyeballs" with others now and then. It tells them you are still with them.

ENDING CONVERSATIONS

Sometimes conversations end on their own. One topic dies, and despite several attempts, nobody agrees on a new one. You may want to end a conversation. Comments like, "I really enjoyed talking to you," carry the message that the conversation is over, but with politeness. Other ways include using more close-ended questions, giving less self-disclosure, or body cues such as less eye contact, less head nodding, and a slight backing away from someone.

Conversational skills are not a mystery. They can be learned, and once learned they must be practiced, for that is what conversation is all about.

THE GOOD LANGUAGE LEARNER

According to current research, good language learners exhibit certain attitudes and behavior.

Read the following list of characteristics. Circle the ones you feel probably belong to the good language learner.

Good language learners:

1. are willing to take risks and make mistakes.
2. look for situations in which they can communicate in the second language.
3. wait until they have looked words up in the dictionary before trying to use them.
4. worry about using the wrong form of the verb.
5. make some comparisons between the new language and their first language, in order to help discover the system of the new language.
6. get upset if they can't understand everything someone says.
7. identify individual problems in their language learning and work on them.
8. wait until someone else speaks first.
9. want to sound just like native speakers when they talk.
10. expect to be perfectly bilingual in one year.

In groups, share and discuss your answers. Consider the following questions: Why are some of the characteristics good and others bad? Which of these characteristics will you incorporate into your portion of the handbook?

The care with which you read any text will depend on your purpose in reading it. Even when you read for academic purposes, a task which usually requires great care, you can still ignore a lot of information. If you can train yourself to select only the relevant information in a text, you'll save yourself both time and energy.

The purpose of this activity is to help you practice the skill of reading for relevant information.

The following case study is taken from *The Good Language Learner,* a book by Naiman, *et al.* This book, published in 1978, contains studies of people who learned languages easily.

Your assignment is to gather information for the handbook as you read this case study of a good language learner. While reading, underline or highlight only those techniques which apply to your section of the handbook. You have 20 minutes to complete the task.

After you have finished, meet with the other members of your group to compare and discuss the techniques you selected.

Case Study

Name: Ms. B.

Age Group: 26–35

Occupation: Ph.D. student of Special Education

Languages Learned and Maintained: Hebrew, French, Latin, German, Italian½

Ms. B. was born in Nova Scotia and brought up in a bilingual family. The languages spoken in her home were English and Yiddish.

Ms. B. had no recollection of her early childhood competence in Yiddish. She was told that she spoke it fluently until the age of seven. Yiddish was the only language in which she could communicate with her grandparents, who at that time lived in her parents' home. Ms. B. reported that at present she understood only a little Yiddish, but that she could use the language actively and generate words and sentences. Despite her bilingual family background she regarded English alone as her native language.

Ms. B. did not come into any contact with other languages until she was sent to Hebrew school at the age of about ten or eleven for a period of five to six years. The focus of instruction was reading the Hebrew script, without attention to meaning. As she did not understand the content of what she had to read, Ms. B. regarded this exercise as completely useless.

The second foreign language Ms. B. attempted to learn was French, which she started in grade 7 of the regular high school. She recalled that the students followed a textbook, learned grammar, did some reading, and memorized a few dialogues. In general, oral production was extremely rare, despite the teacher being a native speaker of French.

Ms. B. continued studying French until the second year of university. The teaching of French at university did not differ greatly from the way French was taught in high school. The focus was on language as a system, and not on language perceived as a means of oral communication. Summing up her achievement in French, Ms. B. reported: ''I discovered later that I could read scientific articles quite well, but I have never been able to speak French.''

During her high school and university years, Ms. B. went through two other similar language learning experiences. She learned Latin from grade 9 to 11 and took German at university for three years. She felt that her achievement in both languages was again very limited, as the emphasis was on grammar and not on communication.

Her experience with language learning, which had previously meant occupying herself with a lifeless academic discipline, was completely revolutionized when she decided to go to Italy for a year and train as a Montessori teacher. From a professional point of view, she could also have been trained in Britain. However, she still regarded learning another language as "a valuable experience," and therefore chose to take a training course in a small town in the north of Italy, deciding to try to learn the language at the same time. The course was to be conducted in both Italian and English.

Ms. B.'s linguistic adventure proved to be extremely successful. Starting from zero competence, she developed more than adequate comprehension and oral production within one year.

Summarizing the outcome of her learning efforts in a self-imposed immersion situation, she explained:

> The travelling I did . . . was . . . to go to Italy knowing absolutely none of the language and coming back a year later able to carry on a conversation with five to six different people simultaneously, not completely idiomatically, but at least, knowing enough about generating words to get myself around a difficult situation.

When asked to elaborate upon the way she approached the new language learning task, Ms. B. revealed many strategies and techniques and showed a great deal of insight into the affective demands made upon her in this unfamiliar situation. In her recollection the first ten days of her stay were rather traumatic. She lived with an Italian family. The other English-speaking students had not yet arrived. "I felt completely cut off . . . I had nobody to talk to. It was an incredible experience." She tried to make herself understood by looking up every word in a dictionary, which she regarded as an "extremely exasperating" way of communicating. Once the other students had arrived, the feeling of being completely isolated decreased.

By following the daily lectures, Ms. B. was amazed to find how much she "picked up" in terms of words, word arrangements, and intonation during the first couple of weeks. As the lecture itself was accompanied by practical demonstrations, she was able to relate language to meaning. "Since you could see what was happening—along with the language—it made a lot of sense." In addition, Ms. B. made lists of useful words by looking them up in the dictionary.

Ms. B. also attributed a great deal of her initial progress in Italian to *Signora*, the lady she was living with:

> I found that *Signora* was a very fine language teacher . . . She was teaching me the way you would teach a younger child to speak the language. She'd be giving me words when I'd stumble. She'd say them for me, I would try and repeat it; it wouldn't be quite right, she'd say it again. She had tremendous patience.

Ms. B. learned a lot of phrases by carefully listening to *Signora:*

> If I knew the words, or at least some of the words in a phrase, when it was used in a practical situation, I'd sort of say "Click, click, that's how you say it". . . . As I had heard, I would imitate.

However, after a while, Ms. B. realized that she was very restricted in the kinds of sentences she could construct. Together with other students, she approached the teachers in the "English Centre" of the town, where English was taught as a second language, and asked them if they would be willing to teach them Italian. One teacher agreed and Ms.

B. attended classes twice a week for a period of three hours each time. The content of instruction was grammar as well as conversation, based upon practical situations. It was fairly easy to learn certain grammar aspects, such as tenses, as she heard them actually being used outside the classroom. Ms. B. emphasized that it was only through formal instruction that she got an insight into the structure of the Italian language. She realized that both formal instruction and an informal immersion situation were essential for her progress in language learning:

> I needed that first few weeks . . . not worrying about grammar, hearing the
> intonation, when it really made very little sense and where I was exasperated
> most of the time, because if I tried to say anything, I would, maybe, get out
> one or two words. I could begin to understand them, but I couldn't make
> them. I had to learn the grammar in order to do that.

When she compared her own competence in Italian with that of her roommate, her belief in the necessity of formal instruction was confirmed. Her friend never reached a high level of grammatical sophistication. She also had more difficulty in expressing her ideas in Italian.

After three and a half months Ms. B. went on a trip with two Italians and one American. It was during this vacation that she experienced her ''linguistic breakthrough.'' As she was the only one who spoke English as well as Italian she became the bridge between the two languages. She was forced to overcome her inhibition and a certain uneasiness with the foreign language as she had to translate constantly. By the time she came back, she had suddenly become fluent in Italian. She had gained confidence in her ability to cope with the foreign language. She tried to speak as much as possible and monitored her language through the feedback she got from native speakers:

> I wasn't afraid anymore, I generated sentences . . . if they weren't correct,
> people around me told me how to say it. I was on the lookout for clues . . . I
> don't suppose there was a lot of correction that I didn't pick up on fairly im-
> mediately and put into the language I was building.

Ms. B.'s attempts at communicating as much as possible very often made native speakers laugh, because of the ambiguity of some of her statements. It was mainly *Signora* who explained to her the double meaning of what she had said. However, it was done in such a way that Ms. B. never felt ridiculed but was able to share the joke.

Ms. B. found that for a long time her comprehension remained ''personspecific,'' in other words, when listening to somebody for the first time her comprehension level dropped. By the end of the year, however, she was able to understand speakers with different accents talking to each other or to her.

Ms. B. attempted not only to learn the language, but also to integrate into the Italian community as much as possible. She would have extended her stay if she had been able to find an acceptable position.

When presented with the chart describing the different proficiency levels and asked to indicate the level of proficiency she had reached within a year, Ms. B. explained that her ability to comprehend and produce was slightly above working knowledge, but that she had never concentrated on reading and writing skills:

> It was always an aural language. Anything that was written I had to read it out loud, unless it was on a very simple level, in order to hear the sound of it, in order to figure out what was said.

With regard to her present knowledge of Italian, Ms. B. indicated that her competence in comprehension and oral production had decreased due to lack of usage.

When questioned if she was satisfied with her achievement in Italian, Ms. B. stated that she was pleased with her progress during her stay in Italy, but that at present there was no need for her to be fluent. She felt very confident, however, that she could reactivate not only Italian but also French if the circumstances required it. On a few more recent occasions, when it would have been desirable to have reactivated her latent French, she discovered that Italian interfered greatly. Similarly, she had experienced some French interference at the beginning of her Italian immersion and had had to suppress French consciously.

In reply to the question of whether she thought she had a gift for languages, Ms. B. emphasized that even though she had to work at learning Italian she nevertheless felt that she had a reasonably good ear for languages as well as a good memory. She also enjoyed analyzing Italian and looking at language as a system.

After having described her main language learning experience in detail, Ms. B. was asked to indicate which factors she would regard as the most influential on her success and her failure in language learning. Ms. B. emphasized that the immersion into an Italian environment, and therefore the motivation for having to learn to speak the language, were the most significant factors at first. In order to develop her language competence further, she had to take recourse to formal instruction. Commenting on her very limited achievement in French and German, she pointed out that she lacked motivation because the languages were learned in a vacuum, without applicability outside the language classroom. She indicated further that she would not hesitate to learn another language and that she felt competent to do so, if, for example, she went to live in another country. "My feeling about learning another language is that it has to be immediately useful."

The Interview

University courses often require students to do primary research—that is, to go to an original source of information. Your original research for this chapter will involve interviewing successful language learners.

1. When you interview the successful language learners, you will want to collect the following information:

   a. the problems they faced in learning English
   b. techniques they found useful in coping with these problems
   c. their reactions to techniques you plan to include in your handbook

   Meet with your group and decide what questions you want to ask.

2. When the interview begins, explain to the person you are interviewing what kind of information you want, and why.

3. During the interview, keep notes; you will need information from the interview for your handbook.

Getting Ready to Write

Now you can begin working on your language learning handbook. Before you begin to write, there are a number of things you can do which will make the actual writing easier.

Evaluating and Selecting Material

Work with your group to plan your section of the handbook. Focus only on your problem.

1. List as many techniques as you can. Don't evaluate them now.
2. Next, discuss each one; make sure everyone in the group understands each technique. Decide which ones you want to include in the handbook.
3. Decide who in your group will be responsible for writing up which technique(s).

Considering Your Audience and Purpose

Before you begin to write, you should consider who you are writing for and why you are writing.

1. As a class, discuss the following questions:
   a. Who is the handbook for?
   b. What do you want your audience to *do* with this information?
2. When you have answered the preceding questions, discuss how your audience will determine:
   a. what kind of information you should include,
   b. how much information you should include,
   c. how you want to organize it, and
   d. what kind of language you should use for that audience.

Preliminary Planning

You will want to make a rough plan of your part before you write.

1. Individually, write down the suggestions you want to include in the handbook. Each piece of advice should include:
   a. the suggestion
   b. supporting detail (elaboration, additional description)
2. As a group, discuss your audience and purpose, and decide how you are going to sequence:
   a. the individual recommendations
   b. the support (details, explanations, examples, etc.)

3. Draw a treelike sketch showing how you have organized your information.
   a. With a partner in your group, discuss in detail what you are going to say in your part.

4. Discuss any gaps or problems in either the information or the organization.

Writing the Handbook

The First Draft: Getting the Information Down on Paper

You are now ready to begin writing your part of the handbook. You will write three drafts of your part. While you write the first draft, you should concentrate on getting the important information written. In a later draft you can correct your grammar, spelling, and punctuation.

1. Write your first draft of your part of the handbook. Double space. Use your sketch as a guide. Don't worry about finding the exact word, spelling, punctuation, etc. Concentrate on getting the information down on paper.

2. Consult with a partner. Read your partner's first draft twice, once for information and once for organization. Ask questions as you read.
   a. Information
      • Is there enough information for readers to know exactly what to do and what to expect?
      • Is everything relevant?
   b. Organization
      • Can readers follow the ideas easily, or must they jump from one idea to another?

3. Share and discuss any problems. Then make any revisions you feel are necessary. You might want to use boxes, arrows, and tape to add, delete, or reorder information.

4. As a class, do the following:
   a. Decide how you will organize the text, how to use headings, capitals, etc., so that your readers will be able to use the handbook efficiently. Discuss how you can help your readers see the major sections and subsections of your handbook.
   b. Develop an introduction and a focus statement that will both tell readers what to expect and interest them in reading at least part of it.
   c. Develop a conclusion that will motivate them to try the techniques.

The Second Draft: Focusing on Clear Language

In this draft you should concentrate on making your text interesting and easy to read. There are several things you should do before you begin writing.

1. Read your first draft aloud to help you find places that may confuse your reader. Make sure your ideas follow logically. Rewrite any sections which you feel need revision. Using scissors and tape, put together your second draft. You have 30 minutes.
2. Write the second draft.

The Third Draft: Editing

This is the draft where you can correct your grammar, punctuation, and spelling errors.

1. Ask your partner to read your draft. Your partner should put an asterisk (*) next to any unclear parts and should underline grammar, punctuation, and spelling errors. Read your partner's paper in the same way. When you are finished, discuss and resolve any difficulties.
2. Revise your section.

Oral Presentations

Preparing

In groups, organize your presentations. As individuals, you'll be teaching your group's section of the handbook to people from other groups. (See the following two paragraphs). So, each person should know all the group's information. Teach one another the techniques you wrote up for the handbook.

Presenting

Form new groups, so that there is one member from each of the old groups in each of the new groups. In this way, the presentations by the new groups will consist of *all* the information in the handbook.

Present your first group's section of the handbook to your new group. Take turns. Your time limit is 10 minutes each, with another 5 to 6 minutes for questions.

Revising

Use what you've learned from your presentations to make last-minute revisions in your text.

Distributing the Handbook

Assemble your handbook and arrange to have it copied and distributed to the students in your class and in other E.S.L. classes.

2

PAIN CONTROL

At some time in our lives, most of us have experienced pain. Scientists and medical researchers have done a great deal of research on what causes pain and how it can be alleviated. In this chapter you will read about some of the research currently being carried out.

Much of the text deals with classifying and describing causes of pain. In the reading part of this chapter you'll discover how authors describe categories. You'll also learn how to take effective notes on what you read.

At the end of the chapter you'll write an essay question on pain control. In order to write a good essay you must select and organize relevant information from the texts you have read. You'll also get practice expressing causal relationships.

THINKING ABOUT THE TOPIC

Answer the following questions as they relate to you individually.

1. Read the following list, checking off the aches and pains you have experienced either chronically or at some point in your life.

    _____ Headache   _____ Earache   _____ Stomachache

    _____ Migraine   _____ Muscle pain   _____ Back pain

    _____ Injury-related pain (please specify) _____

    _____ Other (please specify) _____

2. **a.** What is the worst pain you have ever experienced?

    _____

    _____

    b. What caused it? _____

    c. How long did it last? _____

3. **a.** Which of the following methods of pain control have you tried?

    _____ Popular painkillers such as aspirin, Bufferin (please specify)

    _____

    _____ Other drugs (e.g., Valium, marijuana, heroin, morphine)

    _____ Acupuncture

    _____ Hypnosis

    _____ Relaxation

    b. How effective were they? _____

4. Did any of them cause unpleasant or adverse side effects? If so, please specify.

    _____

    _____

In small groups, compare and discuss your answers.

"MIGRAINE: THE KING OF PAIN"

Read the following questions. Then read the news article on migraines to answer these questions.

1. Define a migraine and describe at least 3 of its secondary symptoms.

2. What is the accepted explanation of migraines today?

3. Briefly describe the 3 main categories of migraines.

4. List 4 different kinds of treatments for migraine headaches.

    a.

    b.

    c.

    d.

5. What forms might treatment by relaxation and stress management take?

Check your answers with your teacher.

6. Reread question 3. Discuss with your teacher the different ways you could make notes on this information to help yourself remember it easily. Try the different ways on the board. Discuss the advantages and disadvantages of each.

Migraine: The king of pain
There's no cure but sufferers can get relief

It's the result of a hit on the head, too many glasses of wine or an argument at the office—for most.

And the cure is time.

But for about 20 per cent of adults, and around four per cent of children, a headache is something completely different.

These people have migraines, an inherited, incurable and little-understood blood vessel disorder that can cause a type of pain the rest of the world simply can't comprehend.

As one sufferer says:

I apply the ice pack and try to sleep but the pounding prevents this. I feel like taking a drill and drilling into my temple or gouging out my eye with my bare hands.

Migraines are democratic—anyone can get them. There are no telltale personality traits, and the only imbalance is the condition seems to favor women victims.

Migraines usually create an intense, throbbing pain that grips one side of the head.

Sufferers also experience a wide sweep of side-effects, or secondary symptoms. These range from the common—dizziness, pallor in the face, nausea, diarrhea and sensitivity to light—to the bizarre—hallucination, speech disorders, memory loss and feelings of déja vu.

Often I won't realize a migraine is about to start. I'm yellowy pale in the face at this point. This is the time when I drop things, use the wrong words, have a fuzziness in my reasoning, and feel detached. This is

also when visual disturbances begin. Then the pain starts.

The response is from one of 650 victims surveyed by Carleton University in a research project now in its second year, which, it is hoped, may come up with information to allow doctors to make a more precise diagnose of migraines.

Migraines have been recognized as a curse for thousands of years.

Ancient Egyptians believed the pain was caused by evil spirits, and drilled holes in sufferers' heads to let the spirits out and relieve the pressure.

A 17th-century scientist, William Harvey, discovered migraines were related to the vessels that supply blood to the brain.

Today, doctors agree migraine is a disorder that seems to cause a sudden constriction, and then enlargement of the vessels supplying blood to the head, causing the throbbing associated with migraine.

The vessel expansion may be caused by changes in the production of body chemicals that affect the blood vessels and produce pain.

There is no cure.

"The point is you can't even hope to be cured," says Dr. Marek Gawel of the Sunnybrook Medical Centre's headache clinic in Toronto.

"You can only hope it will go away from time to time."

"We're not looking for a cure," he says of his team of neurologists, psychologists and psychiatrists doing clinical research into headaches. "We're just looking for a decrease in headaches."

The incredible cost of migraines to the health care system may have played a role in accelerating research.

Gawel says recurring headache pain sends sufferers through a dizzying round of medical treatment, as they seek out the opinion of doctor after doctor, trying to find a solution.

Gawel, a neurologist, estimates about half of the people he sees are headache sufferers.

Gawel estimates between 85 and 90 per cent of victims can be helped.

Preventive medications, painkillers, relaxation techniques and stress management are used along with treatments such as acupuncture and hypnotherapy.

Relaxation and stress management to avoid headaches involves not only learning to relax physically, but mentally. Some people with migraines are taught to take a nap before an attack, while others learn to take a long walk or have a massage.

Mental therapy or psychological changes to avoid attacks can include trying to avoid the thought patterns or behavior that can initiate stress and trigger an attack.

For example, extremely passive people who feel stress because they can't resolve situations on their own, learn to be more assertive.

At Carleton, psychology professor Jim Campbell is trying to categorize into distinct groups those sufferers who have common symptoms and can be treated effectively.

Now there are three categories: classic migraine, common migraine, and cluster headaches.

The classic migraines warn their victims, who experience what is known as an aura, usually a visual disorder; a flash of light or a zigzag pattern across the vision.

My auras are often in blazing, painfully bright Technicolor—so beautiful. I seem to go into some sort of trance during the aura. Sometimes I'm so busy admiring it that I forget to take my medicine.

Common migraine headaches are like the classic version, but without the startling aura, and cluster headaches are almost always suffered by men in bouts. For example, a sufferer might get very severe headaches quite often over a two-week period and then be without a headache for months or even years.

Campbell says if he can break these categories down even further, his research could allow doctors to make more precise diagnoses, prescribe the best treatment and predict the odds of success.

Campbell and his research team have asked the 650 surveyed to describe what the pain feels like, how intense it is, and their symptoms.

He is trying to find out, for example, if people who have visual disorders also experience dizziness.

So far he's come up with four distinct types of headaches which cover about 40 per cent of the people in the project.

Since he began his research, Campbell's list of symptoms has expanded from 71 to 250.

People tell of trying to write a cheque in a bank and forgetting where they are, others says they experience strange emotional swings and have a distorted sense of sound.

The indignity of the side-effects was horrible. I used to pass out in stores and was taken for a drunk or a dope addict.

Some have strange thought patterns when they have a migraine. A jingle heard on the radio earlier in the day or an incident from earlier on will stick in their memories.

The same thought or course of action will repeat itself over and over. After playing bridge one night and getting a migraine, I replayed the same hand for about six hours in my mind. I couldn't stop or change thoughts.

Campbell thinks it's possible some of these symptoms may arise because the neurological changes creating the headache are happening in the part of the brain that controls a specific function. For example, in the excerpt above, the change might be happening in the area that controls motor skills and speech.

At the Children's Hospital of Eastern Ontario, a team has been researching child migraines for four years.

Dr. Pat McGrath, the spokesman for the six-member group including neurologists and psychologists, says children sometimes suffer from unusual forms of migraines, such as the "Alice in Wonderland" syndrome.

Like Alice who grew small and then tall, children may have no headache but experience unusual sensory disorders and hallucinations.

Results of a recent study at the hospital concluded that children with migraine can benefit from relaxation techniques adults adopt to relieve and prevent headaches.

Children also learn to recognize when their muscles are tensing up in

a way that will lead to a headache.

"We want them to control the migraines rather than have the migraines control them."

Right now the group is working on a research program comparing two different types of preventive medication commonly used for adult migraine sufferers.

There is a wide range of prescription medication that prevents migraine. Some is taken regularly to ward off attacks, while others are taken at the first warning of a migraine, usually after a classic migraine sufferer has an aura.

Wendy Richardson, a psychology PhD student at the University of Ottawa, is now just beginning a study comparing the effectiveness of clinical stress management by adults to self-help techniques.

One group is to attend weekly sessions for eight weeks, learning ways to relax, and recognize the thought patterns that provoke a migraine.

She says students who panic at exam time claiming they don't know the material, learn to take a more positive approach.

Exam-scared students "learn if they fail the exam it's not going to be the end of the world."

While this group is taking traditional clinical work, another group will have two clinical sessions and will take a manual and cassettes home to learn the same things.

She hopes the study will show whether self-help is as effective as clinical treatment.

So far, Richardson has about seven or eight people enrolled in her two-year project, and is aiming for about 60.

"HEADACHES MAY BE TRIGGERED BY THE FOOD YOU CRAVE MOST"

Quickly read the accompanying news article and answer the questions below.

1. List Rosemary Dudley's four main categories of migraine precipitators.

   a.

   b.

   c.

   d.

2. Outline the arguments for and against the two most disputed triggers.

	Trigger	Arguments For	Arguments Against
a.	*Food*	*Research by Jim Campbell + R. Dudley shows foods such as chocolate, red wine, etc can trigger an attack*	*research is inconclusive* *no proof*
b.	*Weather*	*Dudley: migraines more frequent when barometer drops* *Phillips: not just barometric pressure, also shifts in many weather exp. unsettled weather, a passing front*	*no proof drop in pressure causes migraine* *stress during rainy weather which causes migraines*

Headaches may be triggered by the food you crave most

While no one knows exactly what physical factors make a person prone to migraine, certain irritants have been singled out as villains.

Almost all migraine sufferers are born with a little-understood vessel disorder, but it takes an irritant, or a trigger to provoke an attack.

"Consider migraine as a gun: heredity loads it and points it at your head; the trigger causes it to fire," says Rosemary Dudley, executive vice-president of the Migraine Foundation in her book *How to Find Relief from Migraine*.

Dudley categorizes countless triggers into major groupings: food; weather; hormonal changes, particularly in women; stress, and changes in sleep patterns.

She says there are so many variables, only two rules of thumb apply to all migraine sufferers: Never change your sleep patterns by more than an hour, and never go more than five hours without food.

The triggers that have grabbed the most attention are food and drink.

While some experts say research is so inconclusive there is no proof food will start an attack, there are those who point to universal culprits: Chocolate, red wine, scotch, old cheese, nuts, heavily salted snacks, fried foods, pork, onions and citrus fruits.

Dudley found alcohol set off her headaches.

She says most people who experience food-triggered migraines suffer a cruel irony at the hands of Mother Nature—they crave the very thing that will set off their headache.

Jim Campbell, a Carleton University psychologist researching migraines, says migraine sufferers back up this finding.

Dudley says the foundation, a Toronto-based group with 280,000 members, urges people to identify the culprit foods and try to stop eating them. The foundation provides information, conducts research and gives assistance to people who have migraines.

However, Dr. Marek Gawel of the headache clinic at Toronto's Sunnybrook Medical Centre, says research there appears to indicate that while getting rid of a trigger may reduce headaches, victims seem to develop new triggers.

The weather has also been suggested as a trigger of migraines, but the suggestion arouses controversy among medical experts and meteorologists.

Some doctors say there is no proof. Rather that the stress associated with rainy, gray weather may be at fault.

Dudley says foundation research shows a direct link: the incidence of headache rises dramatically with a drop in barometric pressure.

In cooperation with the migraine foundation, David Phillips, a meteorologist with Environment Canada's Toronto office, conducted research on the link between weather and migraines.

Migraine sufferers filled out a headache log, indicating when they had headaches and how severe they were.

Phillips says the findings showed it wasn't just barometric pressure that triggered attacks, but rather a dramatic shift in many weather factors.

Days of unsettled weather or when a weather front moves through an area appeared to produce the most complaints.

Those same weather characteristics, he says, however, are also linked to suffering among rheumatism and arthritis patients.

Phillips says the difference between his findings and what the foundation says may lie in the public's lack of understanding about the weather. He says while people associate changing weather with barometric change, it is really only one of a number of weather elements shifting with radical weather developments.

Stress is the trigger about which all the experts agree.

Anticipation of a stressful situation, experiencing stress, and even trying to relax after stress can all set off an attack.

Dudley says some migraine sufferers get "Saturday morning headaches" either from sleeping in or altering regular sleep patterns, or from trying to wind down too suddenly from a stressful week.

For women one of the most common triggers is hormonal change. Some migraine sufferers experience migraines during menstruation, others at the time of ovulation.

Almost all women who get hormone-triggered migraines find pregnancy a relief.

Classification

The authors of the readings you have just completed have given the reader important information about the different types of migraines and migraine triggers. In order to read effectively, you need to recognize the statements of classification used to identify the various types.

1. In "Migraine: The King of Pain," find the sentence in which the writer classifies migraines. Write it on the lines below.

_____

_____

_____

2. How does the writer then help the reader distinguish the three categories?

3. In "Headaches May Be Triggered by the Food You Crave Most," find the sentence in which the writer classifies migraine triggers. Write it below.

_____

_____

_____

4. When deciding to use a particular rhetorical form, a writer usually does so for a purpose. For what reasons did the writer choose to classify or group migraines and their triggers (i.e., How was the writer trying to help the reader?)?

Now it's your turn to practice writing statements of classification. Look at the following diagram to review ways of classifying.

USEFUL EXPRESSIONS

X	can / may / might	be	classified / divided / grouped	into	n	groups: categories: types: divisions: categories:

You	can	divide / group / classify	X	into	n	groups: categories: types: divisions:

There are	n	(major) (minor)	categories types groups groupings classes divisions	of X

Write a statement of classification using the chart above. Use a different form each time.

1. Types of magazines: weekly, monthly, bimonthly.

_____

_____

2. Faculties: arts, social sciences, science, medicine.

_____

_____

3. Body types: endomorphs, mesomorphs, ectomorphs.

_____

_____

4. Write a statement classifying each of the following items into 3 or 4 categories. Watch your punctuation.

a. Music _____

_____

_____

b. Examination questions _____

_____

_____

c. Restaurants _____

_____

_____

As a class, share and discuss your answers.

"THE SKIN SENSES"

Textbooks are organized to help the student find important information easily. As a result, the first sentence in a paragraph frequently tells the reader what the focus or central idea of a paragraph will be, and whether this is a new idea or the continuation of the idea from the previous paragraph. Thus, reading the first sentence in a paragraph often helps you outline the information in general terms before you read for specifics. Reading only these parts is called skimming.

The following article, "The Skin Senses," was taken from a first-year psychology text. Skim the article, highlighting the first sentence in each paragraph. As you skim, decide what the focus is for each paragraph. Then, on the lines below, write one or two words to help you remember these central ideas. You will then have a brief outline of the information contained in this section.

"The Skin Senses"

1. _____

    a. _____

    b. _____

    c. _____

2. _____

Which paragraph is not represented separately in the outline? Why not?

Now read the article carefully, highlighting or underlining the important information.

Then take notes using the information you highlighted or underlined.

THE SKIN SENSES

The sense of touch is actually a combination of at least three sensations: pressure, temperature, and pain. If you unbend a paper clip and probe an area of your skin lightly, you will feel pressure at certain points where the wire contacts your skin, but not at every point. If you do the same thing with a cold wire, you will feel cold at other specific points. If you probe your skin with a warm wire, you will feel warmth at still other points. A pin point will produce spots of pain. Thus, different points on the skin are serviced by receptors that are sensitive to different kinds of stimuli.

The experience you have when you are touched lightly with a single hair is called *pressure* or *touch*. The amount of pressure required to produce this experience varies for different parts of the body. The tip of the tongue, the lips, the fingers, and the hands are the most sensitive areas. The arms, legs, and body trunk are less sensitive. People experience pressure not only when an object touches the skin, but also when the hairs on the body are slightly moved.

In addition to pressure receptors, the skin contains receptors for both *heat* and *cold*.

There are about six times as many cold receptors as heat receptors in the skin. These temperature receptors are more concentrated along the trunk of the body, which is why the hands and feet can withstand greater temperature extremes than can the bare back. Hot and cold are relative terms: Anything that you touch that is colder than your skin will be perceived as cool; anything you touch that is hotter than your skin will seem warm. Interestingly, a really hot stimulus excites both cold and heat receptors.

Here's an experiment you can try. Place one hand in a bucket of cold water and the other hand in a bucket of warm water. In a little while you will be aware that the feeling of warmth or cold comes only from the area where the hand meets both water and air. Now, put both hands in a third bucket filled with lukewarm water. This water will feel warm to the hand that was in cold water and cold to the hand that was in warm water. The sensation from the hand depends on the temperature to which the skin was previously adapted.

A third type of receptor in the skin is the *pain* receptor. Psychologists are still debating whether pain is a separate sense with its own nerve structures or whether it results from a pattern of intense stimulation to any of a number of receptors. Pain seems to be received by a variety of nerve endings—not only in the skin but in other organs as well; very bright lights, loud noises, high or low temperatures, or great pressures all yield pain sensations.

Pain serves to warn us of tissue destruction. However, most internal organs of the body do not have sense receptors for pain and are unable to inform us when they are in trouble.

How do we experience pain? According to the *specificity theory* there are specific pain receptors that relay signals of pain to the spinal cord, and from there to the brain. A person should therefore feel pain exactly where the stimulation occurs, and the amount of pain felt should depend on the amount of stimulation at the pain site. But this theory does not account for the phenomenon of *acupuncture,* in which the insertion of needles into various sites on the body surface sometimes relieves pain in body regions quite distant from the needle site. Ronald Melzack and Patrick Wall came up with a new theory of pain that would account for the effects of acupuncture (Melzack, 1973). They propose that the transmission of pain signals depends on *gate-control mechanisms,* which permit or block the transmission of pain signals to the central nervous system. Stimulation of certain areas will open the gate to allow pain signals to pass; stimulation of other areas will close the gate, so that pain signals from any part of the body cannot reach the pain reception areas of the brain. In the case of acupuncture, Melzack and Wall believe, the needles themselves are inserted at the sites that activate the reticular formation of the brain stem—one of the gate-control areas of the nervous system. As a result, pain signals are blocked before they reach the brain, and no pain is perceived.

Using only your notes, *not* the text, write brief answers to the following questions.

1. The sense of touch is made up of 3 different sensations:

_____, _____,

and _____.

2. Name 4 body areas very sensitive to pressure.

a. _____

b. _____

c. _____

d. _____

3. Because of the higher number of receptors, the body is more sensitive to

_____ (heat/cold).

4. Two examples of pain-inducing stimuli are:

a. _____ and **b.** _____

5. What function does pain have?

_____

6. Why don't we feel pain when some of our internal organs are infected?

_____

7. What phenomenon is not taken into account in the "specificity theory"?

_____

_____

8. Look carefully at the following diagram.

a. According to the "gate-control theory" of Melzack and Wall, which stimulus, A or B, will cause pain? Why?

A ⟶ G | CNS

B ⟶

b. Name G in the diagram and state one area in the body where it is located.

In small groups, compare and discuss your answers. Resolve any differences by referring to the text.

"FRONTIERS OF PAIN CONTROL"

Do this activity in groups of 5, if possible. Read your instructions carefully. You have one hour to complete steps 1 to 5.

1. Read the introductory paragraph in order to discover the focus of the article.
2. Divide the treatments equally among the group members.
3. Read your section, highlighting or underlining the following information for each treatment:

   a. A brief description of the method or treatment
   b. How it works
   c. What kinds of pain it has been used to treat
   d. Successes
   e. Disadvantages

   (Note: Not all information may be available for each treatment.)

4. Put the required information in the appropriate spaces on the table on page 32.
5. After you have finished, share your information (ORALLY) with the other members, so that everyone has as complete a table as possible.

Frontiers of Pain Control

One of the greatest human miseries is chronic pain—continuing, often severe pain caused by such maladies as lower-back problems (slipped or ruptured disks), arthritis, and cancer. The pain is sometimes so great that it is incapacitating, and physicians are often at a loss in treating it effectively. In recent years, however, researchers have been developing some revolutionary treatments for chronic pain. Although most of these treatments are still in experimental stages, they hold great promise for success.

Acupuncture

Really an old rather than a new treatment, *acupuncture* was developed centuries ago in China. In this method, needles are inserted at specific points on the body's surface in order to relieve pain in other parts of the body. Indeed, Chinese physicians regularly use acupuncture as the only form of anesthesia (painkiller) in major operations. As noted in the text, Melzack (1973) believes that acupuncture works by closing off the "gates" that allow pain signals to pass from the afflicted area of the body to the brain. Recent studies have suggested that acupuncture may also stimulate the production of enkephalins or endorphins, newly discovered chemicals that are thought to be transmitter substances in the brain and spinal cord. It is now believed that several other painkilling techniques, such as electrical stimulation, may also work by causing the release of these chemicals in the brain and spinal cord (Iversen, 1979).

Electrical Stimulation

Another approach to the control of chronic pain is the implantation of an electrical stimulator in the patient's back, just above the point at which nerves from the body part experiencing pain enter the spinal column. When the patient feels a stab of pain, he holds a tiny antenna over the stimulator. This produces a volley of electrical signals that can counteract the pain signals (Wang, 1977). In an even more dramatic procedure, a stimulator is implanted in a portion of the patient's brain stem, and he can then use self-stimulation for pain relief. In recent studies, this technique has relieved pain in the majority of patients being tested. (Arehart-Treichel, 1978).

Hypnosis

Not everyone can be hypnotized, but for those who can be, hypnosis can sometimes provide dramatic pain relief. Major surgery, including leg amputations, has even been done under hypnosis. More commonly, hypnosis has been used in childbirth and in dentistry, both cases in which the patient's fear and anxiety concerning the procedure can be a major contributor to the pain she suffers. Even severe chronic pain will sometimes respond to hypnosis (Goleman, 1977).

CAN HYPNOSIS REDUCE PAIN?

There is no question that some people can free themselves from even severe pain through hypnosis. Dental patients, burn victims, women in childbirth, and terminal cancer patients have all been relieved of pain through hypnosis (Hilgard and Hilgard, 1975). One method of studying pain in the laboratory uses the *cold pressor response,* which is the pain experienced when the hand and forearm are placed in circulating ice water. The pain is quite severe for most people and increases very rapidly over 30 to 45 seconds. But hypnotized subjects placed in this situation and given suggestions to the effect that the experience is not painful report very little pain. Instead they may describe what they feel as "a slight tingle" or "like a cold wind blowing on my arm."

While subjects in this situation report very little pain, physiological measures such as heart rate and blood pressure are extremely

high. Ernest Hilgard (1977) views this phenomenon as a *dissociation,* or separation between different aspects of consciousness. Hilgard considers pain to be a complex state with at least two separable components: the sensory aspect (such as the sensation of extreme cold) and the emotional aspect (the feeling of suffering that commonly accompanies the sensation). Hilgard concludes that the hypnotic suggestion primarily affects the emotional component and not the sensory component. This type of dissociation is very different from the mechanism of pain reduction found with certain pain-reducing drugs. The drugs appear to act by blocking the transmission of pain signals to the brain, especially to the areas that control thought and emotion. Hypnosis apparently does not cause this sort of blocking. Instead, the pain information does reach the brain but the emotions that are produced are kept from conscious awareness.

Drugs

Narcotic drugs, such as morphine, have long been used as painkillers. But patients develop increasing tolerance for these drugs, which means that larger and larger doses are needed to be effective. In addition, narcotics are highly addictive and in rare instances can be lethal. Scientists have continually been trying to develop drugs that will relieve pain more safely. So far these efforts have not been notably successful. For example, heroin was introduced by a German drug company in the 1890s as a "nonaddictive" form of morphine. But it soon proved to be even more addictive than the drug it was designed to replace. More recently developed drugs, such as methadone, have also given rise to disappointment.

Pharmacologists are now testing several new synthetic drugs of a class called antagonist-analgesic opiates. (Two of them, butorphanol and nalbuphine, have been approved by the Food and Drug Administration and are available to physicians in injectable form.)

These drugs have as much painkilling power as morphine but are safer and much less addictive. Nevertheless, large doses have been found to cause psychological disturbances in some patients, and researchers are keeping their fingers crossed (Tucker, 1979). Other researchers are trying to develop synthetic forms of enkephalins and endorphins that could be administered to patients. Because these chemicals occur naturally in the brain—in fact, *endorphin* means "the brain's own morphine"—they should not be dangerous or addictive. For most everyday purposes, the most effective painkiller remains aspirin, which has one of the best ratios of benefits to harmful effects. Unfortunately, for severe pain aspirin isn't enough.

Placebos

Sometimes patients suffering from severe pain can be helped by "drugs" that aren't really drugs at all but rather sugar pills that contain no active chemical agents. The surprising effectiveness of placebos testifies to the psychological aspects of pain: if the person *believes* the treatment will work, it just might. But recent research suggests that placebos, too, may work by altering brain chemistry. In one study, volunteer dental patients—mostly college students—were given only placebos to relieve pain following tooth extractions. For some patients, the placebos worked. But for these individuals, the administration of maloxone, a chemical that is known to block the effects of enkephalins and endorphins, worsened the pain. This result clearly suggests that the placebo worked by stimulating release of the brain's own painkillers (Fields, 1978).

A question of tremendous interest to scientists and pain-sufferers alike is whether people can learn to activate the brain's pain-suppressing systems voluntarily, thereby bringing the powers of the mind to bear on the sometimes painful workings of the brain.

Treatment	Brief Description of the Method	How It Works	Kinds of Pain Used for	Successes	Disadvantages
ACUPUNCTURE					
ELECTRICAL STIMULATION					
HYPNOSIS					
DRUGS					
PLACEBOS					

"THE MIND CAN BE TRAINED TO CONTROL ACHES AND PAINS"

Read the questions below. Then read the following article, ignoring any information that is not required by the questions. Finally, answer the questions in the spaces provided.

1. Diagram a chain reaction illustrating how losing a dime in a phone booth can kill you.

2. In this article, the author proposes both causes of and remedies for the aches and pains listed below. For each ailment, fill in the chart with the necessary information.

Ailment	Cause	Treatment
A PULSATING HEADACHE		
SIMPLE HEADACHE AND BACKACHE		
CHRONIC PAIN		

BIOFEEDBACK

The mind can be trained to control aches and pains

VANCOUVER (CP)—Almost half Canada's adult population will use a drug this year to relieve pains that could be relieved by using their bodies' own pain-killing system, says Dr. Kenford Nedd.

A few specific techniques, involving both the mental and physiological processes of the body, could eliminate many chronic aches and relieve a large amount of the pain that accompanies a pulled muscle or serious operation, says Nedd, a Vancouver physician.

What must be learned is a way to send the blood rushing to the extremities, how to recognize a pulsating heartbeat in the fingertips, and how to stop tensing muscles, he explains.

Many forms of pain are caused by tension that comes from small irritations such as losing a dime in a pay telephone or waiting in line.

The stress causes a reaction in the body which raises blood pressure, and speeds up the heart beat as well as the ventricular ectopic beat which causes the heart to beat out of phase with normal impulses. That reaction is a significant cause of death, says Nedd.

There is a physical reaction to mental stress, causing certain hormones to be produced which in turn cause physiological arousal of the body's internal organs, he says.

This wears out the person's natural protection and sets him up for several stress-related disorders.

"Every time we come across one of these situations, our body responds in a negative way and we don't even realize it.

"Like being stuck in a traffic jam. We tend to pull on the muscles of the neck, temple, jaw and forehead which are all connected to the aponeurosis (tendons) of the skull.

"The muscles are held so tightly that they prohibit the flow of blood to the brain, bringing on a pulsating headache."

Nedd explains several responses that result in a form of chronic pain.

The most common is bracing, which can be as subtle as a wrinkled brow or as intense as strained leg muscles. The worst damage is done when only one set of muscles is tensed.

To reverse this response, Nedd says, a patient is taught a six-second mental check to determine which muscles are tensed. With practice the relaxation process becomes automatic.

Another contributor to simple pains of headaches and aching backs is poor breathing. Deep, even breathing is the cure.

Tenseness also creates poor circulation to the hands and feet. By concentrating, a patient can be trained to open up the veins and pump blood to the extremities, Nedd says.

North Americans live in a state of general hyper arousal, waiting for the worst to happen, Nedd said.

"We never try to adjust an environment, like telling a person to slow down his pace, because people like to be busy. We just teach them to avoid making the mistake of allowing their heart beats to speed up with their jobs."

Preparing for a Take-Home Exam

During the next section of this chapter, you will prepare to write an essay question for a take-home exam.

In an essay of approximately $1\frac{1}{2}$ to 2 pages, examine the relationship between stress and pain. Your essay should address the following areas:

a. Stress as the cause of certain kinds of pain
b. Pain control through relaxation techniques and stress management

This task will allow you to review the writing process, this time applied to a much longer text. To help you do this, your teacher will share the task with you. Your teacher will write the first part of the essay, and you, the second part.

You and your teacher will complete the task following a series of steps. For each of the seven steps, the teacher will first do his or her part. Then you'll do yours.

1. Reread the question on page 34.
   a. What is the general topic?
   b. What two areas will you need to focus on?
   c. What is the professor really asking for in each area?
      • What thesis will your teacher have to prove in the first part?
      • What thesis will you have to prove in the second part?
   d. What subsections will there be within those areas?
2. Go over your notes and readings. Highlight all the relevant information. Using a separate sheet for each subsection, take point form notes.

For steps 3 to 6, your teacher will do his or her part. Then you'll do yours.

3. a. Your teacher will begin organizing his or her information, stating the main point in one sentence.
   b. Now you should start organizing your information. State the main point for each subsection in one sentence.
4. a. Your teacher will look at the information collected on the main point and decide which ideas are closely related. He or she will decide how this information will be sequenced.
   b. Now look at the information you collected. Decide which ideas are closely related, and how you will sequence them.
5. a. Your teacher will draw a tree diagram for his or her part, showing

   the information
   the sequencing
   the relationships among the ideas (how the ideas are related)

   b. Now draw a tree diagram for your part, showing

   the information
   the sequencing
   the relationships among the ideas (how the ideas are related)

6. a. Your teacher will tell the entire class about his or her part of the essay, using the sketch. This activity will help your teacher clarify the ideas. The class will make sure that the information is correct and easy to follow. Discuss any changes that need to be made in the tree. Then your teacher will revise the sketch.

b. Now work with a partner. Show your partner your sketch and say what you'll include in your part of the essay. Discuss anything that needs to be deleted or clarified, any definitions, examples, or details that need to be added. Then revise your sketch.

Writing a Take-Home Exam

Before the next class, write the first draft of your part of the exam questions. Bring it to the next class.

Now you need to combine the two parts of the essay into a coherent answer.

1. First read your teacher's part of the essay. Consider the following:
   a. Information:
   - Is the thesis the one required for the question?
   - Is there enough information to prove the thesis?
   b. Organization:
   - Can you see the organizational principle?
   - By skimming, can you get the main idea?
   - Does this sequencing help you follow these ideas more easily?

   Discuss any problems. Your teacher will revise as necessary.
2. Reread your part. Consider the same questions you did for your teacher's part. Make any revisions you want.
3. Now you need to combine the two separate parts, using what your teacher has written and what you've written. This involves writing a transition statement, as well as an inform-and-focus section.

   Read the first part of your section. How can you help your professor see that you have switched from the first to the second half of the essay? Write the transition.
4. With your teacher, develop an inform-and-focus section that announces your topic in general and then focuses the reader's attention on the 2 areas you will deal with in the essay.

Causality

The essay question requires that you be able to express causal relationships clearly. This section will help you to do this.

Causal relationships are involved in the analysis of a problem as well as in predicting the outcome of a particular set of circumstances. The certainty of any causal relationship depends on two things: how much proof there is to support it and the person's attitude toward it. For example, some psychologists might consider violence in young people as the direct result of the amount of violence on TV; others might postulate a very weak or nonexistent relationship between the two.

There are many ways in English to express causal relationships, most of which you have already met in the texts of this chapter. The purpose of the following exercises is to help you systematically review these structures and expressions.

Conjunctions

1. In each of the sentences below, put a single line under the cause, a double line under the effect.

   a. Because these chemicals occur naturally in the brain, they should not be dangerous or addictive.

   b. In the case of acupuncture . . . the needles themselves are inserted at the sites that activate the reticular formation of the brain stem . . . As a result, pain signals are blocked before they reach the brain.

2. Which conjunction precedes the cause? What other conjunctions behave in this way?

3. Which conjunction precedes the effect? What other conjunctions do you know that behave in this way?

so . . . that

1. Again, in the sentences below, underline the causes and effects as you did before.

   a. The pain is sometimes so great that it is incapacitating.

   b. The muscles are held so tightly that they prohibit the flow of blood to the brain.

2. What similarity in structure is evident in these two sentences?

3. What 2 kinds of words may come between "so" and "that"?

4. Why do you think the author chose to use this particular structure?

5. Using the "so $\begin{Bmatrix} \text{adjective} \\ \text{adverb} \end{Bmatrix}$ that" structures, write sentences combining the ideas below to show the causal relationship.

   a. The heart attack was very severe ⟶ she had to stay in hospital for six weeks

   b. He tensed his neck very strongly ⟶ he developed a blinding headache

Causal Verbs

1. For each sentence below, state the cause and effect.

   a. The stress causes a reaction in the body.

   b. Many forms of pain are caused by tension that comes from small irritations.

   c. Several responses result in the form of chronic pain.

   d. This tiny antenna produces a volley of electrical signals.

   e. The stress raises blood pressure and speeds up the heartbeat.

   f. This wears out the person's natural protection and sets him up for several stress-related disorders.

2. In the articles you have read, find three other examples of verbs that indicate causal relationships. Write the sentences in the following space.

   a.

   b.

   c.

3. In small groups, discuss your answers.

Draw a diagram illustrating the information given in the following sentence:

There is a physical reaction to mental stress, causing certain hormones to be produced which in turn cause physiological arousal of the body's internal organs.

Using a different verb each time, write sentences of cause and effect for each of the following diagrams.

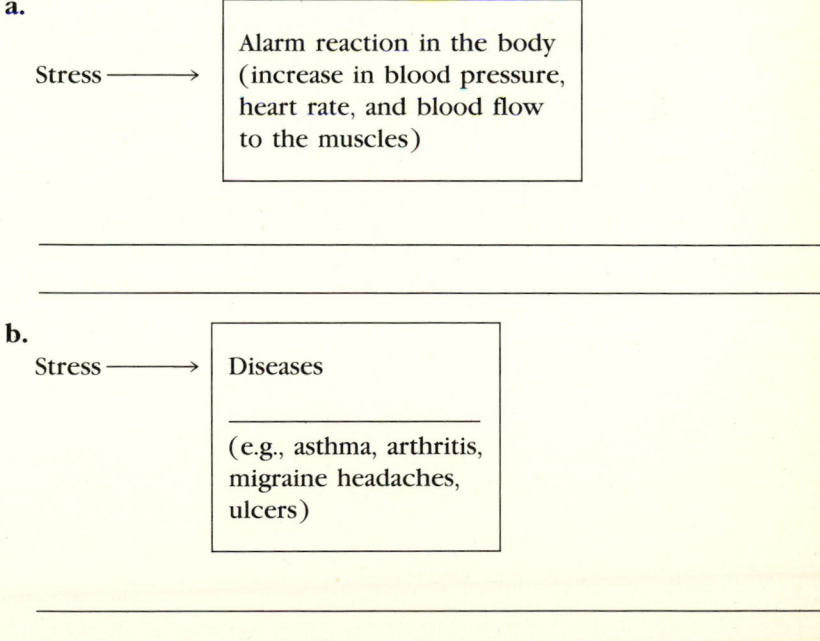

a.

Stress ⟶ Alarm reaction in the body (increase in blood pressure, heart rate, and blood flow to the muscles)

_____

_____

b.

Stress ⟶ Diseases

_____

(e.g., asthma, arthritis, migraine headaches, ulcers)

_____

_____

c.

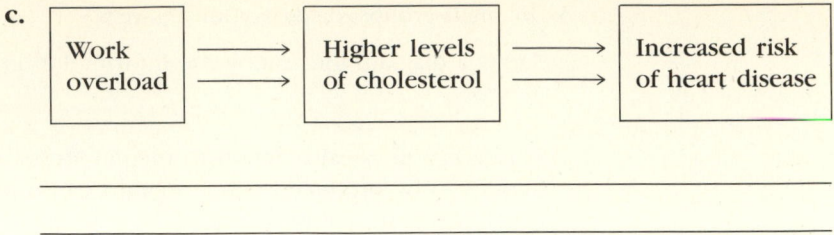

_____

_____

Conditionals

Statements of condition are frequently used to express causal relationships.

The verb in the effect clause indicates the strength of the causal relationship as determined by the evidence supporting it as well as the writer's attitude toward it.

1. If you unbend a paper clip and probe an area of your skin lightly, you will feel pressure at certain points.
2. If you do the same thing with a cold wire, you will feel cold at other specific points.
3. If you probe your skin with a warm wire, you will feel warmth at still other points.

    a. For each sentence above, find the following:
      (1) The _condition_ that will produce a particular effect
      (2) The _effect_ that will be produced by that condition
    b. In each _condition, underline_ the _if_ and the _verb._
    c. In each result or effect, circle the complete verb.
    d. How certain is the author that each condition will produce that particular effect? How do you know?

Notice the difference in certainty between the earlier sentences and the ones that follow:

1. If you probe some areas of your arms and legs, you might not experience pressure.
2. If you put a cold wire on your body trunk, you could feel warmth.

In each of the following pairs of ideas, you will find one condition and one result. Reread the section "The Skin Senses" to find out how definite the connection is between the two. Then, combine the ideas into one conditional sentence, using an appropriate modal—will, may, might, could.

CONDITION	RESULT
1. If (you touch something hotter than your skin)	it (seems) warm.
2. If (you touch something very hot)	you (excite) both cold and heat receptors.
3. If (hairs on the body are slightly moved)	you (experience) pressure.
4. According to the specificity theory, if (you stimulate point x)	you (feel) pain at that point.
5. According to Melzack and Wall, if (you stimulate certain areas of the body)	pain signals (reach) the brain.

Writing the Final Draft

Now that we have reviewed how to express causal relationships, you are ready to write your final draft. Include the inform-and-focus section as well as the transition sections. After you write a section, read each sentence out loud. Listen to make sure each idea is clear. Pay particular attention to causal structures.

Hand in the essay.

3 DREAMING

CHAPTER CONTENTS:

In this chapter you will read about why people dream. You will review some of the current research being done on sleep and dreams.

The major reading in this chapter is from a first-year university psychology text. This is, of course, the type of text you'll use when you begin academic courses. The activities that go with this text will show you how to read quickly and efficiently using textual clues, such as headings and subheadings.

The writing task in this chapter is a short-answer exam question. Professors expect students to give concise but complete answers to such questions. You'll first be taught how to select and organize information in order to write summaries and then how to use these summaries in order to answer short exam questions.

THINKING ABOUT THE TOPIC

Sleep and Dream Survey

Briefly answer the following questions.

1. As a rule, how frequently do you dream?

2. How often do you wake up in the middle of a dream?

3. How frequently do your dreams affect your behavior the following day?

4. Are your dreams usually pleasant or unpleasant?

5. Are your dreams ever in color?

6. Do you have a dream that recurs? If yes, what is the subject of your dream?

7. Do you ever have nightmares?

8. Have you ever tried to analyze your dreams?

9. Have you ever dreamed about something that has been bothering you?

10. Have you ever gained any insight into a problem through dreaming? If so, what?

In small groups, compare and discuss your answers.

"THE INTERPRETATION OF DREAMS"

Good writers help their readers by signaling in various ways both the information coming up in the text and its organization. Good readers actively use these signals to help themselves grasp the main ideas.

In Chapter 1, you practiced using focus statements, headings, and subheadings. In this chapter, you'll practice another reading strategy—skimming certain paragraphs and sentences to find main ideas. This will help you focus on the important information.

You'll also see how writers use *italics* to signal important terms you should know.

1. Beside 1. in the following outline, write the main heading for the section of the text, "Dreaming," which begins on page 45.
2. Quickly flip through pages 45–47 of the text. Beside A, B, and C in the outline, write the three subheadings you find in boldface.

I. _____

   A. _____

   B. _____

   C. _____

3. Skim the introduction to find the two statements that announce what the text is about. Does this information agree with the three headings?

Now you have a general idea of both the kind of information you will find in this section and how it's organized. The next step is to look for the main ideas.

Looking for the Main Ideas

Writers often use certain places in the text to signal topic and organization. The first paragraph of a text and the first sentence of a paragraph frequently announce the thesis, the main point that the paragraph will develop. The last paragraph in a text and the last sentence in a paragraph frequently summarize or criticize what has gone before.

Reading these parts first prepares you to read text more efficiently.

Read the first and last paragraph in the text, then the first and last sentence of each of the intervening paragraphs. As you read, note the thesis of each paragraph in the margin.

Now read the text, underlining or highlighting important information. Pay attention to any terms in italics; the authors chose to emphasize them for a reason.

After you have finished reading, turn to pages 48 and 49 to check the main ideas.

Dreaming

(1) *I have a key that opens a closed drugstore. I go in as if I'm looking for something. I am a sweet, young, responsible girl, like Teresa Wright in* Shadow of a Doubt. *I also have a key to the beauty parlor next door. I go in in order to leave something (a comb and mirror?) in the window. I come back to the drugstore when it is open and decide to have a dessert. I inquire about a letter I sent to myself at this address but it hasn't arrived. I finally find it on a counter—this is what I have been looking for in the drugstore—and I leave. Next I am playing hopscotch with some little girls as it grows dark. Police come and arrest me. They ask me why I killed the little girl (some days earlier, I assume). I say it was because she was very unhappy. They take me away.*

(2) This account, taken from one woman's "dream diary," emphasizes the fact that in dreams we do things that we cannot do in real life. We fly, we change identities, we even kill people. Through most of the world's history, humans have regarded dreams as magical states, as ways of exchanging one's worldly identity and limitations for new selves and new capacities, and as messengers of divine instructions and prophecies. In many cultures people who were thought to have the ability to interpret dreams were likely to be highly respected leaders. Today we are still fascinated by dreams and their meanings. One approach, the interpretation of dreams and their symbols, was given new impetus by Sigmund Freud, who saw dreams as the "royal road to the unconscious." More recently, systematic studies are exploring the physiological bases of dreaming, as well as its contribution to our emotional well-being.

The Interpretation of Dreams

(3) Sigmund Freud came into prominence with the publication of *The Interpretation of Dreams* in 1900. In this work, Freud stated dreams represent the fulfillment of unconscious impulses, unacceptable on a conscious level. He also thought that dreams function to preserve sleep by disguising these wishes and impulses through the use of symbolism, condensation, and displacement.

(4) By *symbolism* Freud meant that unacceptable ideas are presented in a more acceptable—symbolic—form in dreams. Freud focused primarily on sexual symbols, suggesting that sharp, elongated objects (umbrellas, swords, sticks) were symbols of the penis and that containers (cups, boxes, houses) were symbols of the vagina. By *condensation* Freud meant that one image in a dream could represent several elements in a person's life. For example, a dream about scoring a touchdown in a football game may bring together a man's feelings about competition, fame, and sexual accomplishment. By *displacement* Freud meant that events in a dream could focus unacceptable wishes on an object or thing different from the real object of the wishes. For instance, dreaming of hitting a tiger with a baseball bat might represent a displaced wish to harm an authority figure in one's life.

(5) While we sleep, Freud believed, our repressed wishes—especially sexual desires—thrust to the surface and are fulfilled. Disguising these impulses is necessary so that the guilt associated with the disturbing impulse will not perturb the sleeper. If the meaning of the dream were to become known to the

45

dreamer—if a woman actually dreamed of having sexual relations with her father, for instance—she might awaken in order to get rid of such unacceptable thoughts.

(6) Freud distinguished two types of content in dreams: the latent content and the manifest content. The *latent* content is the underlying meaning of the dream. The *manifest* content is the disguised form of the dream that we remember when we wake up. For example, a woman may dream that she is playing a carnival game where she tosses a ring onto a bottle and wins a giant teddy bear. That is the manifest content of the dream. The latent content may be that she wishes she could conceive and have a baby.

(7) Freud's specific approach to the interpretation of dreams can be—and has been—criticized. Because sexual impulses play a central role in Freud's theory of personality, Freud almost always found sexual desires in the latent content of dreams. Other dream theorists do not give sex such important status in their interpretations. In addition, Freud's approach was based on analyzing the dreams of his patients, and he concentrated on those dreams that could be interpreted meaningfully in his framework. Today, most dream analysts feel that dreams can have a much wider range of meanings and functions than Freud believed. Calvin Hall (1966), a leading dream researcher, suggests that we view a dream as "a personal document, a letter to oneself." Hall has also pointed out that gathering and interpreting a series of dreams—looking at the common themes that run through them—can be more helpful than focusing on a single dream.

Where Do Dreams Come From?

(8) People in some cultures have believed that dreams come from the travel of the soul outside the body. Freud believed that dreams originate in unconscious wishes. But recent research provides a different perspective: the idea that dreams originate in the activity of different portions of the brain during REM sleep. According to the *activation-synthesis model* of dreams recently put forth by Allan Hobson and Robert McCarley (1977), the dream process begins with the periodic firing of nerve cells known as *giant cells* in the brain stem. This firing leads to the rapid eye movements and brain waves characteristic of REM sleep, and it also leads to high levels of *activation* in other areas of the brain, including those areas concerned with sensation (especially vision), motor activity, and emotion. At the same time, this neural firing greatly reduces the tone of the major muscles of the body, such as in the arms and legs, producing a kind of paralysis.

(9) During a dream, of course, the activation of sensory areas of the brain does not correspond to actual events, as it does when we are awake. And the inhibition of muscles during REM sleep prevents the actual acting out of motor impulses. Instead, we *synthesize* a dream mentally, coming up with content that corresponds to the pattern of brain activation. For example, stimulation of brain centers for vision, as well as feedback from rapid eye movements, may lead to the rapidly shifting scenes that are characteristic of dreams; stimulation of the brain centers of the vestibular senses (sense of balance) may lead to sensations of spinning or floating. According to the activation-synthesis model, it is the unusual intensity and rapidity of the brain stimulation, often activating simultaneously areas of the brain that are unlikely to be activated simultaneously when we are awake, that accounts for the highly changeable and sometimes bizarre content of our dreams.

(10) Although the Hobson-McCarley model helps to link physiological events with the events of dreams, it raises more questions than it answers about the content of dreams. What leads a person to synthesize a dream that includes specific persons and incidents? Our

memories, emotions, and personality styles, as well as the previous day's events are all likely to play a prominent role. In the dream quoted at the beginning of this section, for instance, the woman might have seen Hitchcock's *Shadow of a Doubt* on the day before she had the dream or she may have gone to the drugstore. Dreams may still serve as wish-fulfillments, as Freud believed, even as they correspond to patterns of physiological activation.

The Functions of Dreaming

(11) The need to dream appears to be as basic as the need to sleep. Young adults dream about two hours a night on the average—whether or not the dreams are remembered. In one experiment, people were awakened for five consecutive nights just as the periods of REM sleep began (Dement, 1960), so they were prevented from dreaming. These dream-deprived individuals became anxious, irritable, and angry; they had difficulty concentrating, and some began to hallucinate. Moreover, as subjects were deprived of REM sleep their need for it seemed to build. When they went back to sleep, they entered REM sleep more often. And for as many as five nights following REM deprivation, the subjects spent more time in REM sleep than usual—sometimes as much as double the normal amount.

(12) Why do we have such a strong need to dream? Freud believed, as we have seen, that dreams provide for the expression of repressed impulses, albeit in disguised form. Carl Jung (1964) took another view of the function of dreams. He argued that dreams compensate for things that we lack when we are awake and thus serve to restore our overall psychological balance. Wish-fulfillment may sometimes be a part of this balancing mechanism. If a woman has a strong desire to punch her boss in the nose but can't actually do it in her waking life, she can do it in her dreams. In other cases, Jung believed, dreams can bring us messages from our unconscious minds, including warnings of personal weakness.

(13) Recent research has begun to document the ways dreams can help people deal with problems in their waking lives. Rosalind Cartwright (1978) has found that people seem to handle emotional situations more realistically after dreaming. In one study, she presented students with incomplete "problem stories" before bedtime in a sleep laboratory. The stories dealt with common concerns of young adults, such as separation from home. The subjects then went to sleep. Some were allowed to dream (they were awakened only during non-REM sleep), while others were not (they were awakened only during REM sleep or were not allowed to sleep at all). In the morning, when asked about possible solutions to the problem posed in a story, the subjects who had been allowed to dream were better able to acknowledge the realistic dimensions of the problem. The results of this and other studies have led Cartwright to propose that dreams provide "a kind of workshop for the repair of self-esteem and competence."

(14) In a book called *Creative Dreaming* (1974), Patricia Garfield suggests that we can train ourselves to dream about specific issues that are troubling us. Such methods have apparently been used for generations by the Temiar, a Malaysian people who teach their children to report their dreams each morning, to control the frightening ones, and to take their dreams into account in their waking lives. There is no solid evidence to date that people in the Western world can, in fact, control their dreams, at least in experimental situations in a sleep laboratory. Nevertheless, if further research bears out current speculation about the functions of dreams, such attempts to "take our dreams in hand" may benefit many people.

This activity will help you measure your ability to select and understand the main ideas. Most of the questions ask you to choose summaries or paraphrases. One of the questions will test your ability to rephrase or summarize.

"The Interpretation of Dreams"

1. Check the statement that best summarizes the main ideas in the first four paragraphs.

    _____ **a.** Freud believed that the unacceptable desires found in dreams, especially the sexual ones, might interfere with sleep.

    _____ **b.** According to Freud, dreams are a form of wish-fulfillment in which the unacceptable content is disguised so that the sleeper can continue sleeping.

    _____ **c.** Freud believed that dreams are an attempt to fulfill our unacceptable desires, especially sexual ones, through the disguises of symbolism, condensation, and displacement in order to preserve sleep.

    _____ **d.** Symbolism, condensation, and displacement are the processes by which unacceptable, unconscious desires are disguised in order to preserve sleep.

2. Match the process to the explanation by writing the correct letter in the blank.

    PROCESS

    a. Symbolism

    b. Condensation

    c. Displacement

    EXPLANATION

    _____ Combining several aspects of your life into one

    _____ Using a harmless object to represent a threatening one

    _____ Directing an unacceptable impulse against someone or something other than the actual object of the hostility

3. Fill in the blanks with words that could summarize the criticisms leveled against Freud. Choose from the list provided.

a. too _____
b. too _____

violent
sexual
morbid
simplistic
narrow
personal
broad

"Where Do Dreams Come From?"

4. Fill in the blanks with words that best complete the following passage. Choose from the following list.

activation	nerve cells	process
simultaneously	inhibition	brain stem
giant cells	sporadically	content
activity	sensitivity	frequently

Unlike Freud and people from other cultures, Hobson and McCarley (1977) suggest that dreams originate in the _____ area, with the periodic firing of the _____ there. In their model, dream _____ is synthesized mentally according to the pattern of increased _____ occurring _____ in such areas of the brain as those involving sensation, motor activity, and emotions.

"The Functions of Dreaming"

5. For the researchers listed below, summarize in a few words their conclusions about dreaming.

Dement _____

_____

Cartwright _____

_____

Either in small groups or with your teacher, compare and discuss your answers and then resolve any differences.

Assertions

The text you have just read contains many assertions; that is, positive statements of observations, findings, opinions, or beliefs. In order to complete the writing task in this chapter, you will need to report on the theories and research of the people discussed in the readings. This exercise will help you discover how to write assertions.

1. Read the assertions reported below. Then fill in the blank with the appropriate source or authority.

   a. _____ stated that dreams allow us to fulfill our unacceptable, unconscious desires.

   b. _____ suggests that a dream should be viewed as "a personal letter to oneself."

   c. _____ feel that Freud's dream interpretation theory was too narrow.

   d. _____ have proposed that dreams originate in the brain stem.

   e. _____ believed that cups, umbrellas, and sticks were sexual symbols.

   What similarity in form exists in all these assertions?

2. In the text, find 3 other examples of assertions that take this form. Write them on the following lines.

   a. _____

   _____

   _____

   b. _____

   _____

   _____

   c. _____

   _____

   _____

3. List all the verbs of assertion that you have found. The list has been begun for you. Use the *unmarked* (simple) form of the verb.

state
find
think

Which verbs are particularly weak?

Which verbs are particularly strong?

4. Another way to report assertions is to use the introductory phrase "According to X . . . ," where X is the source or authority. Find the examples of this form in paragraphs 8 and 9. Write them on the following lines.

Paragraph 8: _____

_____

_____

Paragraph 9: _____

_____

_____

5. Write complete sentences reporting the following assertions. Be sure to cite the authority. Do 2 with verbs of assertion, 2 with "According to . . . ."

* Unacceptable sexual desires are disguised by the processes of symbolism, condensation, and displacement.
* Dreams make up for things we don't have in real life.
* Dreams help people cope better with everyday problems.
* Dreams are the key to the unconscious.

a. _____

_____

_____

b. _____

_____

_____

c. _____

_____

_____

d. _____

_____

_____

Coherence

One important quality in good writing is coherence, the smooth flow of ideas from one sentence, paragraph, or section to the next. Good writers use several strategies to help readers follow their ideas easily. Let's look at two of these strategies:

1. Parallel structure
2. The logical sequencing of old and new information

Parallel Structure

Parallel structure, the arrangement of similar ideas in similar forms, is really a disguised list. The punctuation shows the reader at a glance how many items are in the list.

Answer these questions, quoting the entire sentence from the text.

1. Give 3 examples of things we do in dreams that we do not do in real life.

_____

_____

2. Over the centuries, how have people viewed dreams?

_____

_____

_____

3. How do dreams help us to keep sleeping?

_____

_____

_____

Now examine the sentences for:

1. parallel forms
2. how the forms help the reader organize and remember the information
3. economy of expression

Using parallel structure, combine each group of ideas below into one economical, emphatic sentence.

1. **a.** Dreams can be affected by our memories.
   b. Dreams can also be shaped by our personalities.
   c. Emotions can influence dream content.
2. **a.** Dreams can tell us about our unconscious desires.
   b. From dreams we can learn about the functioning of our brains.
   c. Dreams can provide insight regarding our day-to-day troubles.
3. **a.** People who are deprived of dreaming become anxious.
   b. Dream deprivation can also cause us to become grouchy.
   c. Depriving people of an opportunity to dream can cause hostility.

In pairs or small groups, compare and discuss your answers.

The Logical Sequencing of Old and New Information

Another way to guide the reader easily through your ideas is to order the information so that it moves from the old to the new, from the known to the unknown.

Reread the introductory paragraph of "Dreaming."

Now read the following statements, a and b.

a. In dreams we do things we cannot do in real life. We fly, we change identities, we even kill people. This fact is emphasized in the account above, taken from one woman's dream diary.

b. This account, taken from one woman's dream diary, emphasizes the fact that in dreams we do things we cannot do in real life. We fly, we change identities, we even kill people.

Now answer the following questions.

1. Which version do you prefer as the logical follow-up to paragraph 1? Why?

2. Which one did the author use? How does the author's choice help the reader proceed from one idea to the next?

3. Using the logical sequencing of events in the following passage, insert the sentence (a, b, or c) you feel best fits in the blank.

During the nineteenth century, a scientific approach to the dream became evident. _____

_____

_____. These socially repressed impulses were assumed to rest in the unconscious.

a. There was a developing conviction that the material expressed in dreams often dealt with unacceptable impulses, and that the dream would provide important insights into the dreamer's personality.

b. Dreams could provide insights into the dreamer's personality, and the material expressed often dealt with unacceptable impulses. This, at any rate, was the conviction that was developing.

c. There was a developing conviction that dreams would provide important insights into the dreamer's personality, and that the material expressed often dealt with unacceptable instincts.

In pairs or small groups compare and discuss your answers.

Summaries

A summary contains the essential information from a text. It is helpful to write summaries for two reasons:

1. A summary can be read much more quickly than a textbook passage or an article.

2. Writing a summary is a good way to check your reading comprehension. You have to understand what you've read in order to write a good summary.

When writing a summary, you will want to include only important information. This means eliminating detail such as examples or lengthy explanations.

Reread this paragraph from "Dreaming."

Recent research has begun to document the ways dreams can help people deal with problems in their waking lives. Rosalind Cartwright (1978) has found that people seem to handle emotional situations more realistically after dreaming. In one study, she presented students with incomplete "problem stories" before bedtime in a sleep laboratory. The stories dealt with common concerns of young adults, such as separation from home. The subjects then went to sleep. Some were allowed to dream (they were awakened only during non-REM sleep), while others were not (they were awakened only during REM sleep or were not allowed to sleep at all). In the morning, when asked about possible solutions to the problem posed in a story, the subjects who had been allowed to dream were better able to acknowledge the realistic dimensions of the problem. The results of this and other studies have led Cartwright to propose that dreams provide "a kind of workshop for the repair of self-esteem and competence."

A summary of the paragraph might read as follows:

Recent research by Cartwright (1978) suggests that dreams help people deal with problems. She found that (1) people are better able to handle emotional situations after dreaming and (2) people who are given a problem and then allowed to dream found better solutions than subjects who were not allowed to dream.

The original paragraph has seven sentences and gives details such as who the subjects were and what the problem to be solved was. The summary contains information only on the results of the research and a brief description of the experimental procedure.

The following articles will provide additional information on dreams.

1. "Dreams: A Key to the Workings of Our Brain?"
2. "The History of Dreams"
3. "The Dream Environment"

Form groups; each student in a group should choose one of the supplementary readings.

Read the instructions and questions for the readings *before* reading your article. After you read the article, answer the questions and write the summary.

"DREAMS: A KEY TO THE WORKINGS OF OUR BRAIN?"

This article reports an experiment on why some people remember their dreams and others do not. Authors who write reports of scientific research include the following information:

Purpose of the research

Hypothesis

Experimental procedure

Findings

Answer the following questions.

1. What was the purpose of the research described in the reading?

2. What hypothesis was tested?

3. Briefly describe the experimental procedure.

4. What findings are reported?

Using the answers to questions 1–4, write a summary of the article. When you've finished, give a copy of the summary to the other students in your group.

Dreams: A key to the workings of our brain?

Most of us in North America remember dreaming once or twice a week. In other cultures, however, it is more common for people to recall several dreams in one night. Bob Hoffmann, Al Moffitt, and Roger Wells of Carleton's psychology department are interested in why North Americans don't remember their dreams. Is it that we simply don't dream as much as other people, or are we somehow conditioned not to remember?

To find the answers to their questions, Professors Hoffmann, Moffitt, and Wells have spent the past four summers inviting people to spend a few nights in Carleton's sleep research laboratory. Located in the Loeb Building, the laboratory centers around an Anechoic chamber, a specially designed, sound-proof and light-proof room, with only a bed. Undergraduate students and acquaintances of the researchers have been used as subjects. Few people have trouble falling asleep in the lab.

Subjects bring along their own pillow, are hooked up to an EEG machine, which records brain waves, and to machines for recording muscle and eye movements. Then they settle down to sleep. During the night, they are wakened several times, and asked to report what they have just been dreaming.

Later, researchers match the dreams reported by the subjects with brain waves and muscle and eye movements recorded at the time. Eventually they hope to use the data to find out how the brain functions.

It is generally accepted that we think and use our brains quite differently when we are asleep than when we are awake. It is not uncommon, for example, for people to wake out of a deep sleep with the solution to a problem that seemed insurmountable when they were awake. Reasons for this, and other differences in thought processes when asleep, are disputed by theorists, however.

One hypothesis being tested by Carleton's sleep researchers is that activity in the two hemispheres of the brain is more balanced when we dream than when we are awake. When we are awake, the right and left sides of the brain handle different functions, one side generally being more active than the other. If data bear out the suggestion that brain activity is more balanced when we dream, it may be that we are tapping the potential of our entire brain, rather than only part of it, to solve a problem. This may account for our ability to do a totally different kind of thinking at night.

By comparing brain waves from the two halves of the brain with the type of dream experience the subject reports, researchers hope to discover whether specific thought processes are associated with activity in one hemisphere, or with balanced activity in the whole brain.

Several interesting, though as yet unexplained, findings have already been made in the sleep research laboratory.

Subjects report several different types of dreams, ranging from simple emotions, to re-enactments of daytime experiences, to sensations like flying or falling, to full-fledged dreams with bizarre, surrealistic plots. Each of these categories of dreams is associated with a different stage of sleep, and frequently with a different time of night.

For example, although subjects report dreams during periods of rapid eye movement (REM) and non-REM sleep, dreams during REM sleep tend to have plots, strange characters and intense experiences, whereas those during non-REM sleep often deal with scenes reminiscent of everyday life. In the middle of the night, however, dreams during both types of sleep tend to be similar.

Subjects who recall a high number of dreams tend to have more people in their dreams than people who remember few, or none, of their dreams. Many people who claim they never dream remember several dreams at night in the sleep laboratory, suggesting that external factors may somehow normally make them forget their dreams. The researchers have as yet found no personality correlations with the type of dreams a person recalls, or with the frequency of recall.

A system for transforming EEG readings into a series of numbers that can be fed into a computer for analysis has been developed in the sleep research laboratory.

Until now, when a subject was hooked up to an EEG machine for the night, the researcher ended up with a thick stack of paper, each page covered with wavy lines visually describing the subject's level of brain activity during the night. It takes a researcher four to five hours to analyze the print-out for one night; and each time a particular aspect of brain activity is to be analyzed the entire print-out has to be reexamined.

Now that a method has been developed for transforming the data in the visual print-out into figures, a night's findings can be dealt with much more easily and quickly.

Last year, Carleton researchers published two papers on computer analysis of EEG readings. Even with the use of a computer, Dr. Hoffmann says, the research is still a long, slow process. Data obtained from last summer's 16 subjects still occupies a shelf in Dr. Hoffmann's office, awaiting analysis.

Although sleep and dream research is also being carried out elsewhere, Dr. Hoffmann says the work being done at Carleton is unique. Most other researchers are concerned with the medical aspects of sleep, with problems of sleeping, the effects of drugs on sleep, or with the interpretation and meaning of dreams.

In contrast, researchers at Carleton are interested in the psychological aspects of dreams, their organization, the senses involved in each dream experience, and the stage of sleep in which different types of dreams occur.

We spend approximately one-third of our lives sleeping and a great deal of that time dreaming. Even so, Dr. Hoffmann says, we know remarkably little about the mechanics of dreaming, or how our minds work when we are asleep.

In North America, we live in a technological culture, in which emphasis is placed on the physical world, and on quantitative things. As a result, we pay little attention to our dreams. However, the fact that our dream world is so different from the external world and that our minds work so differently when we sleep may give us a valuable insight into how the human mind and brain operate.

"THE HISTORY OF DREAMS"

The information in this article is arranged in chronological order. This type of information can best be summarized in a chart or table.

1. Read the article and then design a table or chart which will efficiently present the information in the article.
2. Fill in your chart or table. Make sure you have included the important information.
3. Use the chart or table as the basis for your summary. Write a brief introduction and conclusion for the summary.
4. Give a copy of the summary to the other students in your group.

The History of Dreams

As far as we can determine, dreams have fascinated people throughout the ages. For example, a large collection of Babylonian and Assyrian dream books dating back to about 5000 B.C. was found in the library of the Assyrian king Ashurnasirpal, reports R.L. Van de Castle in the anthology *Dreams and Dreaming,* edited by Lee and Mayes (Penguin, 1973).

The Egyptians, too, were deeply interested in dream interpretation. To them, dreams were messages from the gods. One such message to the Pharaoh Thutmose IV (1425–1417 B.C.) is recorded on the chest of the Great Sphinx. There were dream temples located throughout Egypt. Here, dream incubation (the practice of deciding what you're going to dream about and then doing it) became a highly developed art. Researchers believe that 300 or 400 dream temples in honor of Asclepias, the Greek god of healing and medicine, existed in the ancient world and were actively engaged in dream incubation for nearly 1,000 years. Some of these sanctuaries are still standing today, after being out of use for more than 15 centuries.

The Romans borrowed extensively from the Greeks—in dreams as in most things. They, too, practiced dream incubation. Even their caesars took dreams very seriously. Van de Castle reports that Caesar Augustus once went about begging alms because he had been told to in a dream.

In the Middle Ages, prominent Christian theorists of dreams included both Saint Augustine and Saint Thomas Aquinas. During this time, demons came to play a progressively greater role in theorizing about the origin of dreams. A common belief, writes Van de Castle, was that the devil had many disguises available to him and could thus pass easily into a person's dreams. Martin Luther apparently became so fearful that he would not be able to distinguish divine from demonic messages that he prayed to God not to speak to him in his dreams.

As the Age of Reason gradually began to dawn, the concern with the demons of darkness began to disappear. The prevailing dream theory was exemplified by the often quoted phrase of the 17th-century social philosopher Thomas Hobbes, to the effect that dreams were mere reflections of "distemper of the inward parts."

During the 19th century, a scientific approach to the dream became evident. There was a developing conviction that dreams would provide important insights into the dreamer's personality and that the material expressed often dealt with unacceptable instincts. These socially repressed impulses were assumed to lodge in the unconscious. This line of thinking was subsequently developed by Freud into an elaborate theory of dreams and personality.

Van de Castle notes, however, that many of the building blocks of Freud's theoretical structure were already available.

Extravagant praise from some of his disciples, who were to address him in letters as "Dear Master," has left us with the erroneous impression that Freud was the original discoverer of the unconscious, that he was the first to note that dreams dealt with repressed material, and that he alone recognized that dreams contained a meaningful and intelligent message.

Lately, Freud's theory of the purely repressive function of dreams has been challenged. Fascinating and more benevolent theories are being advanced, following research that shows we all dream in a highly predictable cyclic fashion, whether or not we have any personal problem at the time.

"THE DREAM ENVIRONMENT"

This article reports on recent dream research. The author reports several general findings and then supports these findings with results from experiments on dreaming.

Read the article carefully and then answer the following questions.

1. What support does the author give for the following generalizations?

   a. "We all dream."

   b. "Mental activity is continuous during sleep."

   c. " . . . we apparently *have* to have these periods of increased brain activity."

   d. "The relationship between dream life and waking life has been studied intensively."

Using the answers from the preceding questions, write a summary of the article. When you've finished, give a copy of the summary to the other students in your group.

The Dream Environment

The latest laboratory investigations of dreams strongly indicate that *everyone* dreams, and that we never lose consciousness when we sleep. How do scientists know this?

It all began with REM. This acronym refers to the rapid eye movements that almost invariably accompany the dream state, as scientists discovered in 1953. This discovery allowed dream researchers in many countries to know exactly when their subjects were dreaming and therefore to study dreams as they were happening. They found that all individuals studied spent approximately 20 percent of their sleep in REM periods, which appeared in a highly predictable cyclic fashion. The average adult has four or five REM periods every night. These periods typically occur every 90 minutes during sleep, beginning with a short 10-minute REM and ending with a 30- to 45-minute REM toward morning.

We all dream. It's just that some of us don't remember our dreams. In fact, most of us apparently forget most of our dreams. Dr. Garfield reports in *Creative Dreaming* that only five minutes after a dream, our recall of it is almost if not completely gone. However, "So-called nonrecallers of dreams can be converted to recallers in the laboratory," as Carolyn Winget and Milton Kramer report in *Dimensions of Dreams* (University Presses of Florida, 1979). People can also train themselves, without benefit of laboratories, to wake up after each dream. You can find many good pointers in Dr. Garfield's book on how to do this.

To me, the most fascinating finding about our nocturnal adventures is this: Mental activity is continuous during sleep. That is, you never really lose consciousness—you merely alter it when you fall asleep. Dream researcher and editor Dr. Charles Tart reports in *Altered States of Consciousness* that we all have a sleep-dream cycle with two predominant mental states. One state is experienced by sleep subjects as dreaming, the other as being more like thinking. They report the two states as distinct and different types of experience.

What you remember in the morning may therefore be a dream or a fragment of a dream; but it may also be a fragment of the "thinking" you did while you were asleep. Sleep laboratory reports of "thinking" are almost as frequent as the reports of dreams. These scientific findings reflect what we probably already know. We just don't know that we know. Consider, for example, the full implications of the folk wisdom to "sleep on it" when we can't figure something out. It doesn't really imply that we will think better after a good night's rest; it implies that we will awake with the problem already solved.

There are numerous spectacular instances of our ability to solve problems while asleep. One of the most famous is the often told story of how the German chemist Kekulé hit on the concept of the benzene ring, an idea that revolutionized organic chemistry. He reported his discovery to his colleagues at a scientific convention in 1980. He was writing his chemical textbook, he said, "but it did not go well…I turned the chair to the fireplace and sank into a half sleep. The atoms flitted before my eyes . . . wriggling and turning like snakes. And see, what was that? One of the snakes seized its own tail and the image whirled scornfully before my eyes. As though from a flash of lightning I awoke: I occupied the rest of the night in working out the consequences of the hypothesis." He concluded, "Let us learn to dream, gentlemen, and then we may find the truth."

So, we are not mentally inert when we sleep. On the contrary, as Dr. Ann Faraday reports in *The Dream Game,* brain-wave records indicate that the dreaming brain is even more active than the waking brain. This may mean that we may be capable of more mental work asleep than awake.

What's more, we apparently *have* to have these periods of increased brain activity. Tart reports on one study, which found that if, on several consecutive nights, a subject was awakened whenever REM dreaming began, the person would have to be awakened more and more frequently to prevent REM dreaming as the nights went on. Furthermore, if the subject was then allowed several undisturbed nights of sleep after this, his REM dream time was significantly increased for several nights. The study concluded that we have a need for a given amount of dreaming each night. Whether this is a need for the experience of dreaming, however, or for the physiological state represented by REM is still apparently unknown.

Popular belief about when and why we dream is probably heavily influenced by Freud. The idea being that we have "nasty" (Freudians, read "sexual") wishes during the day. Because they're not nice, we repress them—only to have them break out in our dreams. But because we really *do* want to repress them, we have our dream language hide the truth from us by a set of weird symbols. Thus the need for dream interpreters other than ourselves.

That's not how it works, however. The latest dream research indicates that Freud misjudged the conditions under which dreaming occurs. We do not dream to compensate for the number and intensity of our repressed personal problems. Instead, we spend about two hours dreaming every night, no matter what we may have done and felt during the day.

The relationship between dream life and waking life has been studied intensively. From their survey of dream content research, Winget and Kramer conclude that the "content of dreams has most often, but not always, been found to be continuous with, rather than compensatory to, waking life. . . . It has been found that dream content is remarkably stable over long periods. . . . Yet within this stability, the dream is reflective of the ebb and flow of mental life, the vicissitudes of daily existence, and the biological rhythm of the human condition."

In other words, our dreaming appears to be a continuation of daytime situations rather than a reaction to the repression of what we should have dealt with, or should not have felt, while awake. Our dreams can comment on, highlight, and otherwise interact with our waking mental life. We dream about unimportant daily events and not merely about our problems. And our dreams can accurately detect, sometimes even prescribe for, unhealthy physical conditions we might not notice in the hubbub of daily living.

What I conclude from all this is that we humans live in two mental environments, a waking one and a sleeping one, and that we are conscious in both of them. The laws of the dream universe appear to be quite different from the laws of the waking universe. My hunch is, however, that they are what modern physicists call "continuous"—meaning that they do not contradict each other but exist in a harmonious whole. Also meaning that we seem to be far more interesting than orthodox dream theory would have us. ∎

Short Answer Exam Questions

Professors frequently require their students to write "short answers" (about half a page in length) to questions on tests and examinations.

The following steps will help you do this well.

1. Select the necessary information from what you have read.
2. Organize the information.
3. Express the information clearly and effectively in your own words.
4. Observe time limits.

The purpose of this exercise is to help you develop strategies for writing short summaries in an exam. You will answer the following test question.

"Briefly summarize the evidence suggesting that people have a real need to dream."

When you are asked to summarize the evidence, you must give the essential information and organize it so that you state the general information and then present the evidence. You need to use your own words as far as possible, and put quotation marks around words and phrases that you quote *verbatim* from the text.

Writing the Short Answer

The following steps will help you complete the short-answer questions within the time limit given. Do this exercise in 25 minutes. Then you will have 20 minutes to write the answer to the question.

1. Reread the question. What general assertion must you state? Write it on the line.

_____

2. Skim your readings and notes, especially the parts you underlined or highlighted, noting only what you need to use to answer the question.
3. In the space below, write down the key words to help you remember the important information for each piece of evidence. Don't forget the name of the researcher.

4. Go over your notes. Ask yourself: Is everything relevant? Have I forgotten anything?
5. Decide how you will sequence the supporting evidence. Use numbers, arrows, etc. to help you plan.
6. Ask yourself: How strong is the supporting information? How strong will the general statement be?
7. Now, on the next page, write your answer, beginning with the assertion.

TEST QUESTION

Briefly summarize the evidence suggesting that people have a real need to dream *(20 minutes)*.

Hand in your essay.

Evaluating Your Answers

When professors read and grade answers, they are looking for *complete information, coherent organization,* and *clear language.* They want to know if you know the necessary information, and if you can express your ideas clearly and comprehensibly. For this reason, the evaluation scale focuses on these three criteria.

Complete Information

With your teacher, develop a point form list of the *information* required in:

1. the general statement about the biological need to dream.
2. the evidence that supports this claim, including the procedures of both Dement and Tart. Do this part in two columns, one for each researcher.

Coherent Organization

1. Your answer must begin with the general statement. This will tell the professor what thesis you are going to prove.
2. With your teacher, group those ideas which focus on the same point. Then, determine the logical relationships among the ideas (cause and effect, time, exemplification, etc.).
3. Sequence the ideas.

Clear Language

1. The assertion—look at both the question and the evidence. How strong should your general statement be? Make sure your assertion reflects this strength.
2. The evidence—explore some of the possibilities available in English for expressing relationships that you found in Coherent Organization (e.g., parallel structure for similar ideas, etc.).

Now you should have an answer for which the professor would award full marks.

The following exercise will give you an idea of how professors evaluate answers. In this exercise, you will assume the role of professor.

1. Exchange papers with a partner.
2. Read your partner's answer 3 times: once for information, once for organization, and once for language. Assign points for each criterion, using the following table. In the Comments column, note any problems you found in the answer.

	Points	Comments
INFORMATION	/10	
ORGANIZATION	/5	
LANGUAGE	/5	
TOTAL	/20	

3. When you have finished, discuss your evaluation with your partner.

As a class, discuss the two or three best answers.

4

ANIMAL COMMUNICATION

CHAPTER CONTENTS:

Thinking About the Topic
Reading I: "Animals That Try to Talk"
Reading II: "Translating Bird Song"

Oral Presentations
Preparing for an Exam
Writing an Exam

In Chapter 1 you focused on adults learning a second language. In this chapter you will deal with another aspect of language: how animals communicate and the differences between human and animal languages.

In this chapter you will practice strategies that help you read large amounts of text. You will also focus on how authors compare and contrast information. After completing the readings, each member of the class will give a short oral presentation.

In the writing section you will learn ways to prepare for an exam. The most important skills here are predicting the questions a professor is going to ask for an exam and preparing answers for those questions.

THINKING ABOUT THE TOPIC

Briefly answer the following questions.

   a. What's your mother tongue? _____

   b. How many languages do you speak? _____

   c. List your languages in Column A. Then, in Column B, write the word
   that best describes how well you speak each language. Choose from:
   fluently, fairly well, adequately.

                    A   **B**

   _____   _____

   _____   _____

   _____   _____

   Question 1 concerned verbal language. Now let's consider nonverbal
communication, the communication of ideas using gestures and posture.

2. Discuss the gestures or postures used in your culture to express the
following instructions:

   Come here.

   Relax.

3. Discuss the gestures or postures used in your culture to express the
following emotions:

   Impatience

   Surprise

4. Discuss how you get across the following messages:

   Okay.

   You're late.

   I don't understand.

   In groups of 3 or 4, compare your answers.
   Even though no speech is involved in these nonverbal actions, communication does take place. In the following chapter, we'll focus on the nonverbal communication of animals.

"ANIMALS THAT TRY TO TALK"

The first reading in this chapter is from a book entitled *The Articulate Mammal.* Refer to the text as you read the following instructions.

1. Read the title and subtitle. What question will this chapter focus on?

2. Introductions to chapters have a function very similar to the introductions of essays: they tell the reader what topic or problem will be addressed, what sections the problem has been divided into, and in which order these sections will be presented. This kind of overview prepares the reader to read efficiently.

Read the introduction (paras. 1–4) to find out these three pieces of data for this chapter. Note how the author has used questions for some of them to draw your attention to the information. Then write a brief outline of your overview of the chapter.

Problem:

Topic 1

Topic 2

3. Check the boldface headings in the chapter to see if the writer keeps the contract with the reader.

We'll be concerned with only the first half of this chapter: natural animal communication, especially the part of the text that compares animal communication systems to human language, in order to find out if animals do in fact have a true natural language. Let's turn now to this part of the text, "Do animals talk naturally?"

"Do Animals Talk Naturally?"

Again, the text is organized to help the reader follow the ideas step by step. Read your instructions to this part carefully. You have 20 minutes to complete questions 1 and 2.

1. a. Skim this section (paras. 5–33), reading only the *first* and *last paragraphs,* as well as the *first* and *last sentences* of the paragraphs in between. Highlight these parts. Note that the first paragraph prepares the reader for a preliminary discussion of two problems that will precede the comparison of human and animal communication.

b. Also, as you skim each paragraph, ask yourself the following questions:

(1) Does this paragraph begin a new idea? (If so, what?) *or*
(2) Does this paragraph focus on a different aspect of the previous idea? (If so, what?) *or*
(3) Does this paragraph continue the idea discussed in the previous paragraph?

c. In the margin, note key words about the focus of each paragraph. You have only 20 minutes, so *don't* try to read the complete text.

2. When you finish, complete the tree diagram outline on the next page by filling in the blanks with key information from the text.

Animals that try to talk

Is Language Restricted to Humans?

An ant who can speak
French, Japanese and Greek
Doesn't exist.
Why ever not?
Robert Desnos

(1) Judging by newspapers and popular books, there appear to be a vast number of animals which 'talk'—talking budgerigars, talking dolphins—even a talking fish:

Anne, Anne, come quick as you can
There's a fish that talks in the frying pan.

(Walter de la Mare)

(2) Clearly, the word ''talk'' can be used in two totally different senses. On the one hand, it can mean simply ''to utter words,'' as in ''Archibald's got a talking parrot which says *Damn* if you poke it.'' On the other hand, it can mean ''to use language in a meaningful way.'' We already know that animals such as budgerigars can ''talk'' in the first sense of the word. Psycholinguists would like to find out whether animals can ''talk'' in the second sense also. They are interested in this problem because they want to know the answer to the following question: are we the only species which possesses language? If so, are we the only species capable of acquiring it?

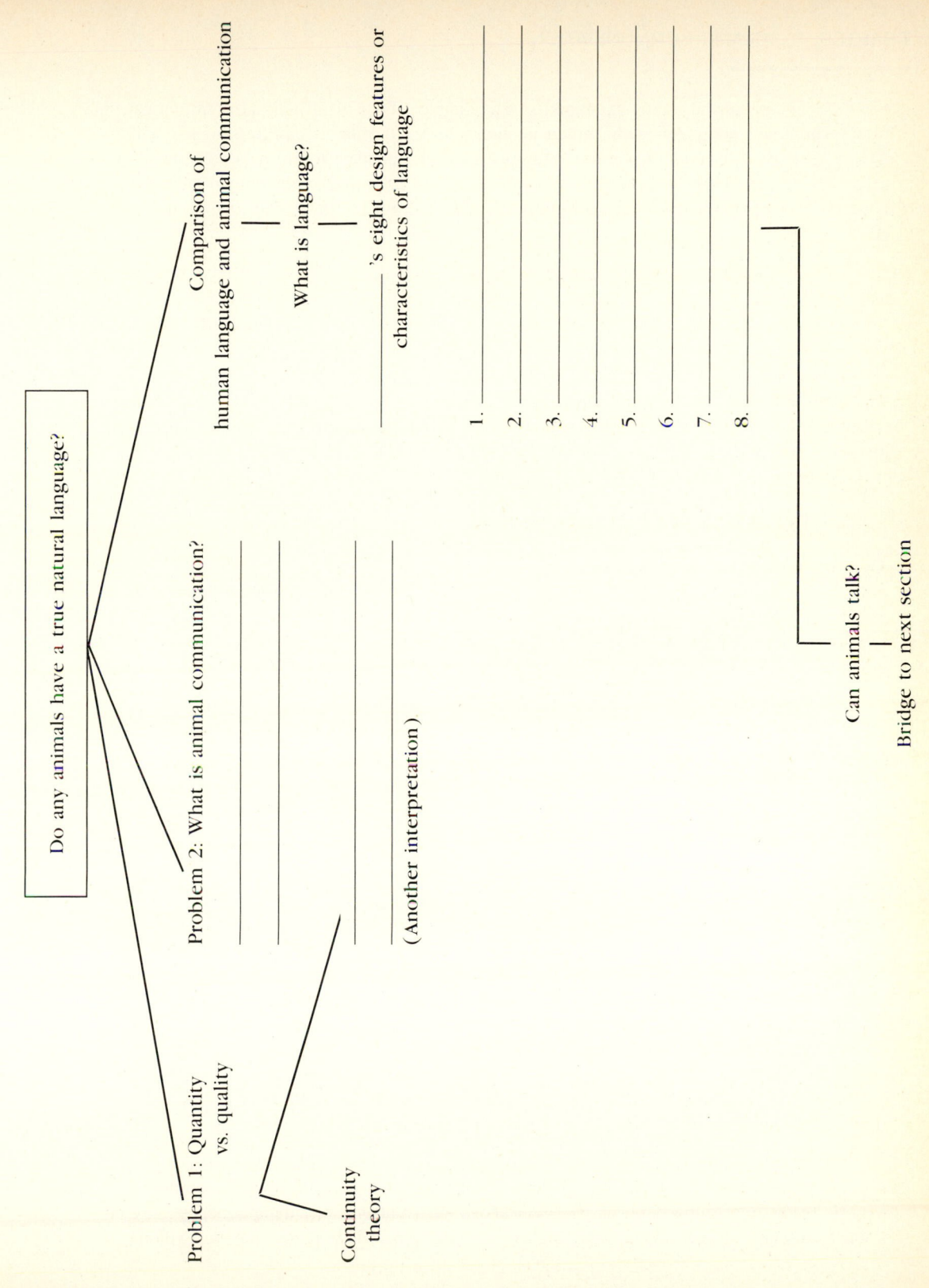

(3)   These are the topics examined in this chapter. First of all animal communication systems are compared with human language to see if animals can be said to "talk" in any real sense. Secondly, various attempts to teach language to animals are considered. The overall purpose behind such inquiries is to find out whether humans alone have the power of speech. Are we biologically singled out as "articulate mammals" or not?

(4)   Of course, if we discover that animals *do* talk, then we shall not have learned anything useful, just as the fact that we can do the breast stroke does not tell us anything about a frog's innate swimming ability. Or, as Fodor, Bever and Garrett acidly note, "The fact that a dog can be trained to walk on its hind legs does not prejudice the claim that bipedal gait is genetically coded in humans. The fact that we can learn to whistle like a lark does not prejudice the species-specificity of birdsong" (Fodor, Bever and Garrett, 1974:451). If, on the other hand, we find that animals do *not* talk, this will provide some support for the claim that language is "innate" in humans.

Do Animals Talk Naturally?

(5) Our first task is to find out whether any animals naturally have a true "language." In order to answer this question, we must compare human language with animal communication. But such a comparison presents a number of perhaps unsolvable problems. Two in particular need to be discussed before we can start to give a coherent reply to the query, "Do animals talk naturally?"

(6)   The first problem we must consider is this: are we comparing systems which differ quantitatively or qualitatively? On the one hand, human language may have gradually evolved from a more primitive animal means of communication in a continuous line of growth—a viewpoint sometimes known as a "continuity" theory. On the other hand, human language may be something quite different from our basic animal heritage, and superimposed on it. This is a "discontinuity" theory.

(7)   Supporters of continuity theories suggest that language grew out of a primate call system, like the ones used by apes today. They assume that humans started out with a simple set of cries in which each one meant something different, such as, "Danger!" or "Follow me!" or "Don't touch that female, she is mine!" These cries gradually became more elaborate, and eventually evolved into language. A possible intermediate stage is seen in the cries of the vervet monkey. This monkey has several alarm calls which distinguish between different types of danger (Struhsaker, 1967). The *chutter* announces that a puff adder or cobra is around. The *rraup* gives warning of an eagle. A *chirp* is used for lions and leopards. A less panic-stricken utterance, the *uh!*, signals the presence of a spotted hyena or Masai tribesman. According to some, it is a very short step from an alarm call warning of a poisonous snake to using the *chutter* as a "word" symbolizing a poisonous snake.

(8)   But another interpretation of these signals is possible. The monkeys could merely be distinguishing between the *intensity* of different types of danger. They may be more frightened of puff adders than eagles—or vice versa. This is a plausible explana-

tion, since the monkeys sometimes give a *chirp* (used for lions) when they see an eagle. So it is likely that eagles and lions represent the same degree of danger—unless you conclude that monkeys cannot tell the difference between them. This suggests that a discontinuity theory may be better than a continuity one.

(9)   Proponents of discontinuity theories claim that man still retains his basic set of animal cries, which exist alongside language. Yelps of pain, shrieks of fear, and the different types of crying observed in babies may be closely related to the call systems of monkeys. If this view is correct, then it is fairly difficult to compare human and animal means of communication. It may be like comparing two things as different as the Chinese language and a set of traffic lights. But at the moment the question is an open one. We do not yet know whether the continuity or the discontinuity theorists are correct. But we must keep both possibilities in mind when discussing the main topic of this chapter.

(10)   The second major problem we face is that it is not always easy to decide what counts as communication in animals. As one researcher notes, "Students of animal behavior have often noted the extreme difficulty of restricting the notion of communication to anything less than every potential interaction between an organism and its environment" (Marshall, 1970:231). So that, at the very least, sticklebacks mating, cats spitting, and rabbits thumping their back legs must be taken into consideration—and it isn't at all clear where to stop. It is sometimes suggested that this problem could be solved by concentrating on examples where the animal is *intentionally* trying to convey information. But such distinctions are difficult to draw, both in humans and animals. If a woman repeatedly flutters her eyelashes when an attractive man walks into the room, is this an unconscious response? Or is she doing it intentionally in order to attract his attention? In the sea, so-called "snapping shrimps" can produce loud cracks (which are capable of upsetting naval sonar devices) by closing their claws sharply. But no one has yet discovered the significance of the snaps. They may be informative—but they may not. There is no way yet in which we can be sure about making the right decision when it comes to interpreting such a phenomenon.

(11)   Having outlined these fundamental problems—which show that any conclusions we draw are only tentative—we can now return to our main theme: a comparison of human language and animal communication. How should we set about this?

(12)   A useful first step might be to attempt to define "language." This is not as easy as it sounds. Most of the definitions found in elementary textbooks are too wide. For example: "The faculty of language consists in man's ability to make noises with the vocal organs and marks on paper or some other material, by means of which groups of people 'speaking the same language' are able to interact and co-operate as a group" (Robins, 1971:12). This definition, if one ignores the word "man" and the phrase involving "marks on paper," might equally well apply to a pack of wolves howling in chorus.

(13)   Perhaps the most promising approach is that suggested by the linguist Charles Hockett. In a series of articles stretching over ten years he has attempted to itemize out

the various "design features" which characterize language. For example: "*Interchange-ability:* Adult members of any speech community are interchangeably transmitters and receivers of linguistic signals"; "*Complete Feedback:* The transmitter of a linguistic signal himself receives the message" (Hockett, 1963:9). Of course, such an approach is not perfect. A list of features may even be misleading, since it represents a random set of observations which do not cohere in any obvious way. To use this list to define language is like trying to define a man by noting that he has two arms, two legs, a head, a belly button, he bleeds if you scratch him, and shrieks if you tread on his toe. But in spite of this, a definition of language based on design features or "essential characteristics" seems to be the most useful proposed so far.

(14) But how many characteristics should be considered? Two? Ten? A hundred? The number of design features Hockett considers important has changed over the years. The longest list contains sixteen (Hockett, 1963), though perhaps most people would consider that eight features capture the essential nature of language: *use of the vocal-auditory channel, arbitrariness, semanticity, cultural transmission, duality, displacement, structure-dependence* and *creativity*.

(15) Let us discuss each of these features in turn, and see whether it is present in animal communication. If any animal naturally possesses *all* the design features of human language, then clearly that animal can talk.

(16) The use of the *vocal-auditory channel* is perhaps the most obvious characteristic of language. Sounds are made with the vocal organs, and a hearing mechanism receives them—a phenomenon which is neither rare nor particularly surprising. The use of sound is widespread as a means of animal communication. One obvious advantage is that messages can be sent or received in the dark or in a dense forest. Not all sound signals are vocal—woodpeckers tap on wood, and rattlesnakes have a rattle apparatus on their tail. But vocal-auditory signals are common and are used by birds, cows, apes and foxes, to name just a few. The advantages of this method of producing the sound are that it leaves the body free to carry on other activities at the same time, and also requires relatively little physical energy. But this design feature is clearly neither unique to humans, nor all-important, since language can be transferred without loss to visual symbols (as in deaf-and-dumb language, or writing) and to tactile symbols (as in Braille). Patients who have had their vocal cords removed, and communicate mainly by writing, have not lost their language ability. It follows that this characteristic is of little use in an attempt to distinguish animal from human communication. So let us proceed to the second feature, arbitrariness.

(17) *Arbitrariness* means that human languages use neutral symbols. There is no connection between the word "dog" and the four-legged animal it symbolizes. It can equally be called UN CHIEN (French), EIN HUND (German), or CANIS (Latin). GÜL (Turkish) and RHODON (Greek) are equally satisfactory names for a "rose." As Juliet notes:

> What's in a name? that which we call a rose
> By any other name would smell as sweet.
>
> (Shakespeare)

Onomatopoeic words such as CUCKOO, POP, BANG, SLURP and SQUISH are exceptions to this. But there are relatively few of these in any language. On the other hand, it is normal for animals to have a strong link between the message they are sending and the signal they use to convey it. A crab which wishes to convey extreme aggression will extend a large claw. A less angry crab will merely raise a leg: "Extending a major chaliped is more effective than raising a single ambulatory leg in causing the second crab to retreat or duck back into its shell" (Marshall, 1970). However, arbitrary symbols are not unique to man. Gulls, for example, sometimes indicate aggression by turning away from their opponent and uprooting beakfuls of grass. So we are forced to conclude that arbitrariness cannot be regarded as a critical distinction between human and animal communication.

(18)   *Semanticity,* the third suggested test for language ability, is the use of symbols to "mean" or refer to objects and actions. To a human, a CHAIR "means" a four-legged contraption you can sit on. Humans can generalize by applying this name to all types of chairs, not just one in particular. Furthermore, semanticity applies to actions as well as objects. For example, to JUMP "means" the act of leaping in the air. Some writers have claimed that semanticity is exclusively human. Animals may only be able to communicate about a total situation. A hen who utters "danger" cries when a fox is nearby is possibly conveying the message "Beware! beware! there is terrible danger about!" rather than using the sound to "mean" FOX. But, as was shown by the call of the vervet monkey who might or might not mean "snake" when he *chutters,* it is difficult to be certain. We must remain agnostic about whether this feature is present in animal communication.

(19)   *Cultural transmission* or *tradition* indicates that human beings hand their languages down from one generation to another. The role played by teaching in animal communication is unclear and varies from animal to animal—and even within species. Among birds it is claimed that the song-thrush's song is largely innate, but can be slightly modified by learning, whereas the skylark's song is almost wholly learned. Birds such as the chaffinch are particularly interesting: the basic pattern of the song seems to be innate, but all the finer detail and much of the pitch and rhythm have to be acquired by learning (Thorpe, 1961, 1963). However, although the distinction between man and animals is not clear-cut as regards this feature, it seems that a far greater proportion of communication is genetically inbuilt in animals than in man. If a child is brought up in isolation, away from human beings, he does not acquire language. In contrast, birds reared in isolation sing songs that are sometimes recognizable (though almost always abnormal).

(20)   The fifth property, *duality* or *double-articulation,* means that language is organized into two 'layers': the basic sound units of speech, such as P, I, G, are normally meaningless by themselves. They only become meaningful when combined into sequences such as P—I—G PIG. This property is sometimes claimed to be unique to humans. But this is not so. Duality is also present in bird song, where each individual note is itself meaningless—it is the combination of notes which convey meaningful messages. So once again we have not found a critical difference between animals and humans in the use of this feature.

(21)   A more important characteristic of language is *displacement,* the ability to refer to things far removed in time and place. Humans frequently say things such as "My Aunt Matilda, who lives in Australia, cracked her knee-cap last week." It may be impossible for an animal to convey a similar item of information. However, as in the case of other design features, it is sometimes difficult to decide whether displacement is present in an animal's communication system. A bird frequently continues to give alarm cries long after the disappearance of a cat which was stalking it. Is this displacement or not? The answer is unclear. Definite examples of displacement are hard to find. But it is undoubtedly found in bee communication (von Frisch, 1950, 1954, 1967). When a worker bee finds a source of nectar she returns to the hive to perform a complex dance which informs the other bees of its location. She does a "round dance," which involves turning round in circles if the nectar is close to the hive, and a "waggle dance" in which she wiggles her tail from side to side if it is far away. The other bees work out the distance by noting the tempo of her waggles, and discover what kind of flower to look for by smelling its scent on her body. After the dance, they unerringly fly to the right place, even if it is several miles away, with a hill intervening.

(22)   This is an unusual ability—but even this degree of displacement is considerably less than that found in human speech. The bee cannot inform other bees about anything further removed than the nectar patch she has just visited. She cannot say "The day before yesterday we visited a lovely clump of flowers, let's go and see if they are still there"—she can only say, "Come to the nectar I have just visited." Nor can she communicate about anything further away in place. She could not say "I wonder whether there's good nectar in Siberia." So displacement in bee communication is strictly limited to the number of miles a bee can easily fly, and the time it takes to do this. At last, it seems we may have found a feature which seems to be of importance in human language, and only partially present in non-human communication.

(23)   The seventh feature, *structure-dependence,* was discussed in Chapter 1. Humans do not just apply simple recognition or counting techniques when they speak to one another. They automatically recognize the patterned nature of language, and manipulate "structured chunks." For example, they understand that a group of words can sometimes be the structural equivalent of one:

SHE THE OLD LADY WHO WAS WEARING A WHITE BONNET	GAVE THE DONKEY A CARROT

and they can rearrange these chunks according to strict rules:

A CARROT	WAS GIVEN TO THE DONKEY	BY THE OLD LADY WHO WAS WEARING A WHITE BONNET

As far as we know, animals do not use structure-dependent operations. We do not know enough about the communication of all animals to be sure, but no definite example has yet been found.

(24) Finally, there is one feature that seems to be of overwhelming importance, and unique to humans—the ability to produce and understand an indefinite number of novel utterances. This property of language has several different names. Chomsky calls it *creativity,* others call it *openness* or *productivity.* A human can talk about anything he likes—even a platypus falling backwards downstairs—without causing any linguistic problems to himself or the hearer. He can say *what* he wants *when* he wants. If it thunders, he does not automatically utter a set phrase, such as "It's thundering, run for cover." He can say "Isn't the lightning pretty?" or "Better get the dog in" or "Thunder is two dragons colliding in tin tubs, according to a Chinese legend."

(25) In contrast, most animals have a fixed number of signals which convey a set number of messages, sent in clearly definable circumstances. A North American cicada can give four signals only. It emits a "disturbance squawk" when it is seized, picked up or eaten. A "congregation call" seems to mean "Let's all get together and sing in chorus!" A preliminary courtship call (an invitation?) is uttered when a female is several inches away. An advanced courtship call (a buzz of triumph?) occurs when the female is almost within grasp (Alexander and Moore, quoted in McNeill, 1966). Even the impressive vervet monkey has only thirty-six distinct vocal sounds in its repertoire. And as this total includes sneezing and vomiting, the actual number used for communication is several fewer. Within this range, choice is limited, since circumstances generally dictate which call to use. An infant separated from its mother gives the lost *rrah* cry. A female who wishes to deter an amorous male gives the "anti-copulatory squeal-scream" (Struhsaker, 1967).

(26) But perhaps it is unfair to concentrate on cicadas and monkeys. Compared with these, bees and dolphins have extremely sophisticated communication systems. Yet researchers have reluctantly concluded that even bees and dolphins seem unable to say anything new. The bees were investigated by the famous "bee-man," Karl von Frisch (1954). He noted that worker bees normally give information about the *horizontal* distance and direction of a source of nectar. If bee communication is in any sense "open," then a worker bee should be able to inform the other bees about *vertical* distance and direction if necessary. He tested this idea by placing a hive of bees at the foot of a radio beacon, and a supply of sugar water at the top. But the bees who were shown the sugar water were unable to tell the other bees where to find it. They duly performed a "round dance," indicating that a source of nectar was in the vicinity of the hive—and then for several hours their comrades flew in all directions *except* upwards, looking for the honey source. Eventually, they gave up the search. As von Frisch noted, "The bees have no word for 'up' in their language. There are no flowers in the clouds" (von Frisch, 1954:139). Failure to communicate this extra item of information means that bee communication cannot be regarded as "open-ended" in the same way that human language is open-ended.

(27) The dolphin experiments carried out by Dr. Jarvis Bastian were considerably more exciting—though in the long run equally disappointing. Bastian tried to teach a male dolphin Buzz and a female dolphin Doris to communicate across an opaque barrier.

(28) First of all, while they were still together, Bastian taught the dolphins to press paddles when they saw a light. If the light was kept steady, they had to press the right

paddle first. If it flashed, the left-hand one. When they did this correctly they were rewarded with fish.

(29)   As soon as they had learned this manoeuvre, he separated them. They could now hear one another, but they could not see one another. The paddles and light were set up in the same way, except that the light which indicated which paddle to press first was seen only by Doris. But in order to get fish both dolphins had to press the levers in the correct order. Doris had to *tell* Buzz which this was, as only she could see the light. Amazingly, the dolphins "demonstrated essentially perfect success over thousands of trials at this task" (Evans and Bastian, 1969:432). It seemed that dolphins could *talk!* Doris was conveying novel information through an opaque barrier! But it later became clear that the achievement was considerably less clever. Even while the dolphins were together Doris had become accustomed to making certain sounds when the light was flashing and different sounds when it was continuous. When the dolphins were separated she continued the habit. And Buzz had, of course, already learnt which sound of Doris's to associate with which light. Doris was therefore not "talking creatively."

(30)   So not even dolphins have a "creative" communication system, it seems—though it is always possible that more is known about "delphinese" than has been made public. The high intelligence of dolphins has obvious implications for naval warfare, and so has attracted the attention of military authorities, with the result that much research is shrouded in official secrecy. But on the whole it seems unlikely that there exist hidden tanks of "talking dolphins" (as was suggested in a recent film). Most researchers would agree with the comment of the psychologist John Morton: "On the question as to whether dolphins have a language, I would like to comment parenthetically from the evidence I have seen, if they do have a language they are going to extraordinary lengths to conceal the fact from us" (Morton, 1971:83).

(31)   It seems, then, that animals cannot send truly novel messages, and that Ogden Nash encapsulates a modicum of truth in his comment:

> The song of canaries
> Never varies.

And so does Alice in her complaint about kittens:

> It is a very inconvenient habit of kittens that, whatever you say to them, they always purr. If they would only purr for "yes" and mew for "no," or any rule of that sort, so that one could keep up a conversation! But how *can* you talk with a person if they *always* say the same thing?
>
> (Lewis Carroll)

(32)   It is now possible to answer the question, can animals talk? If, in order to qualify as "talkers" they have to utilize all the design characteristics of human language "naturally," the answer is clearly "no." Some animals possess some of the features. Bird song has duality, and bee dancing has some degree of displacement. But, as far as we know, no animal communication system has duality *and* displacement. No animal system can be proved to have semanticity or to use structure-dependent operations. Above all, no animal can communicate creatively with another animal.

(33) But although animals do not "naturally" talk, this does not mean that they are *incapable* of talking. Perhaps they have just never had the chance to learn language. The next section examines the results obtained with animals which have had this opportunity.

Teaching Animals to Talk: Washoe and Sarah

(34) In discussing attempts to teach language to animals it is important (as we have already noted) to distinguish mimicry from "true" language. Parrots and mynah birds can imitate humans with uncanny accuracy. But it is unlikely that they ever understand what people are saying. There are reports of a grey parrot which could say "Good morning" and "Good evening" at the right times, and "Goodbye" when guests left (Brown, 1958). But most talking birds are merely "parrotting" back what they hear. For example, a budgerigar I knew heard a puppy being trained with words such as "Sit!" "Naughty boy!" and used to shriek "Sit!" "Naughty boy!" whenever anyone went near its cage, whether or not the dog was present.

(35) Although psychologists have spent considerable time experimenting with mynah birds, it is perhaps not surprising that the results have been disappointing. Apes seem more promising candidates. Over the past forty years several attempts have been made to teach human language to chimpanzees.

Now read the text carefully in order to answer the following questions.

1. What is the main difference between the continuity and discontinuity theories?

2. What is meant by the problem of *intention* in studying animal communication systems?

3. What is the author's test of whether or not an animal can talk?

4. For each of the design features or characteristics suggested by Charles Hockett, find the following information:
   a. The name Hockett gave the feature
   b. An explanation of the characteristic
   c. An example of its presence in human language
   d. Its presence or absence in animal communication

5. On a separate page, construct a table showing this information.

6. Form groups of 3 or 4. Compare your table with the tables of the rest of the group. Decide whose is the most complete and the most easily understood.

7. In groups, discuss the following two questions:

   a. According to the text, which are the 3 most distinguishing features of real language?
   b. Which creatures appear to give researchers the most difficulty in deciding how closely their communication systems approach human language? Why do you say this?

"*T*RANSLATING *BIRD SONG*"

This reading is excerpted from the book *Eloquent Animals*.

1. Read the first sentence to find out the focus of this excerpt.
2. Now read the entire excerpt carefully. Beside each paragraph, write a few words to indicate the point(s) of comparison focused on there. Try to come up with a general heading or topic for each paragraph.
3. Discuss your notes with a partner and try to reach a consensus about the topic of each paragraph.
4. With your partner, look at the organization of the information in each paragraph. How has the writer made it easy for the reader to follow the comparisons?

As a class, discuss the answers to questions 3 and 4 with your teacher.

Translating bird song

When one considers the way birds learn to sing and the way babies learn to talk, some of the similarities are so obvious that they're easy to overlook. Just as birds learn the song of their kind and not that of some other species, so babies learn to speak and not to bark or to chirp. And just as some birds learn dialects, humans learn different languages—and, of course, local dialects of those languages. Furthermore, people—like birds—can recognize a neighbor by his or her voice or tell the sex of a stranger just by listening.

In infants, babbling seems to serve the same function that subsong serves for birds: it's a chance for the baby to exercise her vocal equipment and to try to match her own sounds to words she has heard spoken by adults. Early babbling (like early subsong) sounds much the same for all babies, but late babbling (like late subsong) shows evidence of learning: an older Chinese baby sounds different from an older French baby.

The drive to learn to speak or to sing seems to be present in both babies and young birds almost from birth. And just as some birds have a critical period for learning song, many linguists believe there is a critical period for humans—that if a child isn't exposed to language during the early years, he will never learn to speak.

There are parallels, too, in the problems faced by children who become deaf before they have begun to speak and those of young deafened birds, since both are unable to match the sounds they make to sounds they've heard (or to an inherited template). But the most fascinating correspondence of all is the anatomical one: both the ability to speak and the ability to sing reside in the left hemisphere of the brain. And the similarity doesn't stop there. An adult human with left-hemisphere damage often loses the ability to speak or to understand language, though very young humans with similar damage generally grow up to talk quite normally, since the right hemisphere takes over the tasks of the left. In much the same way, if an experimenter cuts the nerves that connect an adult bird's vocal equipment with its left hemisphere, afterward it can sing only the most fragmentary song, while if the same operation is performed on a young bird, it eventually comes into song quite normally.

Marler* suggests that humans may also have something very like the template he has postulated for song birds: there may be innate mechanisms that first focus the infant's attention on speech sounds as opposed to nonspeech sounds and that also provide an orderly frame of reference as the baby listens to those around him.

*Dr. Peter Marler, a professor at Rockefeller University in New York City, is perhaps the world's foremost authority on bird song.

Oral Presentations

During this part of the chapter you will give a brief oral presentation summarizing information you have read. The class will be divided into small groups: each person in a group will be given an excerpt from a book on animal communication.

In order to prepare the oral presentation you must choose and organize information from the reading.

According to current literature, animals use one or more forms of communication (sounds, touch, visible signals, smells, or any combinations of these) for a variety of purposes (survival, including warning and distress signals; breeding; rearing of young; and social life).

1. Form groups of three or four and look at the excerpts you have been assigned. Each excerpt focuses on a particular animal or group of animals. Assign the articles as evenly as possible among yourselves. The readings focus on the communication systems of the following animals:
   a. Canids: Dogs and wolves
   b. Ants
   c. Chimpanzees
   d. Small mammals, including bats
   e. Marine mammals
   f. Birds
2. For the next class, you will present the following information to your group:
   a. the forms of communication used by these animals
   b. the purpose(s) for which each form is used

3. The following guidelines for oral presentations can help your listeners take notes efficiently. When you prepare your presentation, remember to follow these guidelines.
   a. First, tell your listeners in advance what your topic is.
   b. Tell them what sections you have divided your information into, and their order.
   c. Use one introductory sentence per section to guide them through your talk.
   d. *Talk* to your group instead of reading your information.
   e. Stay within your 15-minute time limit.

Each group member should prepare six sheets of paper set up as follows for taking notes:

Forms and Purposes of Communication

Animal	Sounds	Touch	Visible Signals	Smells

While you listen to each presentation, take notes on the sheets you have prepared.

1. CANIDS: DOGS AND WOLVES

He came out of a doze that was half
nightmare, to see the red-hued she-wolf
before him. She was not more than half a
dozen feet away, sitting in the snow. The
two dogs were whimpering and snarling
at his feet, but she took no notice of
them. She was looking at the man, and
for some time he returned her look.
There was nothing threatening about her.
She looked at him merely with a great
hunger. He was the food. Her mouth
opened, the saliva drooled forth, and she
licked her chops with the pleasure of anticipation.

—WHITE FANG,
by Jack London

I first met Michael Fox at a seminar he gave at Rockefeller University in New York back in 1975. His subject was wild canids—wolves, coyotes, foxes, and the like—and he had some fascinating things to say about canine communication. However, what I remember most clearly was the way he ended the lecture—with a strong plea for conservation. Since wolves are in danger of extinction, he said, scientists can't afford to simply sit back and look on, holding to their traditional objectivity. From comments I overheard as the audience of graduate students filed out the door, I gathered that such a plea from a research scientist is rare; but then Dr. Fox is an unorthodox sort of man, a veterinarian and psychologist, author of popular books as well as texts. In fact, by now he has moved on from research to become head of the Institute for the Study of Animal Problems, which is a new division of the Humane Society of the United States.

Over the years, Dr. Fox has observed wolf packs in the United States and wild dogs (called dholes), in India, and he has owned foxes, jackals, coyotes, and wolves, as well as a number of dogs. He has written about dog communication, drawing on both his own observations and on insights gained from studies of wild canids. It was primarily dogs that I wanted to talk to him about when I interviewed him, some months after his Rockefeller University lecture, in the Manhattan apartment of a mutual friend. It seemed to me that a book on animal communication should include something about the animals who live most closely with humans.

However, it turned out that we may know more about the signals of birds and bees than we do about those of dogs, for dogs haven't been studied as much. Perhaps *Canis familiaris* doesn't seem a "real" canid to scientists, as a canary didn't seem a "real" bird to Donald Kroodsma. Animals evolve to fit their natural habitat, and when humans step in and domesticate them, breeding them for particular purposes, they corrupt the delicate and fascinating relationship between animal and environment. By studying pigs or cattle, dogs or canaries, we might learn what humans want of such species, but not what evolution has demanded.

Studies of wolves and coyotes, however, have been forging ahead. Realizing that wolves are a threatened species, scientists have rushed to observe them while there's still time. What makes them particularly fascinating is the fact that in some ways they're similar to humans: they're hunters who live in packs that are rather like extended families; they're intelligent; they share food and cooperate in the business of survival; they teach their young and display deep affection for one another. And if wild canids are fascinating in themselves, knowing something about them is also a help in understanding dogs, for the dog is not only related to the wolf but is believed to have descended from it or to share a common ancestor.

Both wolves and dogs communicate primarily in three ways: with pheromones, with sounds, and with body language. In his book *Understanding Your Dog*, Dr. Fox pointed out that one of the things that's so appealing about dogs is that their emotions and reactions are easy to read: they seem straightforward, honest, utterly incapable of deception. Dogs have no trouble reading people, either, and in fact they may be better at interpreting us than we are them. Dr. Fox also said that wolves he has had have been even more expressive and more sensitive to human nuances than most dogs are.

There are several reasons why humans and dogs can communicate so comfortably. One that's often overlooked is the fact that individual dogs train their owners to respond to particular signals. For example, one dog I know notifies her people that she wants to go out by popping up and down like a kid on a pogo stick in front of the door. (Cats do the same sort of thing. One of mine uses the classic Lassie technique to tell me she's hungry: she runs ahead of me toward the kitchen, looking back to make sure I'm following. My other cat conveys the same information with an even more effective signal—when her dinner is late, she steps in front of me and trips me.)

However, the most important reason that dogs are easy to read is that their body language is in many ways similar to ours. This is particularly true of facial expressions. The delighted grin a dog wears when greeting its owner or a canine friend looks very much like a human smile. The dog's play face—which also involves a grin but with a wide-open mouth and ears pricked forward—resembles human laughter, and though humans rarely produce a full-fledged, teeth-baring snarl, the impulse is there, and it helps make the threat in a dog's snarl unmistakable.

Canid postures are also hauntingly familiar. Dr. Fox has photographs of wolves, for example, in which it's easy to tell the pack leader from his subordinates. The alpha male stands tall and holds his head high and his ears forward. The others seem hunched and wary—ears back, tails down, obviously avoiding their leader's eye. In some cases, heads are down as well, just as humans bow their heads in submission. Canids out to dominate or threaten make themselves appear larger and more dangerous by raising their hackles and walking stiff-legged—they seem almost to stand on tiptoe. To signal submission, they make themselves smaller. Perhaps this is simply the logic of the body, since many animals, from wasps to humans, share the same tendencies.

In canid society, a direct stare is a threat, and again this is a signal many species share. Dr. Fox explained that in a wolf pack, the dominant animals can control the others from a considerable distance with eye contact. All they have to do is stare intently at a subordinate, and it will generally assume a submissive posture. Ethologist

Konrad Lorenz, observing that a threatened animal will often turn its head sharply aside, suggested that it is offering its throat to the aggressor, which would be, perhaps, the ultimate in conciliatory gestures. However, Dr. Fox believes that all that's involved is an exaggerated looking away. In any case, he recommends that when humans are threatened by a strange dog, they should definitely not return stare for stare.

Canids are, of course, intelligent animals, and so their signals are flexible and sometimes even subtle. For example, though looking away is usually a sign of submission, on rare occasions it can be a bid for dominance instead. Dr. Fox recalled a particular wolf who was once introduced to a captive pack. On previous occasions, newcomers had been attacked by the pack in spite of the fact that they assumed submissive postures and facial expressions. In this case, however, the stranger refused to cringe and instead simply ignored the other animals, staring off into the distance as if they didn't exist. Surprisingly, the attack was aborted. Dr. Fox explained that it can actually be more intimidating to ignore threats and look away. ''It's like a man wearing sunglasses or a mustache,'' he said. (He was at the time sporting quite a luxuriant mustache himself.) ''The lack of expression creates distance, and that distance creates social control and dominance.''

I asked Fox how you can tell, when you're out walking a dog and a strange animal approaches making threatening noises, whether a real fight is likely to develop. He said that animals who are serious about fighting don't generally make a lot of noise or display very much—snarling with hackles raised, for example. Most often, when dogs threaten, all they do is stand over the other and shove: the aggressor dog will place itself perpendicular to the other animal, shoulder to shoulder, and push. In fairly short order, one individual or the other gives up, rolls over, and starts whining. When this kind of ritualized wrestling match is all that's involved, it's often best to just let it happen, since by intervening, you might start a real fight. In fact, on a quiet street, you should probably drop the leash and move away so that your dog won't take it into its head to defend you as part of its mobile territory. If you're really afraid a serious fight might break out, you can always ostentatiously pick up a rock, even an imaginary one. Most dogs will get the point.

Body signals to beware of, on the other hand, are those typical of the fear-biter: the animal puts its ears back and tucks its tail between its legs as if in submission, while at the same time, the hackles are up and dog is growling. It may actually grin—and simultaneously expose its teeth in threat. Believe the growl, not the grin, Fox said, and steer clear of the animal. A wagging tail is also not always what it appears to be. Though it's usually a token of friendliness, a tail carried high and waved stiffly and rapidly often accompanies other signs of aggression.

Some of the signals in the dog's repertoire are, in effect, baby talk, infantile behaviors carried over into adult social relationships. For example, for the first few weeks of life, a dog can't empty its bladder or bowels without help from its mother. When the mother returns to her litter, she will nose the puppy's groin. It responds by holding perfectly still so that she can lick the inguinal area and thus trigger evacuation. In general, she then tidily laps up the urine or feces. In adulthood, many dogs will still become momentarily immobile if touched on the groin, and a dog that has been scolded by her human will often raise one forepaw, not to shake hands, but in the old wolf-pack signal that she intends to roll over. Then she may roll onto one side, exposing her genitals just as a puppy does for her mother. She may even urinate a bit as she did when she was small. This is a sign of extreme deference, and in such a situation, a dog who piddles at her owner's feet is really presenting a bouquet, according to Dr. Fox. (Similar occurrences take place in wolf packs between adult wolves, and there the dominant animal may actually lick up the urine afterward, just as a parent would.) When a dog directs such signals to a human, it's because it relates to its owner as if he were the pack leader. In fact, a dog's human family *is* its pack.

Among wolves, there are other signals as well that linger after babyhood. Once the cubs are a few weeks old, the adult wolves begin to bring food home to them from the hunt. Since they're not supplied with pockets, they carry it in their stomachs and regurgitate it when the cubs lick them about the face and mouth. (Mother dogs also sometimes regurgitate to their litters.) Low-ranking adult wolves often use this cub gesture as a sign of submission, poking at the muzzle of a dominant animal, behaving as if they were cubs and the other animal were the parent.

Just as canids use baby signals in adult situations, so they sometimes use aggressive displays to express ritualized allegiance and affection, or so Dr. Fox believes. He once watched while several wolves came up to their pack leader and made submissive gestures. The alpha male got up in leisurely fashion and pinned them to the ground, one at a time; then he gave a big yawn and sat down again. Dr. Fox believes that this was a case where aggressive signals functioned instead as bonding behavior, and he thinks this may often happen.

Obviously canid body language is versatile and complex, and the more sociable the species, according to Dr. Fox, the richer the signal system. Foxes, which are fairly solitary animals, seem to have no submissive behavior—most of the time, they simply avoid one another—and they also lack subtle gradations of intensity in their facial and body displays. Wolves, within the complex social structure of the pack, have the most impressive signal repertoire of all.

Remembering Roger Fouts, who believes he communicates with his chimps in a kind of pidgin language, part signing and part Chimpanzeese, I asked Dr. Fox whether he ever communicated with canids in their own terms. He immediately recalled the one and only time he was ever attacked by a wolf. He went into the animal's cage, he said, not realizing that its female was in heat. Inadvertently he came between the two—and suddenly found himself pinned against the cage with the huge male standing over him. "I looked away and whined," he recalled. The wolf stopped attacking and someone else pulled him away.

Dr. Fox often communicates with dogs in a dog way. "It sometimes freaks them out," he said. "I use their body postures, facial expressions, vocalizations. I paw at them, touch them on the groin, bite them on the muzzle, make the play-inviting bow wearing the play face. Some of them bristle, yelp, run away, get very disturbed—for them, it's a schizoid space. Others get right into it. Though I'm sorry when they're disturbed, it's fun when they play along."

Though body language is important to dogs, they also rely on pheromone communication, to what extent we really don't know. It may be impossible for humans to understand or even imagine the olfactory world of a dog—a world in which odors linger on for hours to tell their stories.

Dogs come well equipped for sending odor messages. Each has a special scent gland near its tail—which explains the avid canine interest in that area—and there are other glands between the toes. Dr. Fox explained that when a dog urinates and then scrapes at the spot with its paws, it's marking the site visually, but it's also adding to the scent message from those interdigital glands.

With their system of marking with urine, canids can communicate across time. The spaniel lifting his leg beside a tree trunk is leaving a calling card that probably conveys several different messages. It may be a territorial marker or an aid to finding his way home; probably it also identifies him to other dogs who know him, and it may even specify his sex and tell them how long ago he was there. But we haven't really broken the code of canine urine yet—we can only guess what the messages are.

I asked Dr. Fox why, when you're walking two dogs, one sometimes insists on sniffing interminably around a tree or bush while the other remains indifferent. He explained that the animal more interested in sniffing and marking may be the more dominant of the two, since these activities seem to be more important to a dominant animal. Then again, the difference might be simply one of gender: male dogs are usually more interested in sending and receiving odor messages than females are—though females in heat do engage in a lot of marking.

Dogs also signal, of course, with a variety of sounds, and to a surprising extent, they can understand human speech. Dr. Fox estimates that many dogs can understand forty words or so; sixty are possible but would be exceptional.

Dr. Norman Bleicher, now at International College in Los Angeles, recently completed a study of dog vocalizations. Using the classic method, he observed behavior as he recorded sounds to be analyzed later with a spectrograph, and he found that there were indeed sounds that seemed to go with particular situations. Puppies, for example, vocalize differently according to whether they're hot, cold, hungry, hurt, playing, and so on. Dr. Bleicher also noted that dogs bark and growl both in play and to threaten, and that although some dog owners claim they can hear the difference, it doesn't show up on a spectrogram. This could be because the human nervous system is in some ways capable of making finer distinctions than the spectrograph can, or it could be, as Bleicher suggests, that barks in particular may serve merely to announce that the dog is there, while the animal signals its intentions with body language. At any rate, the bark is usually a long-distance threat, and so when two dogs who are face to face bark at one another, it's safe to assume they're playing—unless theirs was a sudden and unexpected confrontation.

Scientists are also trying to decipher the vocalizations of wild canids, and the great mystery there is group howling. Dr. Erich Klinghammer has been studying and recording the sounds of a captive wolf pack in Indiana, and at the Animal Behavior

Society meeting in 1976, he warned me, "Don't let anyone tell you we know what the wolf chorus is about, because we don't.

"Solo howls are not difficult to figure out," he said. "They apparently serve to attract a mate in the breeding season and to make contact with other wolves at any time. Probably the wolves can recognize one another's voices, just as I can, and in fact group howls may be one way wolves learn the voices of other pack members. They may also serve in territorial defense, to warn off other packs, as Harrington and Mech suggest, although this has not really been proven to my satisfaction. When humans howl in wolf territories, they rarely come to investigate, so we do not really know how wolves see this."

Why do so many people have such strong feelings about the wolf, pro and con—even city people who have never really seen one? I suspect that there are those in both camps who tend to project human values onto the animal. Some see the wolf as a wild creature that is intelligent, affectionate, courageous, self-sufficient. Others see a cunning and dangerous animal who kills without mercy. The wolf seems to embody both our negative and positive feelings about our own role as predators.

Conservationist that he is, Dr. Fox is sometimes turned off by the way the wolf's case is argued. "I'm getting very annoyed with people who feel they have to justify the existence of wolves or whales or whatever by demonstrating their superior intelligence or sociability, in other words, their similarity to us humans," he told me. "Everything is precious—whether it's humanlike or not. What right have we to destroy *any* animal? That's why it's important to realize that animals communicate and feel much as we do. Perhaps out of that, we can develop what we really need: a biospiritual ethic, a reverence for all life."

2. ANTS

The Chemical Language of Olfactory Signals

This is the way certain ant species behave, but not necessarily all, for myrmecologists (specialists who study ants) are continually finding new methods of communication between different species. According to whether the ants are African, Asiatic, European, etc.—and 6,000 different varieties have now been classified—each behaves in a distinct fashion.

Dealing specifically with ant scouts, Hingston in 1928 drew attention to a distinct variant in the *Crematogaster auberti* ant, from the neighborhood of Baghdad. When a scout finds fragments of an insect's carcase, it returns to the nest and—like other species—recounts its adventure. But it does not remain there. Excitedly jostling other members of the colony, it offers them a little of its nutritious find (with which it has already gorged itself), then accompanies a work party back to the scene of its discovery. Who selects this party and decides on the number of participants? And how is this done? We do not know, but the size of the work party always corresponds to the value and number of fragments of the prey.

Modern myrmecologists have tried to interpret this ''language,'' but the behaviour of the *Crematogaster auberti* ant seems less rigid than that of other ants. The question is whether the *Crematogaster auberti* (and probably other varieties) possess a ''symbolic'' language adaptable to the circumstances. According to a number of American entomologists this is by no means impossible. Certain ant species can exchange information in a still more sophisticated manner than the *Crematogaster auberti*. Discussions seem to take place between the informant ant and the rest. They form little groups, touch each other lightly with the tips of their antennae or legs, then separate again, repeating this until a final selection of ''commandos'' is ready to march forth. One gets the impression that the ants have come to a decision and that the ''scout,'' having been questioned, has, by virtue of its superior knowledge, prevailed as leader. Obviously, there is no proof of this, and to regard the impatient or hesitant movements of the forager ants as the action of a discussion group is pure anthropomorphism. We must beware, therefore, of regarding what is probably purely an instinctive reaction as conscious reasoning.

Nevertheless, in the view of E. O. Wilson, one of the greatest authorities on the subject in the United States, all ants can transmit different signals according to circumstances. Certain species, so he claims, are even able to emit signals at variable and successive intensities, just as we join words to form sentences.

What is the nature of these signals? To what exactly do they refer? On this point not all myrmecologists agree. It has been known for a long time that, because of their dark habitat, ants cannot rely on visual stimuli to any great extent, but transmit certain information by touch—by tactile pulsations of their antennae. Rémy Chauvin has never been convinced—unlike Szlep and Jacoby—that these confused pulsations and trembling of antennae form a code (for example, to induce the forager ants to leave their nests).

Chauvin, the foremost French myrmecologist, attaches more importance to olfactory signals. This is a ''chemical language'' so rich that among the *Solenopsis sævissima* (a species of ''fire ant''), no fewer than seven different olfactory means of communication have been observed. There is the scent of the nest, scent for marking out a trail, scent for a summons to battle, and so on.

These odoriferous liquids—or pheromones—are secreted in glands whose anatomical position and physiological functions are becoming better known. Among other glands, as Rémy Chauvin tells us, is Dufour's gland from which a colorless secretion flows along the length of the ant's sting. This secretion is used to mark out a trail, the ant touching the ground with its sting at regular intervals, leaving a sort of dotted line. Other glands close by secrete liquids which are substances of alarm. Fewer than a dozen of these different pheromones are enough to control the whole organization of an ant nest.

However, to explain the complex and various ways in which this ''chemical language'' is employed by different ant species—at least, those most familiar to us— one would have to make a complete résumé of the works of Rémy Chauvin.

Wireless Among the Ants

Apart from these olfactory signals, ants have other quite different signals which a study of the remarkable *Solenopsis sævissima* has revealed. The *Solenopsis* was first observed some forty years ago in Texas and immediately made its presence felt. Not only is its sting extremely painful, but, worse still, it is poisonous enough to kill a child.

It was obviously necessary to rid society of this pest but the most potent insecticides were useless against it. Even Dieldrin, the effects of which are both rapid and irreversible, failed to destroy the offspring although it massacred the fully grown ants. It was then that Wilson, digging deep into the soil, discovered that the females, after the first dusting with Dieldrin, immediately took evasive action by hurriedly removing all their eggs and burying them many feet underground. Thus, unexposed to the poison, the future ants were safe. But why did the female ants in neighboring colonies, unaffected as yet by the poison, follow their example?

Intrigued, Wilson and his pupils set out to get at the truth. Just as von Frisch had studied bees, day after day Wilson and his companions now patiently devoted themselves to deciphering the code of these intelligent ants.

It had already been shown that, apart from olfactory signals, ants emitted sound signals on frequencies between 20 and 100 millihertz (which are inaudible to the human ear). When research was continued on these lines, it was soon discovered that these highly acute sounds, produced by the ants rubbing one segment of their abdomen against another, were transmitted by vibrations through the ground. Not only could these sonic emissions alert the whole ant nest but they could also warn other colonies, even those relatively far away.

These few illustrations reveal the danger of comparing the innate methods of communication among certain social insects, not only with the intelligent language of men, but even with means of communication between other insects which merit a study of their own.

For the sake of clarity, therefore, we can say that patient research has now yielded details of the sensitivity of various species of insects: termites and butterflies are mainly olfactory; dragonflies are visual; bees, both olfactory and visual; ants, tactile and olfactory; and finally, crickets are auditory in the extreme. This relative classification will give the amateur entomologist a simple guide to the different ways in which insects emit signals and answers; in short, how they "communicate."

3. CHIMPANZEES

Because the highest apes seem so much like man, their behavior has been carefully observed for a long time. Some people have tried to teach them human skills, sometimes with fair success. But although apes have complex languages of their own, they have been unable to copy more than a word or two of human language and then only with sounds that are somewhat similar, never the same. One chimpanzee was raised in a family that intended to teach it to speak if possible. The chimpanzee was able to learn only four words in six years, and these words were not very clear. Efforts to teach apes to speak must always fail, not because an ape is incapable of learning but because the root of its tongue is in a different position from that of man's, and an ape cannot use its tongue the same way that man can.

Chimpanzees

At least one chimpanzee has been taught to converse with its trainer in a simple way by using special plastic symbols and letters. It can identify objects and their colors and give instructions for whatever it wishes its trainer to do with them. At the end of two years' training this animal could use 120 words. Another chimpanzee trained in American sign language learned 130 words in signs in four years. This is comparable with the ability of some human children, so chimpanzees are obviously capable of subtle language expression, even though their tongues and throat structure are unsuitable for making words.

Although neither of these chimpanzees could say a word, they could express their ideas in other ways. This is of course what they would do in their natural environment. Chimpanzees have a wide range of calls, posture signals, and facial expressions with which they communicate, just as we use nods, hand gestures, and eyebrow movements to add to our word meanings. These movements were used by man long before he used words, and he has never given up using them in spite of his use of word language. When an ape makes a gesture, however, it may not mean the same thing as when a human being makes the same gesture.

A chimpanzee's facial expressions cover a wide range of feelings, such as relaxation, alertness, aggressiveness, threat, attack, fear, threat with fear, hunger, pain, play, and so on. Most of these feelings also produce voice sounds—some of them very powerful; yet there are times when, like man, the chimpanzee prefers to be silent. If he thinks a fight is coming and he doesn't feel like fighting, he is quite likely to sneak off into the jungle without a sound.

These animals express contentment with low grunts when they are eating, and similar grunts are heard when they play. A low-pitched ''hoo'' will be used to greet another chimpanzee, and occasionally friends will fling their arms around each other when they meet. Sometimes they will just touch hands or grin, or they might give several panting grunts. So much depends on the circumstances and how the two animals feel about each other.

Greetings between two large groups can often build up to loud, excited calls and screams. At the approach of a hunting animal like a leopard or when they are really angry at the approach of another chimpanzee, their calls can be loud, defiant, repeated, and a bit hair-raising. Any juveniles in the area will be giving their own short, sharp screams of fear. When a male leader is about to cross a ridge or a hill, he gives a series of hoots followed by three or four roars to let any groups on the other side know he's coming with his family. This makes certain that their sudden appearance doesn't start a fight because they have surprised the others.

Chimpanzees can be very noisy during their dance sessions. They thump, clap, stamp, scream, tear up vegetation, and even beat on hollow logs or tree trunks. They sway and dance, and the juveniles join in as though they were enjoying a human "rock session." The animals may keep it up for half an hour, their laughter making a kind of panting sound.

Chimpanzees have air sacs in their throats for amplifying sound, and when a chimp grunts, it is thought to be due to the release of air from the animal's air sac. Such air sacs are found in a few species of all other orders. The largest sacs of all primates are found in orangutans. Macaques, baboons, and a number of other monkeys have them, but lemurs do not. None of the sacs are as large as the orangutan's, although the gibbons seem to make tremendous use of theirs.

Quite often chimpanzees will express themselves only with their faces or by contact. The greeting of a juvenile can be a forward protrusion of the lips, while that of an adult might just be a broad grin. Chimps will crouch, grin, smack their lips, chatter their teeth, and pout for various reasons, and when frightened they will draw back their lips and show their teeth with an open mouth. Showing the teeth both with and without sound is common to all apes, and there are many ways of doing this—all with different meanings.

If one chimp approaches another one rather nervously, it will make its mouth into a small opening and raise its eyebrows. Then it will touch the other's hand in greeting. If an ape is frustrated, it will open its mouth and project its lips with great force; but real anger brings the hair on its head upright and bristling.

Contact signals are also very prominent among chimpanzees. If they are nervous, they will reach out and touch each other for reassurance. The first one reaches out palm up, and the other accepts the palm with its palm down. A dominant male will touch the back of another male to give it confidence. A mother will touch her young when she is about to move away, or she will tap a tree trunk when she wants junior to come down to the ground.

A chimpanzee will pat a branch as an invitation to sit alongside him. If he wants to sample another's food, he will hold out his hand palm up. All these silent signals are as useful and expressive as speech, and they serve the same purpose at times when (unless the group is large and powerful) noise will attract the unwanted attentions of the big hunting cats.

4. SMALL MAMMALS, INCLUDING BATS

Small Mammals

We find quite elaborate systems of communication even among the smallest mammals. Some, like the porcupine and some rodents, appear to be quite silent. But many small animals' sounds are so high-pitched that human ears cannot detect them. This is true with mice and many other rodents; the distress calls of their young are much too high for us to hear. But a great many small mammal sounds are within our hearing range, and many of these have been studied.

Prairie dogs, which are not dogs at all but ground squirrels, have been given their name because they utter a warning or danger signal like a dog's bark. Whenever a prairie dog barks in this way, it is really saying, "Get below ground!" All members of its group or family then head for their burrows or at least sit up and look all around them for the cause of the alarm. By changing its pitch a look-out animal can change the meaning of the bark to "all clear."

The yellow-bellied marmot, another squirrellike rodent, uses odor, touch, and visible signals as well as sound. It has six different whistling calls with both long and short pauses between them. There is a quiet whistle that may simply keep members of the group in touch with one another. In another whistle the pauses gradually get shorter and shorter; this is for threatening and scolding. A third whistle with short pauses is used when a group of marmots are close to each other. All these calls are used for some kind of danger or to alert other marmots in the area. Marmots also have a barking whistle used while running, a single extra-loud whistle, and a scream. Visible signals are also used by marmots, and these are seen in their postures and movements.

Prairie dogs and marmots are not active at night, but many other rodents are. A number of these rodents use their vision much less than their other senses for receiving messages. They find it more useful at night to use their noses and their ears. The more an animal's nose and its center for smell in the brain are developed, the more active it is likely to be at night and the more it will use odors for communication. It is not surprising that mice have odors that are so personal they identify the sex, the species, and the individual. The males also produce in their urine a pheromone that conditions females for mating merely by its odor. A pheromone is a glandular secretion that stimulates the opposite sex. This pheromone is capable of making a female seem to be pregnant even if she is not—a false pregnancy.

The gerbil is a desert rat that uses odor from a gland in the middle of its underside for several purposes. This odor also carries both an individual and a species label, and the gerbil uses its odor to mark its territory in the same way as a dog does with its urine.

Bats

There has been a great deal of publicity about the investigations into the echolocation ability of bats, but little has been said about their ordinary voice communication with each other. Many bats have large larynxes and masses of larynx muscles, and perhaps all use their voices for close communication. Although some of their sounds have been recorded, little is yet known of their meanings.

Sometimes the meaning of the sound is obvious because of what happens when it is uttered. For instance, the male white-lined bat of Trinidad barks at every other male approaching his few square inches of roosting territory; this is a challenge. But as soon as a female comes near, he changes to a twittering song consisting of a mixture of chirps, buzzes, and pure notes that our ears cannot separate easily.

One of the most interesting things about this bat's voice signals is the fact that the frequencies of the notes are all multiples of each other. The male calls the female with a note of 6,000 cps. While hovering its sounds are 12,000 cps. It defies other males at 24,000 cps., and it hunts with 42,000 cps. Why all these signals are in frequencies so exactly spaced in multiples of 6,000 cps. is as mysterious as it is remarkable.

There is a very unusual fruit-eating bat called the hammerhead which lives in Gabon. Some of the range of its voice is easily heard by human ears. The hammerhead is very large and ugly with a three-foot wingspan and a head like a moose; and it hangs in dense forest and gives off a loud, metallic honking from sixty to one hundred times a minute. This soon becomes a chorus as other members of the species within hearing range join in.

Such calling in bats is unusual and so is such great power, but the power is not surprising because the animal's larynx occupies 20 percent of its entire body volume. On a similar scale, a man would have a larynx almost half the size of his chest cavity. One can imagine that if anything like that were possible, the volume of noise it would make might shatter windows. The male hammerhead honks to attract females. Once a female approaches, the male stops honking and starts a repeated buzzing sound that is his way of singing a love serenade. But this bat's voice is not used just for mating calls. The bat will snarl quite viciously at any intruder—other than a female—to his roosting place.

5. MARINE MAMMALS

As water is a better conductor of sound than air, it is perhaps natural that marine mammals have learned to use their voices much more effectively than land animals. This ability has probably also been encouraged by the fact that visibility in water is less clear than on land. In the last forty years marine mammals have been very closely studied, and the information that has been obtained shows that they have amazing voice ranges and clever ways of communicating.

Dolphins

The dolphins have been the most rewarding animals used so far in these studies. They show all the emotions of excitement, fear, pleasure, inquisitiveness, welcome, teasing or humor, concern, and distress. They are also able to transmit and receive sounds over several miles, probably much greater distances than man-made underwater sound-detection instruments have been able to measure.

Dolphins have two separate ways of making sound, which are ordinarily used under different circumstances, but in courtship or play they may be used together. They consist of whistles, clicks, and buzzes used for echolocation, and of animal voice sounds. Almost all small-toothed whales—including dolphins—make whistles and chirps. Some also produce squeals.

Not only can dolphins make a wide range of notes, they can also use a wide range of volume, the difference between two sounds sometimes being as much as one hundred decibels. This is almost the limit of what a human ear can stand without discomfort. And the complicated way their sounds are put together varies according to whether the animals are alone or together in groups. One thing that never seems to vary is their distress signal—a repeated double whistle, the first getting louder and the second getting softer. Other dolphins will locate this sound, but the increase and decrease in volume makes it impossible for sharks to track it down.

When they hear this distress signal, all dolphins within hearing range become silent and search for the animal sending it. When they reach the distressed animal, they push it to the surface to breathe, all the while chattering to it in whistle tones. This combined effort will keep a sick dolphin breathing for days, even weeks, and even dolphins that are complete strangers to each other will cooperate to do this without ceasing until the sick or injured animal is well or it dies.

This response to distress is not something unique to dolphins. Many whales will also answer appeals for help—especially sperm whales. It has been noticed, however, that while bulls will help cows, cows will never help bulls except among humpback whales. Cows will only help distressed calves. A film made by Jacques Cousteau on his research ship *Calypso* showed twenty-seven female sperm whales gathering from great distances to rescue an injured calf in answer to its distress signal. On land such a habit is less common, and perhaps the elephant is the only animal to help another of its kind.

Just as there is a definite distress signal like our SOS among dolphins, there is also a very recognizable sound of fear—a loud, sharp crack. Something like this has apparently been identified in other whales too. Each individual dolphin has a personal whistle pattern like a signature; other dolphins it knows recognize it by this whistle. Communication between dolphins is so good that they can even pass each other instructions or organize a herd to kill attacking sharks.

The killer whale, which is actually a giant dolphin, also has a good vocabulary but with entirely different sounds. Instead of the whistlelike squeal used by other dolphins for communication, this animal has much harsher screams. Killer whales have larynxes but no vocal cords. They, nevertheless, have one of the most complex languages in the entire animal world, and hearing is their most important sense. They and the whales have taken full advantage of the fact that sound travels better, louder, and faster in water than in air.

The fact that sound is louder in water is obvious to anyone who lies in a bathtub of water and while keeping an ear under water knocks on the bottom of the tub. The sound will be quite loud, but it will barely be heard if the head is raised out of the water. Similarly, any sound made in the air is hardly heard by a person or animal underwater. If it is to be heard clearly, the sound must be amplified considerably or be high pitched. For this reason whistles have been used for thousands of years to attract whales near enough to be killed.

Very small underwater explosions can be picked up at a great distance. Because such noises are so greatly amplified, the Japanese used to be able to drive whales into bays by beating against the sides of their boats with wooden hammers. Anything falling into the water beside a whale creates enough noise to send the whale off in any direction at high speed.

Sound travels up to a mile a second in water, with slight variations for salinity, depth, pressure, and temperature. This is five times faster than in air, so a sound wave of any given frequency has to be five times longer than it would be in air. Water is therefore an ideal medium for sound communication, and other marine mammals—the seals and sea lions—have taken full advantage of this fact.

If dolphins have no vocal cords, how do they make their sounds? Some scientists believe that the sounds are made by forcing air from small sacs close to the blowhole, and that small pieces of cartilage in the air passage play a part in their soundmaking. Others think that the air vibrates in folds in the linings of the larynx and throat and that sounds are made when air is forced through the larynx, but our knowledge of this is still incomplete.

6. BIRDS

The Rockefeller University Field Research Center in Millbrook, New York, is deep in the countryside. Once the gate house to a large estate, it's a big, handsome place that looks more like a ski chalet than like what it is: one of the major American laboratories for studying bird song. On the inside, the building is a regular warren of short corridors and large, sunny offices. There are walls as thick as those of a Cotswold cottage, and some of the doors are shaped like archways. The ambience is part graduate school, part country estate.

What I remember most vividly, though, is the bird lab on the ground floor. I was shown around the lab by Roberta Pickard, a research assistant, and when she opened the door of one particular room, a sound like steam escaping rushed out at us. The sound is called white noise, and it's used to make sure that no canary arias, no vagrant scrap of swamp-sparrow song, can reach the ears of the birds inside the room, some of whom have been raised from the egg in white noise without ever hearing so much as a peep or a chirp from any kind of bird.

Inside the room, dozens of boxes sat side by side on utility shelves. They looked rather like wall ovens, each with a little window in the front, but they were actually soundproof containers. When Ms. Pickard opened one of them, I saw that it held a large microphone and two long-billed marsh wrens—small, slim, racy-looking brown birds. They were in adjoining cages, and the wren on the right was a young male who hadn't yet begun to sing, while the adult wren on the left was his song tutor. The latter was actually doing double duty, for the microphone piped his lessons on to yet another young bird alone in a cage a few boxes away. Eventually it would be possible to compare the song of the bird who was able to see the tutor with that of the bird who was only able to hear him, to find out if there were differences. But what particularly intrigued me was the fact that the tutor himself originally learned his song not from an older bird but from a tape recording.

More than twenty years ago, scientists in England first proved—by raising young chaffinches in soundproof isolation—that all song birds aren't born knowing exactly what to sing. Peter Marler, the Rockefeller University professor I had come to

Millbrook to interview, was involved in some of those early experiments at Cambridge University, and after he moved to the United States in 1957, he added a great deal to what we know about song learning through extensive studies of California's white crowned sparrow. A solid, thoughtful, slow-spoken Englishman, he's immensely respected in his field.

Professor Marler was in conference when I arrived at Millbrook, so while I waited to talk to him, I rapidly reviewed some of what I'd already learned about bird song. There were, I had decided, seven principal facts one had to know to understand the basics of bird song.

1. In most species, only the male bird sings. As with the cricket, his song identifies him as a member of his species and attracts females. Simultaneously, it warns other males away from his territory.

2. It's also his personal signature. Scientists have found that in many species, one bird can recognize another by his song.

3. Many birds also sing in dialect: all those living within a given area produce the same variations on the basic theme.

4. For some species, there's a critical period for learning to sing. If, during the first few weeks or months of life, scientists and soundproof boxes prevent them from hearing the song of their kind, they grow up to sing abnormally no matter how often they hear that song *after* the critical period is over.

5. A young bird raised in a soundproof box will learn normal song quite readily if he's allowed to listen to recordings of wild birds singing. However, most will learn only the song of their own species, ignoring those of other birds, even if that's all they ever hear.

6. The young male bird, hatched in spring or summer, doesn't begin to sing until his hormones prompt him in the spring of the following year. In the meantime, he practices with something called *subsong,* which is soft and rambling and only gradually crystallizes into the themes of his species.

7. An adult bird that is deafened surgically continues to sing quite normally. If the same operation is performed on a young bird who hasn't yet begun to sing—even if he's old enough to have heard and learned his song—when he grows up, he won't sing at all but instead will make strange, insectlike sounds.

Years ago Professor Marler took all these separate facts and made sense of them with a single theory. He suggested that the male song bird is equipped from birth with a *template,* a rough plan of the song of his species. Unlike the cricket, which is born knowing every note and nuance of its calling song, the young bird often knows only enough to ensure that as he develops, he'll tune in to and learn the themes of his own kind, rather than those of some other species. As he matures, then, he learns from his elders and improves on the template by adding details, including a local dialect and some personal touches. If he's raised in soundproof isolation, of course, he can't learn these details, which is why he sounds somewhat abnormal; and if he's deafened before he has come into song, he can't even approximate the anthem of his kind, because he hasn't been able to listen to his own singing and match it to his template by practicing with subsong.

Not all birds learn to sing in just this way. For some, the song plan is complete at birth, or very nearly, just as it is with crickets. Others use a different learning strategy. The bullfinch, for example, simply acquires the song of the male who tends him, whether that male is a bullfinch or not. But what's important about birds such as the white crowned sparrow and the chaffinch is that there are intriguing parallels between the way they learn to sing and the way human infants learn to talk.

Song learning in birds is, then, a complicated but important subject, and the setup at Millbrook is quite elaborate. When Professor Marler took me around, he began by showing me a formidable array of sound-analyzing equipment.

The problem in studying animal sounds has always been that humans miss so much. Most of the time, we're not aware of the spread of frequencies in a sound or the subtler shifts in pitch and loudness. We can't tell just by listening when a trill in a bird's song is one syllable shorter than usual. The solution has been to freeze sounds by making them visible.

Dr. Marler explained that within about the last five years, there has been a breakthrough in techniques for analyzing sound. For a long time, scientists were dependent mainly on the spectrograph, a machine that graphs short swatches of sound, plotting the frequency (or pitch) along the vertical axis, with time along the horizontal one. Marler showed me a spectrogram of the trills of a swamp sparrow's song, and it looked a bit like a musical score, with the notes of the music drawn as a row of slanting, upsidedown exclamation points. I could easily see the way the pitch shifted upward as the lines did.

The spectrograph, however, has its disadvantages. It's a small machine topped with a revolving drum that's wrapped with a strip of paper. You play bird song into it, and as soon as you hear sounds you want to analyze, you pull a switch. Several minutes later, the machine traces out on the revolving drum a spectrogram of the 2.4 seconds of sound that preceded the pulling of the switch. Patching together a picture of a stretch of sound longer than 2.4 seconds is obviously a tedious business. About five years ago, life became much easier for bioacousticians (those who study animal sounds) when "real time" sound-spectrum analyzers became available. This new machine can provide a continuous display almost instantaneously on a screen or within minutes as a permanent photographic copy.

The research team at Millbrook is also trying to design a machine that can synthesize bird songs. Ron Hoy already has an artificial cricket, and Bob Capranica can dial up a frog's mating call, but crickets and frogs make simple sounds in comparison to bird songs, and it will take some fairly sophisticated equipment, including a computer, to mimic birds. Once the Millbrook synthesizer is perfected, Marler will be able to copy songs and then to alter them at will in subtle ways to find out which features are significant to birds.

Calls With and Without Song

Certain birds make no sounds that we would call song, but they have calls with which they keep in touch with each other. These birds do not usually mark out territory, so they may have less need for song. Just keeping in touch within the group will bring them together for breeding anyway, and calls can be used for that.

Even birds that have territorial and courtship songs also have certain calls of this kind, and their alarm call is usually the one most easily recognized. But their warning signal for invading members of their own species is quite different from the one they give when humans or predators come into view. There are, in fact, many versions of alarm calls; some of them not only alert members of their own species but also alert other birds and animals, which even seem to understand the differences in calls for different kinds of danger. Warning calls can also be divided into those for possible danger and those for definite danger.

Indian mynas have a special danger signal for humans and birds of prey which sends all other birds diving for safety as well, often giving their own alarm calls as they go. The chickadee sounds a different alarm call when danger is overhead than when it is on the ground. Crows have five different danger calls, and jackdaws even have one that brings help from other jackdaws, but this would probably also be considered a distress call.

These alerting calls are always the result of *seeing* an enemy. This fact has been proved in the laboratory by electrically stimulating the vision centers in a bird's brain. This stimulation automatically produces scolding and alarm calls and results from the fact that there are connections in the brain between hearing and vision centers.

Many birds vary the pitch of their danger calls to confuse hawks and other predators, and there is a reason why this is successful. The easiest sound to locate is one that is steady, like a ''clucking'' or ''chirping,'' because these sounds can be timed by the two ears. But when calls are varied by fading or by gradually amplifying them in such a way that they seem to be moving farther away and then coming closer, they are much more difficult to trace.

Identification calls keep a flock together or bring it together, and some birds use a call of this kind when one of them finds a supply of food. Identification is very important between parents and their young as well as between the parents themselves. Thus, these calls are often quite individual, although to our ears the differences may not be apparent.

Penguin calls to their young all sound alike to us—but not to the chicks. Within a colony of many thousands a parent's call will bring only her chick to her, so penguin voices must be as personal to penguins as ours are to us. There are some birds, however, in which individual calls are so different in tone that they can be identified by man; but even in these the species sounds are always present.

It has already been mentioned that certain birds call before hatching from the egg. Sometimes this goes on for hours or even days before final hatching. Air can penetrate an eggshell, and the chick uses air in the space between the inner and outer shell membranes to make the sounds with its syrinx. It responds to outside sounds, to the mother's calls, and to other embryos calling. This is thought to be a provision for making certain the eggs all hatch at about the same time because those in contact with each other do hatch at the same time but more distant ones do not. The hatching of those not in contact may be spread out over a twenty-four-hour period.

The rhea, an ostrichlike, South American bird, has very successful simultaneous hatchings in this way. It probably needs this ability more than many other birds because a number of female rheas visit a male and leave eggs with him to incubate and hatch. By the time he has all he can manage, there may be fifty or sixty eggs. The embryos communicate with each other, however, and although there may be quite some time between the laying of the first and last eggs, all hatch at about the same time.

Some of the bird sounds most pleasing to our ears are quiet conversations that go on between a pair in some species. These conversations appear to be quite personal. Perhaps the most familiar of these is that of the duck; when a female has young around her, she hardly seems to cease her chatter. The Australian magpie converses so tunefully in this way that one cannot help but get pleasure from listening to it. At times the conversation is almost like a quiet little duet.

Many Australian birds talk among themselves all the time because Australia has so many parrots, cockatoos, and budgerigars. These birds also have their calls, which may vary with the seasons, but the chatter continues all the time. The Easten rosella has about twenty-four different calls for warning, distress, aggression, location, and victory in a fight.

Most birds seem to have more danger calls in autumn, when there are more predators about, and more aggression calls in spring, because of mating rivalry. Then as the juveniles and other groups gather together before the winter, aggression calls once again become more frequent.

The more we listen to birds, the more certain we become that most people miss the meaning of their language. Probably all birds have wider vocabularies than anyone realizes. Because the canary is a captive bird, we recognize many of its messages; it has ten or more kinds of sounds for courtship alone, as well as calls for attack, alarm, agitation, anxiety, and surprise. Chickadees have sixteen songs and calls with obvious meanings, and even the humble domestic chicken, which seems so stupid to most of us, has more than twenty. All birds express in one way or another alarm, hunger, identity, finding food, territorial aggression, threat, attack, flight, courtship, and mating.

The Indian myna (one species of which is called the noisy miner in Australia) is another constant chatterer. Some of its calls we can recognize easily. One of these is uttered by the bird when it finds food, to tell a widely scattered group about it. Another is a scolding cry to drive away competitors—larger birds, foxes, and cats—and to warn of snakes. The last call is also used to warn others of another group that have come too close. As explained before, this bird has a separate danger cry against falcons and humans. Another call is a kind of inquiry when danger appears to be past; ''Is it okay now?''

Bird Displays and Signals

Bird display and bird song cannot be separated because in some species the two are so intimately linked that they occur together, reminding us of very similar behavior seen in some mammals. A simple example is the cat, which arches its back and hisses at the same time. This is display and voice being used together. We even see the same thing in young boys who put up their fists and say at the same time, ''Come and get me.'' Yet in describing display we must concentrate on display by itself to some extent, for certain birds display without making sounds.

POSTURES

Many birds signal their feelings or their intentions clearly with the position of the body, tail, bill, head, crest, and legs; frequently combining these with repeated movements, calls, bill-clapping, or quiet sounds. Those birds in which the male performs aerobatics to impress a female often sing at the same time, but not all do. Sometimes these acts do not carry a message at all. They just identify a bird or its species like a signature.

In any species in which the male and female are similarly colored, they may identify their sex only by posture or movement, but when a movement carries a message, it is clear to every member of the species. For instance, it has been noticed in Wales that the sandpiper raises its right wing to a vertical position as a warning, and it would be difficult for any other bird not to see this.

Display is an important part of courtship. While display may seem to us to be something that should be private between a pair of birds, some species congregate in groups on special display or ''strutting'' grounds for their courtship displays. Often these groups include considerable numbers of both sexes, the females watching the males strut around, spread their feathers and tails, and perhaps make throat sounds too. But not all strutting is done in groups. The pigeon, the ostrich, the peacock, the lyre-bird, and many others require no audience at all, although if there is one, this does not affect the behavior of some of them.

Individual displays—that is, those in groups that do not congregate—include postures, movements, and color. These will often but not always go on with song or quiet chatter. Male birds of paradise have vivid displays. They perch, fly, or even hang upside down, spreading their tails, wings, and special feathers or plumes that show colors, shapes, and attitudes while singing or calling their courtship tunes.

Once birds have paired up, the displays change in many species. Greeting (recognition), especially at the nest for identifying each other, and the offering of gifts may take the place of the previous courtship displays. When the two sexes have the same coloring, posture can be most important for recognition. A good example of this is seen in the frigate bird, where the male points his bill up in greeting and the female points hers down. The male penguin may stretch up his neck in greeting, while the female will bow hers.

Postures also convey other information. The black cormorant crouches horizontally with its crest down when at the nest, but when it is away from the nest, its body is upright and its crest is raised. The crest goes down at once, however, to signal danger. It is natural that birds without voices or with syrinxes that hardly function should use visible signals, and this extends to basic things as well as to warnings and greetings. When the voiceless young cormorants are begging, they close their bills for food and open them for water.

THE DRUMMERS

Woodpeckers can communicate in a kind of Morse code by drumming with their beaks on tree trunks; this has nothing to do with their pecking to get at insects. Woodpeckers may make only a single knock or several lasting a few seconds, but these knocks seem to carry a message to other woodpeckers out of sight. Male grouse make drumming noises too, but in their case it is done with their wings for courtship or challenging other males. This bird also makes posture signals by expanding its body and raising its feathers.

OHER SIGNALS

Most attention has been paid in the past to the display and behavior seen in courtship and raising the young, and our knowledge of other visible signals made by birds and their meanings is not yet so comprehensive as it might be. There are probably nearly forty different voice and visible signals in the language of some bird species, and this is many more than would be required just for bare survival in courtship, alarm, and defense. Some signals used in disputes over territory are not displayed by males alone; in some species both sexes display together.

Among the special display features commonly seen are the inflatable pouches of the male frigate bird and the giant bustard, and crests that are invisible until raised in anger or display of the cockatoo. Such moveable crests are used for signaling. There are also crests that are always in a raised position and combs like those of the domestic chicken that are similar to the helmets of the hornbill or the cassowary and the shield of the marsh hen. These are only a way of identifying the species or of separating the sexes.

Some birds open their wings to reveal different colors or special markings when they are about to take flight. It seems that this movement stimulates a whole flock to take off at the same time. Whooper swans bob their heads up and down for the same purpose.

All animals have language of some kind or another and use it effectively.

Preparing for an Exam

Assume that you have just finished the animal communication section of your introductory biology course. Your exam is scheduled for next week. You're fairly sure you know the course content, but you're not sure what kinds of questions the professor usually asks or how students are expected to *use* what they have learned. Also, you aren't sure of your ability to write short answers quickly in an examination situation. The purpose of this exercise is to help you practice answering this kind of question.

To help you with the first part of the problem, what will be on the exam, your library might carry copies of previous examinations. If so, your first step might be to research old exams to find out what kinds of questions are usually asked. If, however, your library doesn't offer this service, or if the professor hasn't taught this course before, the library won't be of much use. In that case, your next best strategy is to try to *predict* the questions he might put on the exam.

Go over your first two readings and your notes. Then answer the following questions.

1. What topics have you covered? List them.

2. Are there any terms you might be asked to define or explain? List them.

3. Understanding and applying information is more important to a professor than your ability to regurgitate. Professors often want to know if you can see connections between topics. Can you see any way of:
   a. applying one set of principles to other information?

   b. comparing and/or contrasting information?

4. Write three questions you think the professor would be likely to ask you on the exam. Be prepared to justify your choices.
   a.

   b.

c.

5. Form groups of 3 or 4. Discuss your questions. Decide on 4 or 5 that stand a good chance of being asked on the exam.

Predicting what questions will be on an exam and then answering them is a good way to review what you have learned. In your group, choose two questions from the ones you wrote above.

Question 1:

Question 2:

Read your questions carefully. In each question, exactly what information is needed? How should the information be organized?

Do the next 6 steps individually.

1. For question 1, go back over your readings and notes, putting boxes around the information you should include.
2. Consider your organization:
   How many sections will your answer have?
   How will you sequence them?

3. On a separate sheet, draw a tree diagram or sketch to show the main topic and subtopics for each section of your answer. Write one or two words for each, just to jog your memory.

4. On the sketch, write one or two words to help you remember any details or examples you want to use to prove what you say.

5. Reread the question. Check the whole sketch to make sure you have a complete answer. With your teacher, discuss a possible introductory sentence.

6. Repeat steps 1–5 for question 2.

7. Reform your groups. Go through the following steps for your question 1:

   a. Take turns. Show your group your sketch, telling them briefly what you will say in each part.
   As you do this, the rest of the group will check:
   • your information, to make sure that you really answered the question
   • your organization, to see if they understand the relationships between your ideas

   b. Decide on the best answer to your question 1.

8. Repeat steps a and b for question 2.

You will be tested on the following readings:

"Translating Bird Song"
"Animals That Try to Talk"

You should also review the table comparing systems of animal communication. During the exam, you will be allowed to use only the table.

Compare and Contrast

Considering the nature of the texts you have read, you will probably be asked at least one question requiring you to compare and/or contrast information.

The purpose of the next exercise is to help you review the structures necessary to do this clearly.

The Structures of Comparison and Contrast

Read each of the following sentences. Decide if it states a *contrast* or a *comparison* or *both*. Write the appropriate term on the line beside the sentence.

_____ 1. " . . . although animals do not 'naturally' talk, this does not mean that they are *incapable* of talking."

_____ 2. "On the one hand, it can mean simply 'in other words,' as in 'Archibald's got a talking parrot which says _Damn_ if you poke it,' On the other, it can mean 'to use language in a meaningful way.' "

_____ 3. "Failure to communicate this extra item of information means that bee communication cannot be regarded as 'open-ended' in the same way that human language is open-ended."

_____ 4. "Among birds it is claimed that the song-thrush's song is largely innate . . . whereas the skylark's song is almost wholly learned."

_____ 5. "Just as birds learn the song of their kind . . . so babies learn to speak. . . . "

_____ 6. In much the same way, if an experimenter cuts the nerve that connects an adult bird's vocal equipment with its left hemisphere, afterward it can sing only the most fragmentary song, while if the same operation is performed on a young bird, it eventually comes into song quite normally."

_____ 7. " . . . an older Chinese baby sounds different from an older French baby."

As a class, discuss your responses with your teacher.

_____

Reread the 2 texts, finding at least 3 other examples of structures expressing either comparison or contrast. Write them below. Share these with others, in groups of 3 or 4. In the appropriate place below, write down any structures you don't already have.

1. Comparison

   a.

   b.

   c.

2. Contrast

a.

b.

c.

Writing an Exam

You will now write the exam on animal communication. You can refer to the table on systems of animal communication.

You will have 40 minutes to complete Part A of the exam.

EXAM
Part A (15 points)

Answer *three* of the following questions. Each question is worth 5 points.

1. How is the continuity theory of human language different from the discontinuity theory?

2. Briefly explain what is meant by two of the following characteristics of language: cultural transmission, arbitrariness, and displacement.

3. What characteristic appears to be unique to humans? How did von Frisch find out that bee communication lacks this feature?

4. What is a critical period in language learning?

5. List three forms of communication other than sounds.

Part B (25 points)

Using your tables of notes, answer the following question. You will have 30 minutes to write your answer.

In an essay of approximately 1 page, compare the use of visible signals in the communication systems of dogs and birds.

Hand in your papers.

With your teacher, decide what a professor would consider complete answers to the essay questions.

You will use this as a guide when your teacher hands back your paper.

5
THE GREENHOUSE EFFECT

CHAPTER CONTENTS:

Some scientists have predicted that, because of a number of environmental conditions, the Earth's climate may become much warmer. This condition is known as the *greenhouse effect*. In this unit you will learn about the causes and consequences of this change.

The text in this chapter will allow you to evaluate and compare information from a number of sources. You will also be asked to summarize what you have read.

The writing task is a short essay question asking you to summarize information about the effects of possible climatic changes.

THINKING ABOUT THE TOPIC

Throughout history, there have been a number of worldwide climatic changes. In this chapter, we'll be investigating one climatic change that many scientists have been predicting.

This activity is designed to help you predict the consequences of a series of possible changes in climate by applying your knowledge of the world. Carefully consider the following questions. Then write point form answers.

1. a. If your country's annual rainfall increased by 50%, how might this change affect your country?

b. What might happen if the rainfall decreased by the same amount?

2. If your country's average winter temperature rose by 5–10°, how might this change affect your country's agriculture, tourism, and/or fishing industries?

3. If your country suddenly developed huge fresh water resources, what effect could this have on your relations with neighboring countries?

In groups of 3 or 4, compare your answers.

"*THE GREENHOUSE EFFECT*"

You can develop strategies that will help you read the large amounts of text in university courses. There are a number of things you can do before you begin to read the entire text.

1. Use the text support the author has provided. Authors often use headings and subheadings to indicate what the text is about and how it is organized. It's a good idea to read these headings first.

   Read the title and subtitle of the following article. Try to answer the following questions.

   a. What is this article about? What kind of information are we likely to find in it?

   b. Does the article adopt a positive or negative attitude toward the topic? Why do you think so?

2. Another strategy that will make you a more efficient reader is to consider what you already know about the topic.

   a. What do you already know about the greenhouse effect? Share your information with the class.

   b. What is a greenhouse? How does it work?

3. If you are aware of the organization of a text, it is easier to remember the information.

   The following list of phrases can serve as an outline of the main points in the article. Skim the text. Which paragraphs talk about each of these points? Put the corresponding paragraph numbers in the blanks.

   _____   Introduction—the possible arrival of the "greenhouse effect"

   _____   Why this has been labeled the "greenhouse effect"

   _____   The recent increase in carbon dioxide

The Green-house Effect

Scientists warn that a blanket of carbon dioxide is causing the Earth to warm up

(1) We've been hearing about the greenhouse effect for years. Now, two U.S. reports predict that it may happen sooner than we counted on. Released separately by the U.S. Environmental Protection Agency (EPA) and the National Research Council (NRC), the reports warn that the first effects may be felt as early as the 1990s.

(2) A greenhouse can produce a tropical climate in sub-zero weather by trapping the sun's rays under glass. Scientists say we're creating the same effect on a global scale by burning fossil fuels (coal, oil, gas). Carbon dioxide is a by-product of the burning. The gas allows sunlight to penetrate the atmosphere but slows the escape of heat back into space. This one-way trip for the sun's rays tends to make our planet a big greenhouse. We are beginning to warm up, just like a pot of violets under glass.

(3) We've been burning fossil fuels for centuries. However, the automobile and heavy industry have speeded up the release of carbon dioxide so much that experts say it's almost too late to prevent the coming results. Even a switch to other forms of energy might do no more than delay changes for a few years.

(4) A warming trend in climate will be the main effect. At first, that seems all to the good, especially for Canadians. But a closer look reveals dangers which may call for major adjustments all over the world. Average temperatures may rise by 2°C by the year 2040, and by 5°C by 2100. Increases up to three times as large may take place at the poles, however, causing the ice caps to melt rapidly. The oceans would then rise, causing flooding of coastal cities such as Halifax. To compensate a little, Halifax could have a climate like Daytona Beach, Florida, by 2100.

(5) Coastal cities will have to plan for the coming changes. The loss of land, houses, and factories can be reduced by planning new building sites, erecting sea walls, and contouring the land. Even so, low-lying countries will suffer. One third of the Netherlands, Florida and Louisiana, and large parts of Bangladesh will be submerged. Many port cities will look like Venice.

(6) The warmer climate will bring changed patterns of drought and rainfall. The desert Sahel area of Africa will get more rain, but the wheat-growing areas of the United States, the Soviet Union, and China will be drier and less productive. More carbon dioxide will likely spur plant growth, but some regions may become too hot and dry for crops.

(7) Earth has gone through temperature swings before, but only slowly over thousands of years. The coming changes may take place in a mere 120 years, and the NRC report says they would have "few or no precedents in the Earth's recent history."

(8) "It is the global environment issue of the century," says Henry Hengeveld of Environment Canada. "For the first time man will change his environment on a global basis." Others like Jack Val-

lentyne, a senior Canadian water scientist, rank the greenhouse effect with nuclear war and the population explosion in terms of its potential impact on humans. (9) Predictions for Canada contain both pluses and minuses. Prince Edward Island will likely be cut in half by the rising Altantic Ocean. On the other hand, warmer temperatures might open the Northwest Passage to summer shipping. Against that advantage we would have to weigh the possibility that foreign warships might challenge our sovereignty in the Arctic Ocean.

(10) A drop in Great Lakes levels due to reduced rainfall and greater evaporation could be disastrous for the millions living around them. Industries would grow thirsty for water needed in production. The reduced outflow of water would cost millions in lost electric generation. Ships would have to carry less cargo, fisheries would suffer, and pollution would be more concentrated. Drought in the central and southwestern U.S., already short of water, would increase political pressure from our neighbor to divert the Great Lakes and other Canadian waters. Wider beaches and less shoreline erosion would be minor benefits in comparison to these negative effects.

(11) The already dry southern prairies would suffer still more from drought. Some crops would be eliminated. Some crops would be eliminated, replaced by rangeland. There would be a potential loss of 19% in wheat, 14% in oats, and 11% in barley. These losses might be offset by spectacular crops in fertile areas of the far north, particularly in Alberta.

(12) Our forests would likely march north to the Arctic Ocean, a dramatic revolution for a major Canadian industry. Against that we would have to balance an increase in forest fires, insects, and disease in dry areas.

(13) Heating bills might drop by 15%, along with taxes for snow removal. Higher demand for air conditioning and for shrinking water supplies could offset these reductions, however.

(14) In Canada, as elsewhere, some will gain and some lose from the greenhouse effect. The NRC report stresses that we need to learn a good deal more about the degree of temperature change, the timing, and the consequences before we jump in with costly plans which may turn out wrong.

Now read the text carefully, looking for answers to the following questions:

1. Why has this phenomenon been termed the "greenhouse effect"?

2. Why is it happening now?

3. What are the two major consequences of a warmer climate for the world in general?

4. What are the main negative and positive consequences for Canada in particular?

"'GREENHOUSE EFFECT' AND METHANE RISE"

It is easier to remember information if you summarize it. One easy way to summarize a process, for example, is to draw a diagram.

Read the article on methane gas from the *New York Times*. Then draw a cause-and-effect diagram on page 117 to illustrate how the increase in world population has contributed to the warming of the earth's surface.

SCIENCE WATCH

"Greenhouse effect" and methane rise

Methane gas, a contributor to the greenhouse effect that scientists believe may be slowly warming the earth's surface, has been increasing in atmospheric concentrations since 1977, a team of researchers at the University of California at Irvine report.

Their worldwide seven-year study has revealed an annual methane increase of 1.1 percent throughout the earth's lower atmosphere, according to the team leader, F. Sherwood Rowland, professor of atmospheric chemistry, in a report recently issued by the university.

Carbon dioxide from the burning of such fossil fuels as coal and gasoline is believed to be the principal substance that acts to reflect the sun's heat back to the earth, causing the greenhouse effect. But, the researchers point out, methane is also a factor because it absorbs infrared rays that act as a barrier to a portion of the earth's thermal radiation. The gas also plays a role in urban smog and depletion of ozone in the atmosphere.

Methane is released into the atmosphere by cows in their digestion of cellulose and by biological action under water in flooded rice paddies and swamps. The pungent odor often present in marshes, bogs and swamps, commonly called swamp gas, is primarily methane.

Dr. Rowland believes that methane concentrations are rising because of the growing need to feed the earth's rapidly increasing human population. This, he said, has led to a 50 percent rise in the number of cattle in the world in the past few decades, and a corresponding increase in the number of high-yield rice planting areas on the earth.

Writing a Short Essay

In this chapter you will practice writing a test question for your professor in physical geography. The question you will answer later in the chapter is:

What is the greenhouse effect? Why are scientists concerned about it?

In order to do this essay, you will have to complete the following tasks.

1. Gather information from articles on the greenhouse effect
2. Choose and organize the information needed for the answer

(This page has been left blank for you to draw a cause-and-effect diagram.)

"'Greenhouse effect' May Cause Havoc in Canada"

"'Greenhouse Effect' Could Hit by 2000"

"Greenhouse Effect May Shrink Lakes, Cut Water Supply"

This next activity will provide you with additional information on the greenhouse effect.

Form groups of three. Each person will select one of the following articles. Your task is to prepare a 5-minute summary of the information in your article. Number the main points so that the other group members will be able to take notes easily. Be sure to pay particular attention to anything relevant to your writing task.

"Greenhouse effect" may cause havoc in Canada

TORONTO (CP)—A predicted warming of the earth's climate—known as the greenhouse effect—could alter the landscape of Canada, flooding some areas and turning others into dustbowls, experts say.

While balmy temperatures will moderate Canada's bitter winters, Prince Edward Island will likely be cut in half by a rising Atlantic Ocean and the Hudson Bay lowlands could become the country's foodbasket, studies predict. The arid southern Prairies would get drier and many crops would be eliminated and possibly replaced by rangeland.

Scientists believe such dramatic changes could occur worldwide because industrial air pollution is forming an insulating blanket around the planet.

The polluting gases—mostly carbon dioxide from the burning of fossil fuels such as coal, oil, gas and wood—permit sunlight to reach the earth, but slow the natural escape of infra-red heat from the planet's surface.

As a result, scientists say the earth will heat up like a pot of flowers in a greenhouse.

Two U.S. studies say the first effect of the global warming may be noticeable in a decade and severe changes will take place in the next century, possibly including mass movements of population.

Henry Hengeveld, advisor to Environment Canada on the issue, says the greenhouse effect "is the global environment issue of the century."

"For the first time, man will change his environment on a global basis."

Although experts predict the amount of carbon dioxide in the atmosphere will double before the year 2100 and likely raise the earth's temperature two degrees, the greatest effect will occur near the poles.

Southern Canada can expect a temperature increase of three to five degrees, while the north will be about 10 degrees warmer.

The greenhouse effect could also mean the loss of hundreds of millions of dollars in electrical generation as the level of the Great Lakes falls because of more evaporation. Lower levels on the Great Lakes could also threaten fisheries and increase the concentration of pollution but reduce erosion and widen beaches.

Agriculture and forestry, two of Canada's major industries, also would undergo a tremendous upheaval as growing areas alter and the tree line moves north.

"Greenhouse effect" could hit by 2000

WOODS HOLE, MASS. (AP)—A new study of atomic fallout and nuclear waste shows the Earth is heating up far faster than earlier thought, and floods, heat waves and monsoons caused by this "greenhouse effect" could strike by the year 2000, a physicist says.

"It should bring some alarm to all of us," said William Jenkins of the Woods Hole Oceanographic Institute. "We will see drastic changes in the next decade that will affect us all."

Jenkins said Monday the conclusions are based on a two-year study of North Atlantic conditions.

Jenkins said the research appears to substantiate the "greenhouse effect" theory, which asserts that warmer temperatures are coming because a buildup of carbon dioxide in the atmosphere will trap the sun's warming rays and hold in heat like a greenhouse.

Jenkins said his findings are more dire than those of an Environmental Protection Agency report released in October, which concluded that the full "catastrophic" impact of the greenhouse effect will be felt by the year 2040.

Shortly after the EPA report appeared, the National Academy of Sciences issued a study that said the world could adapt to the anticipated climate changes without a major crisis.

The academy report did not dispute that added carbon dioxide, produced mainly by the burning of coals and other fossil fuels, could raise average temperatures by several degrees by the third quarter of the next century.

The EPA report said casualties will include farms and the people who depend on community crop production, adding that widespread starvation may accompany the climate shifts.

Some scientists say melting of the polar icecaps could raise ocean levels and cause coastal flooding.

Jenkins, who was awarded the 1983 Rosenstiel Award in Oceanographic Science from the University of Miami, said he believes the effects of the polar melting will be obvious within the next 10—not 100—years.

He said he reached this conclusion after discovering that the North Atlantic is becoming much less salty, and therefore is absorbing less carbon dioxide than in the past.

Scientists had previously assumed that the worst ramifications of the greenhouse effect would be delayed, thanks to the ocean's heavy carbon dioxide intake.

But Jenkins said the ocean can no longer be counted on to decrease the amount of carbon dioxide in the atmosphere.

Greenhouse effect may shrink lakes, cut water supply

INDIANAPOLIS—The greenhouse effect that is gradually warming the earth's atmosphere may be the next big environmental hazard facing the Great Lakes, says the chairman of a bilateral committee studying Great Lake pollution.

Richard Thomas, a member of the International Joint Commission, told a meeting on water quality here Wednesday that the twofold increase in carbon dioxide expected in the atmosphere by the middle of the next century could have serious effects on the lakes, the largest source of fresh water in the world.

"The surface temperature of the earth could rise anywhere from 1.5 to 4.5 degrees. In the next 10 to 20 years, there could be an increase in temperature of two degrees, and a decline in rainfall of about 10 per cent."

"The rainfall runoff to the rivers would decline anywhere from 40 to 70 percent," Thomas said, quoting a recent report from the United States' National Academy of Science.

Based on those figures, even the current use of Great Lakes water could exceed the future supply of water running into it from tributaries.

And scientists feel that if lake water levels decline, pollutants in the water will be more concentrated.

"So the idea that we may be facing a water crisis comes home even more strongly," Thomas told the joint commission.

Thomas is Canadian co-chairman of the commission's science advisory board, which reports on scientific· progress in cleaning up the lakes and identifies new pollution problems.

Saying he wanted to be "a little bit provocative," Thomas told scientists "the decline or collapse of North American society will ultimately be due to the decline in our water supply."

But even as it supported his warning, the science board cautioned that little is known yet about the effects of the predicted carbon dioxide increase.

A major atmospheric pollutant, carbon dioxide traps the sun's rays in the atmosphere, and may lead to dramatic temperature increases worldwide, climatologists theorize.

---

1. Read the following list of possible effects. Find those that are mentioned in your article. (Not all effects appear in all news stories.) Then, using the information that appears in the article, decide how likely it is that each effect will come to pass. Circle the number that best indicates the degree of certainty. Read the following key before you start.

KEY
1. Certain
2. Likely, probable
3. Possible
4. Unlikely

a. The elimination of many agricultural crops grown in the Canadian Prairies   1   2   3   4

b. The appearance of drastic climatic changes within the next 10 years   1   2   3   4

c. Coastal flooding as a result of polar melting   1   2   3   4

d. Widespread starvation   1   2   3   4

e. A water shortage   1   2   3   4

f. Dramatic changes in the Canadian forestry industry   1   2   3   4

g. Extensive population migration within the next 100 years   1   2   3   4

h. A doubling in the amount of CO_2 in the atmosphere by 2050   1   2   3   4

2. Form a group with the others who read the same article. Compare your answers. Discuss and resolve any differences by referring to the text.

3. In your group, share and discuss your answers, using the text to substantiate your claims. Pay particular attention to any differences in the opinions of the experts.

"*HOTHOUSE EARTH*"

1. In column A, list the various consequences of the greenhouse effect as stated in the first article you read. Check this information in groups of three or four.

   Now, scan "Hothouse Earth" to see which paragraph(s) deal with each of these effects. Put key words in the margin of the text to help you remember.

   Read only the relevant paragraphs, comparing the articles to see whether they agree or disagree about the effects, including both the degree of difference and the anticipated date of onset. In column B, write 'agree' or 'disagree', depending on your findings.

   If there is disagreement, note the differences in column C.

-A-	-B-	-C-
Effects	Agree/Disagree	Differences

2. The section beginning "Even if the math is right . . . " deals with scientists' doubts about the mathematical climate models predicting these effects. In the space provided below, state the 3 major sources of the uncertainties, and briefly summarize the reasons why the scientists are reluctant to place total faith in their models.

3. Now reread this section, which contains fairly technical information. How has the author made it easier for the lay reader to understand this information?
Consider the following:

   a. the information the author chose to include
   b. the way the author organized this information
   c. the language the author used to convey the information

   In groups, share and discuss your answers.

Hot-house Earth

Carbon dioxide from fossil fuels will probably cause a "greenhouse effect" that warms the climate. But how drastically, and how soon?

It seems as though some director of disaster movies were writing the news. Headlines warned of rising temperatures and melting polar icecaps. Television newscasters speculated grimly about palm trees sprouting on New York City's Fifth Avenue, and floods inundating Charleston, South Carolina, Galveston, Texas, and other coastal cities.

These apocalyptic visions were not some movie maker's madness. They were inspired by the sober judgments of experts at the federal Environmental Protection Agency. In the same October week, both the EPA and the National Academy of Sciences issued reports warning of potentially severe climate changes resulting from the "greenhouse effect"—the gradual warming of the atmosphere caused by an increase in carbon dioxide levels from the burning of fossil fuels.

The EPA report concluded that average global temperatures could start to rise within a few decades—some say the rise has already begun—and reach levels nine degrees Fahrenheit higher than today's temperatures by the end of the next century. This, the experts said, could wreak havoc with global weather patterns, change annual amounts of rainfall, swell or dry up rivers, and raise the level of the seas. Farming, building, and the political stability of nations could be profoundly disrupted.

While admitting that this forecast was fraught with uncertainty, the scientists warned against treating it as a cry of wolf. "We

are deeply concerned about environmental changes of this magnitude," the staid National Academy of Sciences said. "Man-made emissions of greenhouse gases promise to impose a warming of unusual dimensions on a global climate that is already unusually warm. We may get into trouble in ways that we have barely imagined." Only by planning ahead, scientists said, could disaster be averted.

Although there is considerable debate over how severe the greenhouse effect will be, one thing seems certain: carbon dioxide levels are on the rise. Measurements at the federal atmospheric observatory on Mauna Loa volcano in Hawaii show that the concentration of the gas in the atmosphere has risen steadily from 315 parts per million in 1958 to 340 parts per million today. Air pockets trapped

in glacial ice indicate that in the mid-nineteenth century, the concentration was only about 265 parts per million.

The evident culprit, scientists conclude, is the burning of coal, oil, synthetic fuels, and natural gas. These carbonrich fossil energy sources release an estimated five and a half billion tons of carbon into the atmosphere each year as colorless, odorless CO_2 gas.

The increased carbon dioxide is probably not a threat to health, since normal indoor levels of the gas can run 1,000 parts per million or higher without apparent harm. But it could profoundly affect the way the earth is heated by the sun. The sun's energy strikes the earth principally in the form of visible light. As the earth heats up, it radiates this energy back into space, but at the much longer wavelengths of infra-red light, or heat. Carbon dioxide lets the visible light pass through, but absorbs energy at infra-red wavelengths. Thus, the more carbon dioxide in the atmosphere, the more the earth's heat is blocked from escaping—just as a blanket holds in the heat of a sleeper's body. In the late 1800s the Swedish scientist Svante Arrhenius gave this phenomenon its name when he compared it to the way glass traps air heated by the sun in a greenhouse.

Some scientists think the greenhouse effect already has begun: average global temperatures have risen about one degree Fahrenheit in the past 90 years (with a dip from the mid-1940s to 1970). Others argue that the rise could be due to natural temperature fluctuations.

Nevertheless, most scientists agree that the accumulation of carbon dioxide has reached the point where an increase in temperature is imminent. "We are trying to get people to realize that changes are coming sooner than they expected," says John Hoffman, head of the Environmental Protection Agency office that prepared the EPA report. "Statistically significant changes are likely to be here by the years 1990 to 2000. We need to start considering how to live with them." The EPA study said average global temperatures probably would rise nearly four degrees by the year 2040, and go up another five degrees by the end of the twenty-first century—a total warming greater than that since the last ice age.

Rising temperatures would be just the beginning. The heating would shift global rainfall patterns, the EPA warned, bringing drought to some now-fertile areas and irrigating some deserts. Alpine glaciers and polar ice-caps could melt substantially, causing the seas to rise two feet by the end of the century. Many low-lying communities could be flooded.

Worst of all, the report said, the effect may be irreversible: possibly there is already enough carbon dioxide to start the warming, but the trend is slowed because the ocean is drawing off excess heat. As the ocean heats up, scientists concluded, the atmosphere will warm too—even if governments take steps to discourage the use of fossil fuel. Thus, the EPA esti-mated that a 300 percent world-wide tax on fossil fuels would delay the four-degree warming by only about five years. An outright ban on coal—something the report said was "economically and politically infeasible"—would delay it by only 15 years.

These grim conclusions were seconded, but in more cautious language, by the 496-page report released by the National Academy of Sciences. The NAS echoed some of the EPA's predictions, but saw in them "reason for caution, not panic." True, the study said, a four-degree heating would probably bring a 40 to 76 per cent decrease in the amount of water in Western rivers—including the already overtaxed Colorado. (Higher temperatures would cause more runoff water to evaporate before it reached a river.) But the NAS saw a silver lining in some of the dark clouds. A summer melting of the arctic ice pack, it pointed out, could open the fabled Northwest Passage and spur oil and gas exploration in the Arctic Ocean. Both agencies noted that increased carbon dioxide would make photosynthesis more efficient, increasing crop yields.

Even some of the good effects could have bad consequences, however. The Soviet Union and Canada, for example, would stand to benefit from a warming trend because it would make more of their frigid land farmable. And that fact might make them less likely to cooperate with any worldwide ban on fossil fuels. "Given that these two countries (and the former's allies) burn 25 per cent of world coal," the NAS report said, "it is hard to see how a carbon dioxide control strategy can succeed without them."

News accounts of the two studies focused—predictably—on the worst-case scenarios, thus giving a sometimes exaggerated impression of the bad news. But most scientists agreed with climate modeler James Hansen of the Goddard Institute for Space Studies in New York City that the reports' predictions were "within the range of plausibility." That fact testified to the faith that scientists have come to place in the computer models on which such studies are based. The EPA, for example, used separate computer simulations to predict world fuel consumption, the world distribution of carbon, and the temperature of the atmosphere.

These models achieve a byzantine complexity. The carbon cycle model, for example, must simulate the movement of carbon to and from all the natural sources and repositories (or "sinks") for that element. The principal source of atmospheric carbon is fossil fuel, although carbon may also come from deforestation, decomposing plants and animals, emissions from volcanoes, and carbon-containing gases produced by bacteria that live in the guts of termites and ruminant animals like the cow.

Running a climate model is like creating a world, says Jerry Mahlman, a meteorologist at Princeton's Geophysical Fluid Dynamics Laboratory. "First you turn on the sun, then you put in some oceans, add the atmosphere, and start the earth spinning." Mahlman plays down the Genesis-like quality of his work. "Climate modelers are not ready to call themselves God," he declares. "Our models don't have that kind of precision. It's a big leap from our mathematical toys to the real world." The perils of modelmaking are legion. The Club of Rome, an influential group of international businessmen and scholars, discovered this in 1972 when they published dire predictions of global disaster—only to learn, a year later, that their model contained a fundamental mathematical error.

Even if the math is right, scientists can never be sure that they have included all variables and modeled them accurately. The biggest source of uncertainty in climate models is the ocean, which serves as a repository for carbon dioxide as well as for the heat it generates. The ocean contains perhaps 60 times as much carbon as exists in all the atmosphere. Yet scientists are uncertain how long it will take the ocean to absorb this carbon (in the form of dissolved carbon dioxide gas from the air) or to be heated by the warming of the atmosphere.

"If you only had to warm up the top hundred meters of the ocean, it would take no more than a couple of decades," says Wallace Broecker of Columbia University's Lamont-Doherty Geological Observatory. But this uppermost "mixing layer" of the ocean transfers its heat and carbon dioxide very slowly to the deeper regions. These circulate in a grand pattern: cold water sinks to the ocean bottom near the poles and moves toward the equator. A complete circuit takes half a millennium or more, making somewhat problematical any estimates of how fast carbon dioxide and heat can be absorbed,

not to mention what effect they will have on ocean circulation.

Another major question mark is the role played by other gases that contribute to the greenhouse effect. These include nitrous oxide, methane, ozone, and chlorofluorocarbons. They are present only in minute concentrations, counted in parts per billion or trillion rather than parts per million, as with carbon dioxide.

"Climate modelers are not ready to call themselves God. It's a big leap from our mathematical toys to the real world."

Yet many of them are better infrared absorbers than carbon dioxide, and hence could boost atmospheric heating substantially. "The levels of these other greenhouse gases are increasing so fast that it is absolutely unknown what will happen," says Mahlman.

A third source of uncertainty is the effect of clouds—"the most important natural variable in the atmosphere," according to Robert Schiffer, manager of NASA's climate research program. A hotter atmosphere would increase evaporation, throwing up more water vapor that could condense into clouds. But an increase in cloud cover, says Veerabhadran Ramanathan of the National Center for Atmospheric Research in Boulder, Colorado, might reflect so much sunlight that it would slow the rate at which the earth would be heated. (Ice

sheets and volcanic dust, which also reflect the sun's energy directly, can have a similar effect.) On the other hand, because clouds are good infra-red insulators, they could accelerate the warming by trapping heat. No one knows which effect will predominate.

Scientists say the first priority in dealing with the greenhouse effect must be to resolve such uncertainties. On July 1, an international cloud climatology project, headed by Schiffer, began getting data on cloud cover from five satellites—including one from Japan and one from Europe. "We will produce an atlas of global cloudiness," he says, "that will give long-term statistics on where clouds occur, their height and quantity, what fraction of the sky was covered, and their radiation properties." Other research is under way to determine the effect of the oceans and the infra-red-absorbing trace gases. And scientists are studying whether long-term changes in the earth's orbit and in the amount of radiation given off by the sun will alter the greenhouse effect.

Some critics of this research have maintained that the world already faces such substantial dangers from population growth, diminishing food supply, and the spread of nuclear weapons that the greenhouse threat seems mild by comparison. Others argue that since the earth has endured a long string of ice ages in the last two million to three million years, any warming is likely to be temporary. Even so, those who try to minimize the problem must also explain away the harsh conditions on the planet Venus. There, a runaway greenhouse effect is thought to account for surface temperatures approaching 900 degrees Fahrenheit; Venus's cloud-shrouded atmosphere is about 97 per cent carbon dioxide.

Although few scientists think the earth will go the way of Venus, most agree that planning for the greenhouse problem should start soon. The EPA's Hoffman says, for example, that the estimated $210 million damage that would result from the flooding of Charleston, South Carolina, could be cut in half by such measures as revised city planning and dikes. Similarly, catch basins and reservoirs could be built to supplement water supplies in drying regions. And biologists could breed drought-resistant crops. As Hoffman puts it, "We feel carbon dioxide is a very serious thing, but we think there *is* time to do research, and there *is* time to adapt." Meanwhile, scientists will be keeping an eye on the thermometer for the first unequivocal sign that the greenhouse era has arrived.

Getting Ready to Write

One of the worst strategies students use when writing essays is to try to write everything they know on a topic. This means that they include a great deal of irrelevant information.

The purpose of this task is to help you develop a strategy for dealing successfully with writing essays. You will do this following a series of six steps.

1. Reread the question on page 116, underlining the key words. Discuss these with your teacher.

    a. What are you being asked to do?

    b. How many parts will there be to your answer? What will each focus on?

2. Consider your reader.

    a. What does your professor want to know:

       • about the topic?
       • about you?

    b. Has your professor indicated how the answer is to be organized?

3. Gather your information.

    a. Go over your readings and notes.

    b. Using a separate page for each section of your essay, make point form notes of the information you want to include.

    c. Include main points, examples, details, statistics—anything relevant.

4. Organize your information.

    a. What main points are you trying to make in your essay? Write each one in a general statement.

    b. In what order will you present each main point? Has your professor given you any indication of the sequencing expected in your essay?

    c. Using lines, arrows, brackets, etc., group the point form information on each main point.

d. For each main point, draw a tree diagram showing how you intend to sequence this data. Are there any sections that should be organized in the same way?

5. Exchange sketches with a partner. Read your partner's sketch, then compare it with yours.

   a. Consider your partner's information:

   - What has your partner included that you left out, and vice versa? Discuss which information belongs in the answer.

   b. Consider your partner's organization:

   - Has the thesis been clearly stated?
   - How has the information been sequenced?
   - Is there a logical progression of ideas?
   - Does each section begin with a thesis statement for that part of the answer?
   - Does each paragraph have a clear focus?
   - Has your partner helped the reader to see the relationships between the ideas?
   - Has your partner helped the reader make the transition from one idea to the next?

   Discuss these questions with your partner.

6. How will you introduce your reader to the topic? What focus statement will you use?

   Now you should have all the information you need to do the essay.

Writing the Essay

Write a 1–2 page essay answering the following question:

What is the greenhouse effect? Why are scientists concerned about it?

Writing the First Draft

Using your sketch to help you organize your essay, write your first draft. Remember that you should concentrate on getting your ideas down on paper and not worry about grammar, vocabulary, and punctuation. You can work on these during a later draft. Don't feel that you must write your first paragraph first. Many writers begin in the middle of their text and write the introduction later.

Writing the Second Draft

Writing the second draft will allow you to choose and organize content so that your essay is easy for your audience to read. Before you change anything in your text, read your first draft through. Remember that you are writing this text for a physical geography professor. Ask yourself what the professor would want you to include. Then think about how to organize the information so it is easy and interesting to read.

Next, exchange drafts with a partner. As you read each other's first draft, underline or mark with an asterisk (*) places where the writer needs to change what has been written. When you finish, discuss these problems. Revise as you wish.

Now write an inform section that tells the professor what the essay is about. Also write any necessary transitions to mark changes in the topic.

Write the second draft of the essay.

Strength of Predictions

In this writing task, you must report on the theories and predictions of a number of scientists. When you write your essay, you must ensure that you have accurately reported the certainty of those predictions.

Go through your essay and check where you have used

1. verbs of assertion (see page 50 in Chapter 3).
2. modals such as may, might, will, could.

For example, on page 114, the article reports, "A warming trend *will* be the main effect. This is a certainty." However, later in the same paragraph, the writer reports, "Average temperatures *may* rise . . . *may* take place . . ." This means that the writer is not certain about how much the temperature will increase.

As you read your essay again, make sure you have accurately reported the possible consequences of the greenhouse effect.

Editing the Final Draft

When you write your final draft, make the necessary editing changes. Read your essay aloud. This will help you find grammar errors. Underline words you think may be misspelled and check the words in a dictionary.

Exchange drafts with a partner. Edit each other's work.

Hand your essay in.

Evaluating Your Answers

When evaluating your exam answer, a professor considers several criteria:

1. Information

- Relevance
- Completeness
- Support (details, examples, and statistics) to prove the points you have made

2. Organization

- All information about one part of the topic should be in the same section (*note:* not necessarily the same paragraph).
- Each point should be connected to the last preceding point and should lead to the next point.

3. Language

- Minor errors will be forgiven but your reader *does* want to be able to understand easily what you are trying to say. (If the class has 75 students, and the exam has 5 questions, the professor has to mark 375 answers! If your language is difficult to follow, there might well be a direct relationship between your teacher's humor and your mark.)

Now let's evaluate your answers from all three viewpoints.

Information (*15 points*)

With your teacher, establish a point form list of the information necessary for a complete answer. Consider details and examples, as well as main points.

Organization (*5 points*)

Discuss the following questions with your teacher:

1. What focus statement will your answer need?
2. How many sections will your answer have?
3. What conclusion will your answer need?

Language and Clarity of Expression (*5 points*)

With your teacher, decide what you think the professor would accept in terms of clarity of expression.

Work with a partner. Read your partner's answer three times. The first time, focus on content; the second, organization; and the third, language. Assign points, depending on the level within each category:

	Excellent	Good	Adequate	Poor
CONTENT	15–13	12–9	8–5	4–0
ORGANIZATION	5	4	3–2	1–0
CLARITY	5	4	3–2	1–0

Return your partner's answer. Discuss the evaluation with him or her.

Using the Library for Research

You may want to do some library research on one area of this topic.

The effects of the warming trend will be felt differently in different parts of the world. Your assignment is to research the possible physical impact of the greenhouse effect on your country or area of the world. You might want to use this information to speculate on possible economic and political effects resulting from these physical consequences.

Prepare a 10-minute oral report on this information. You will present your report in class. Feel free to use visual aids to clarify and enhance your presentation.

6 THE NOBEL PRIZE

CHAPTER CONTENTS:

This chapter is a test. You will have a chance to use the reading and writing skills you have learned and practiced in the first five chapters.

The topic of this chapter is the Nobel Prize. A series of readings will show you how Nobel Prize winners are chosen and what characteristics these winners show.

At the end of the chapter you will write an essay which your teacher will evaluate as a professor in an academic class would.

The test question is:

> In an essay of 3–4 pages (double-spaced), discuss those characteristics or qualities of the Nobel Prize winners, as well as any external circumstances, that contributed to their being chosen for the prize. Also discuss factors that may have prevented worthy candidates from winning.

Now do the following readings and exercises so you can answer the question.

"NOBEL PRIZES"

Use information from the *Encyclopaedia Britannica* article on pages 133–135 to answer the following questions.

1. The process of selecting Nobel Prize recipients can be divided into five major stages. The following flow chart outlines the process. Each box in the chart represents one stage. Complete the chart by answering a, b, and c.

   a. In each of the boxes, write two pieces of information

      (1) Who acts
      (2) What this group does

   b. In the boxes for stages III and V write in the important dates.
   c. Complete the title by putting the name of the correct field in the blank.

The following flow chart shows the selection process for the Nobel Prize winner in the field of

_____.

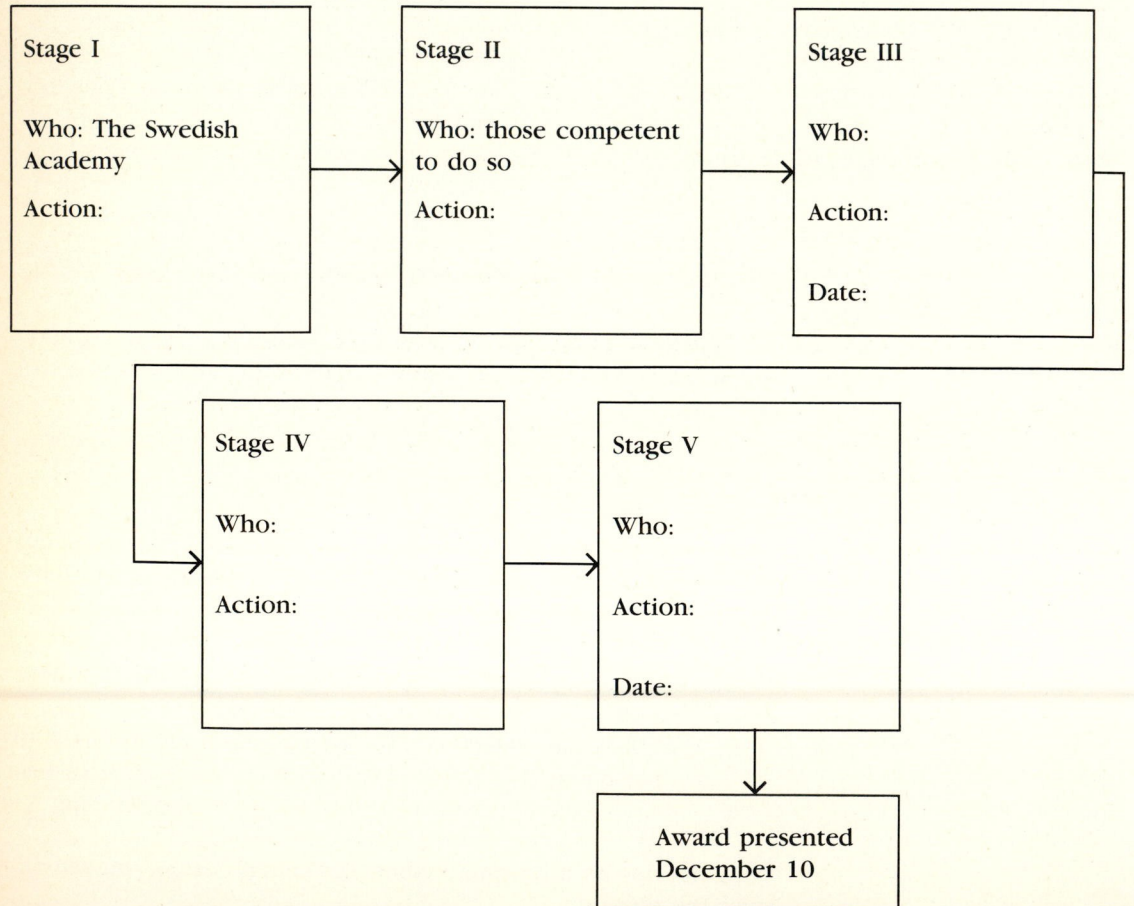

Stage I

Who: The Swedish Academy

Action:

Stage II

Who: those competent to do so

Action:

Stage III

Who:

Action:

Date:

Stage IV

Who:

Action:

Stage V

Who:

Action:

Date:

Award presented December 10

2. A Nobel Prize winner is also called a _____.

3. Check the *true* statements in the following list.

_____ **a.** In 1992, two separate prize winners can be selected in any one field if no worthy recipient is found in 1991.

_____ **b.** If you were the 1992 Nobel Peace Prize recipient, you would probably be in Stockholm on December 10 to receive the award.

_____ **c.** If a group of four researchers were jointly responsible for the discovery of a cure for cancer, they would share equally both the prize and the money.

_____ **d.** If, for example, a recipient has had to decline the prize because of government pressure, it would be possible for the prize winner later to receive the gold medal but not the financial part of the award.

4. For what reason is the economics award given?

(1)   **NOBEL PRIZES.**   These prizes, five in number until 1969 when a sixth was added, are awarded annually by four institutions (three Swedish and one Norwegian) from a fund established under the will of Alfred Bernhard Nobel (*q.v.*). Distribution was begun on Dec. 10, 1901, the fifth anniversary of the death of the founder, whose will specified that the awards should annually be made "to those who, during the preceding year, shall have conferred the greatest benefit on mankind" in the fields of physics, chemistry, physiology or medicine, literature and peace. The additional award, in economic science, was set up in 1968 by the Bank of Sweden, and the first award was given in 1969.

(2)   The institutions mentioned as prize awarders by Alfred Nobel in his will are: the Royal Swedish Academy of Sciences, physics and chemistry; the Royal Caroline Medico-Chirurgical Institute, physiology or medicine; the Swedish Academy, literature (all in Stockholm); and the Norwegian Nobel Committee, appointed by the Norwegian *storting* (parliament), in Oslo, peace. The Academy of Sciences also supervises the economics award. The Nobel Foundation, established in pursuance with the provisions of the will, is the legal owner and functional administrator of the funds and serves as the joint administrative body of the prize awarders, but it is not concerned with the prize deliberations or decisions, which rest exclusively with the four institutions. Each award consists of a gold medal, a diploma bearing a citation, and a sum of money; the amount depends on the income of the foundation and has ranged from about £11,000 ($31,000) to about £30,000 ($72,000). The economics award is administered in the same manner as the others and the monetary value is also the same.

(3)   The selection of the prize winners starts in the early autumn of the year preceding the awards, with the prize institutions sending out invitations to nominate candidates to those competent under the Nobel statutes to do so. The basis of selection is professional competence and international range; self-nomination automatically disqualifies. Prize proposals must reach the proper committee in writing before Feb. 1 of the year of the prize decision.

(4)   On Feb. 1 six Nobel committees—one for each prize group—start their work on the nominations received. If necessary, the committees may call in experts, irrespective of nationality. During September and early October the committees submit recommendations to their respective prize-awarding bodies—only in rare cases has the question been left open. The final decision by the awarders must be made by Nov. 15. A committee recommendation is usually but not invariably followed. The deliberation and the voting are secret at all stages. Prizes may be given only to individuals, except the peace prize which may also be given to an institution. Work cannot be proposed posthumously, but a prize duly proposed may be so awarded, as with Dag Hammarskjöld (for peace; 1961) and Erik A. Karlfeldt (for literature; 1931). The awards may not be appealed against. Official support, diplomatic or political, for a certain candidate has no bearing on an award since the prize awarders, as such, are independent of the state.

(5)   A prize is either given entire to one person, divided equally between at most two works, or shared jointly by two or more (in practice never more than three) persons. Sometimes a prize is withheld until the following year; if not then awarded it is paid back into the funds, which happens also when a prize is neither awarded nor reserved. Two prizes in the same field can thus be awarded in one year; *i.e.*, the prize withheld from the previous year and the current year's prize. If a prize is declined or not accepted before a set date, the prize money goes back to the funds. Prizes have been declined and in some instances governments have forbidden their nationals to accept Nobel prizes. Those who win a prize are nevertheless entered into the list of Nobel laureates with the remark "declined the prize." Motives for nonacceptance may vary, but the real reason has mostly been external pressure; *e.g.*, Hitler's decree of 1937 forbade Germans to accept Nobel prizes because the peace prize to Carl von Ossietzky in 1935 was taken as an affront. Whenever possible later, the one-time refuser has explained his situation and on application received the Nobel gold medal and the diploma—but not the money, which has already been paid back into the funds.

(6)   Prizes are withheld or not awarded when no worthy candidate in the meaning of Nobel's will can be found, or when the world situation prevents the gathering of information required to reach a decision, as happened during World Wars I and II. They are open to all, irrespective of nationality, race, creed, or ideology. They can be awarded more than once to the same recipient. The ceremonial presentations for physics, chemistry, physiology or medicine, literature, and economics take place in Stockholm, and for peace in Oslo, on Dec. 10, the anniversary of Nobel's death. The laureates usually receive their prizes in person.

(7)   The general principles governing awards were laid down by Alfred Nobel in his will. In 1900 supplementary rules of interpretation and administration were agreed upon between the executors, representatives of the prize awarders and the Nobel family, and

confirmed by the king in council. These statutory rules have on the whole remained unchanged, but have been somewhat modified in application; *e.g.,* the ambiguous words in the will, "idealistic tendency" as qualification for the prize for literature, were in the beginning interpreted verbally, but have gradually been interpreted more flexibly, as the list of laureates shows. The basis for the economics award was scientific, *i.e.,* mathematical or statistical, rather than political or social. The first two laureates, economist Ragnar Frisch (Nor.) and Jan Tinbergen (Neth.), were given the prize for their work in econometrics, the analysis of economic activity by means of mathematical expression.

TABLE V.   Nobel Prize winners (Economics), *1969–1970*

YEAR			
1969	Ragnar Frisch	(Nor.)	Work in econometrics
	Jan Tinbergen	(Neth.)	
1970	Paul A. Samuelson	(U.S.)	Work in scientific analysis of economic theory

(8)   The scientific and medical prizes have proved to be the least controversial, while those for literature and peace by their very nature have been the most exposed to critical differences. The peace prize has been most frequently reserved.   (N. K. St.)

"KING PRESENTS PRIZES"

Read the newspaper account of the presentation of the 1983 Nobel Prizes. Then answer the following questions.

1. What *major* change in the awards has taken place since 1901?

2. If we assume that the *Encyclopaedia Britannica* is the ultimate authority on the awards ceremony, what error did the newspaper make regarding the date?

King presents prizes

STOCKHOLM (AP)—Five American scientists who pioneered research in chemistry, physics, medicine and economics, one of them Canadian-born, accepted their 1983 Nobel prizes Saturday from the king of Sweden.

A 72-year-old British writer of dark myth who won the Nobel Literature Prize joined them in the awards ceremony.

The Canadian-born scientist who won the Nobel Chemistry Prize is Henry Taube, a 67-year-old Stanford University professor who is a native of Saskatoon. The Royal Swedish Academy of Sciences, in naming him the winner, described his as "one of the most creative contemporary workers in inorganic chemistry." He became a U.S. citizen in 1942 after obtaining degrees in science at the University of Saskatchewan.

One by one the laureates stepped forward to receive their heavy gold medals, diplomas and checks from King Carl Gustaf. Each prize carried a stipend of $240,000.

Novelist William Golding, 72, is the first Briton to get the literature prize since Winston Churchill won it 30 years ago.

The 1983 prize in medicine went to Barbara McClintock, 81, of New York. William Fowler, 72, of the California Institute of Technology, and Subrahmanyan Chandrasekhar, 73, of Chicago, shared the physics prize.

Theoreticist Gerard Debreu, 62, of the University of California at Los Angeles won the economics prize.

The traditional ceremony this year came on the 150th anniversary of the birth of Swedish industrialist Alfred Nobel, the man who invented dynamite.

"3 *AMERICANS WIN NOBEL SCIENCE PRIZES"*

Quickly scan the article on page 138. Then complete the chart with the necessary information.

Field	Recipient(s)	Country of Citizenship	Contribution—Reason for Award

3 Americans win Nobel science prizes

STOCKHOLM (CP)—Canadian-born Henry Taube, a professor at Stanford University in California, won the Nobel Prize in chemistry today, completing an American sweep of the 1983 Nobel science prizes.

In honoring the 67-year-old Taube, the Royal Swedish Academy of Sciences described him as "one of the most creative contemporary workers in inorganic chemistry." His citation noted "his work on the mechanisms of electron transfer reactions, especially in metal complexes."

Taube was born in Saskatoon on Nov. 30, 1915. He became a United States citizen in 1942 and went to Stanford as professor of chemistry in 1962. Academics had tipped a classical inorganic chemist such as Taube to take the prize, worth $240,000, after a spate of awards to biochemists.

Also, two American astronomers, professors Subrahmanyan Chandrasekhar of the University of Chicago and William Fowler of the California Institute of Technology, won the 1983 Nobel Prize in physics for their work on the evolution of stars.

The Royal Swedish Academy of Sciences, which awards the prize, said the Indian-born Chandrasekhar was honored for "his theoretical studies of the physical processes of importance to the structure and evolution of the stars." Chandrasekhar, who won the award on his 73rd birthday, has been one of the world's top authorities on stellar evolution for four decades.

It said his best-known work was in the 1930s, when he was in his 20s. It dealt with the structures of so-called "white dwarfs," the stellar body left after the collapse of a star.

The academy said Fowler won because of "his theoretical and experimental studies of the nuclear reactions of importance in the formation of the chemical elements in the universe."

Fowler, 72, has studied the nuclear reactions that occur on stars during their evolution.

"Fowler has done extensive work on the experimental study of nuclear reactions of astrophysical interest, as well as carried out theoretical calculations," the academy said.

Chandrasekhar and Fowler are the third and fourth Americans to win science prizes this year. Barbara McClintock of the Cold Spring Harbor Laboratory in New York was chosen for the prize in medicine last week. French-born American Gerard Debreu won the Nobel Memorial Prize in Economics Monday.

The physics and other science laureates along with literature prize winner William Golding will accept diplomas, medals and checks equivalent to $240,000 for each prize on Dec. 10, the anniversary of the death of Swedish dynamite inventor Alfred Nobel.

Chandrasekhar was born Oct. 19, 1910, at Lahore, now part of Pakistan. He took doctorates from Trinity College in Cambridge, England, in 1933 and 1942, then became a U.S. citizen in 1953. He became a member of the Swedish Academy, which awards the Nobel science prizes, in 1973.

Fowler was born in Pittsburgh, Pa., on Aug. 9, 1911. He took his doctorate at Cal Tech in 1936 and has been professor of physics there since 1946.

"NOBEL CLIMAXES SOLITARY QUEST"

"AT LONG LAST—A NOBEL FOR A LONER"

Read the two articles on Dr. Barbara McClintock, winner of the 1983 Nobel Prize for Medicine. As you read, look for any characteristics or qualities of Dr. McClintock that contributed to her being awarded the prize, as well as any external circumstances that enhanced her chances. Also, note any factors which might explain why she did not win a Nobel in 1951. Be prepared to support your claims with references to the text. (Underline or highlight the relevant parts of the paragraphs as you read, and note the contributing factors in the margin.) Take notes in your own words.

Nobel climaxes solitary quest

NEW YORK—For years, Barbara McClintock worked alone in a small cornfield, struggling to uncover a pattern in the delicately shaded reds and browns of Indian corn.

The painstaking research led her 30 years ago to what should have been a triumph: the discovery that the genetic center of a living cell is in constant motion, the genes breaking, moving and recombining like fragmented clouds on a windy day.

The discovery, which earned McClintock the Nobel Prize on Monday, was shocking. The genetic template was supposed to be immutable. Otherwise, how could genetic traits be passed on in such an orderly way?

That was the question her colleagues asked in 1951, when she announced her discovery.

All but a scattering of them concluded that she had made a mistake. And for two decades they ignored her.

By the 1970s, though, things had changed. The same movement of genes had been found throughout the animal kingdom.

The solitary woman bent forward in a cornfield had become a legend.

With the simplest equipment—farmers' tools, carefully catalogued seeds and voluminous notebooks—she discovered a very subtle scientific truth.

She performed her work in isolation, with stubborn single-mindedness. She never had much money, and on a few occasions was almost without a job.

Yet when she learned of the Nobel Prize Monday, she said that it seemed unfair "to reward a person for having so much pleasure over the years."

McClintock, 81, began her career at Cornell University, where she received her PhD in 1927. From 1936–41 she was at the University of Missouri, and then she moved to Cold Spring Harbor Laboratory in New York, where she has been ever since.

She lives in a small apartment on the laboratory grounds, and until recently maintained a plot of land nearby for breeding maize, a close relative of corn known most commonly as Indian corn.

In the 1930s, she was acclaimed for the crucial experiments that confirmed the theory that genes, the carriers of heredity, are themselves carried on chromosomes, fibrous strands visible under the microscope.

In the 1940s, she began the experiments that led to the discovery of transposable, or moveable genes.

She would cross-breed two strains of maize, nurture them through a growing season and examine the progeny. In some cases, the offspring did not carry the characteristics that were predicted by classical genetics. Many such results finally led her to conclude that genes responsible for the color of the kernels were changing position.

She announced the finding in 1951. "She knew what she was proposing was radical," says her biographer, Evelyn Fox Keller, a professor of mathematics and the humanities at Northeastern University in Boston.

The announcement was met with disbelief. McClintock was "stunned," says Keller.

For several years McClintock continued to present her work at scientific meetings. The response was always the same.

Then, in 1953, James Watson (now the head of Cold Spring Harbor Laboratory) and Francis Crick announced that they had discovered the structure of DNA, or deoxyribonucleic acid, the chemical of which genes are made.

Biology raced off in a new direction, leaving McClintock in its wake, far removed from the new mainstream.

For about 20 years, McClintock persevered in her work at Cold Spring Harbor. She gave up her attempts to convince her colleagues. "The less appreciated she was, the more she withdrew," says Keller.

In the 1970s, biologists experimenting with genetic engineering suddenly found that genes move frequently in bacteria. Then, in short order, they found the same thing in fruit flies, in yeast, and elsewhere.

The phenomenon appears to be of primary importance in the normal workings of the cell. Its disruption could account for various diseases. And it may also explain why, for example, some genes are turned off in childhood and turned on at puberty.

Biology had come full circle. McClintock was vindicated.

In 1981, the honors began to pile up. In quick succession, she won a $50,000 prize from Israel's Wolf Foundation, was given an award of $60,000 a year for life by the MacArthur Foundation of Chicago, and won the $15,000 Albert Lasker Basic Medical Research Award.

It was all a matter of luck, she said then. "I saw things nobody else was looking for." And she added: "I saw them too soon."

Since her retirement in 1967, McClintock has been busy cataloguing seeds and recording her findings for future generations of scientists.

At a news conference Monday, she said, "I've has such a good life, a very satisfying life. I couldn't wait to get to the laboratory. I hated sleeping."

A W A R D S

At Long Last— A Nobel for a Loner

At 81, Barbara McClintock leads an all-American parade of science laureates

Barbara McClintock is not pleased with the brouhaha. After agreeing reluctantly to hold a press conference on October 10, the day Sweden's Karolinska Institute announced that she had won the Nobel Prize for her discovery of movable genetic elements in maize, the 81-year-old cytogeneticist retreated to her lab. "On Monday, when the announcement was made, the phone in Barb's lab was ringing all day," says Susan Gensel, a colleague who has known McClintock for twelve years. "Barb would pick up the receiver, hold it in the air, and then put it down, click. She doesn't want all this. She wants to do her work."

For six decades, that is precisely what McClintock has been doing. Poised over the microscope in her spartan lab or turning a speckled cob of maize in her hands, she has looked among corn kernels and their chromosomes for what is contrary and strange. Working alone, without lab assistants or technicians, she has put questions, in the form of experiments, to the maize plant about its genetic make-up and actions, and constructed from its answers a complex descriptive framework—so complex that even some geneticists cannot follow it.

The essence of McClintock's work is her discovery in 1951 that genes are not fixed in place like beads on a string, but can jump around from place to place on chromosomes. These movable genetic elements, or "jumping genes," can cause certain gene functions to cease. When they jump away, the functions begin again. Biologists, having discovered such genes in bacteria and other organisms, now see that her work can provide vital clues to the mechanisms of gene regulation, and thus of heredity.

Over the course of her career, McClintock has been both celebrated and ignored by the worldwide scientific community. In 1944, for instance, she became the third woman to be elected to the National Academy of Sciences. But seven years later, when she published the paper on movable elements that eventually won her the Nobel, she received only three requests for reprints. Even so, her name was never far out of the mainstream. A handful of her colleagues—for example, Marcus Rhoades, also known for his work in maize genetics, and George Beadle, who shared a Nobel in 1958 for his work with enzymes—have always appreciated, if not fully understood, her work. And for the better part of her life, McClintock has been an eminence around Cold Spring Harbor Laboratories, a center for DNA research during the 1950s and 1960s, as it is for cancer research now. Soon after her discovery of jumping genes, says James Watson, the longtime director of Cold Spring Harbor and a Nobelist himself, "there was a steady procession of the world's best geneticists to Cold Spring Harbor to hear Barbara tell her story."

Starting in the 1970s, McClintock began to be recognized publicly for her explorations of gene regulation and expression. In 1981 alone she was awarded eight prizes, among them the prestigious MacArthur Foundation, Wolf Foundation, and Lasker awards. This year her biography was published, *A Feeling for the Organism,* by Evelyn Fox Keller (DISCOVER, July 1983). For days after the Nobel announcement, she was in a state of siege. Reporters traipsed the wide lawns at Cold Spring Harbor, trying to hunt her down in her tiny apartment or at her lab. Two Argentine newsmen dodged about the grounds for days, hoping to snap candid shots of her on one of her two daily ambles. But McClintock is determined to have nothing to do with the press. Explains one friend, "She doesn't give a hoot about publicity."

McClintock has been described variously as a loner, a recluse, a hermit—that "obscure geneticist" out on Long Island. There are stories that her conversation is mainly with inanimate objects. There are stories about her career that could have been taken from the eighteenth century English novel *Pamela:* virtuous young woman overcomes obstacles of gender and rises to deserved wealth and fame. Because she rarely grants interviews, the myths have not often been challenged. James Watson seems to come closest when he talks about her "principled, Yankee" behavior.

McClintock's daily routine has been essentially the same for thirty years. She rises early, does aerobic exercises, breakfasts, then goes for a walk along Bungtown Road and into the woods. By seven she is in the library, photocopying papers and reading the latest journals. From there, she is off to her lab, where she sometimes spends 16 hours, taking occasional catnaps on a cot. In the spring and summer, she plants her maize in a plot a quarter of a mile away. Her original plot, next to the bird sanctuary, is now covered with grass. "It's a lovely little oasis," she says of the area. "So it's a very nice place to be."

For many years McClintock did not have that refuge. In college, graduate school, and for several years after she received her doctorate from Cornell in 1927, she considered Ithaca her home. But then there were eight tedious years when she hopscotched around the country, going from one short-term teaching or research appointment to another. Her professor at Cornell, the maize geneticist R. A. Emerson, had described her as "the best trained and most able person in this country on the cytology of maize genetics." But in large measure because of her sex, she was not offered tenured positions.

Finally, in 1941, McClintock came to the Carnegie Institution of Washington at Cold Spring Harbor, at the invitation of its director, Milislav Demerec. She moved into an unheated, converted garage across the road from the labs. Although Carnegie closed its facilities in 1962, she has stayed on at Cold Spring as a Distinguished Service Member.

By the time she arrived, McClintock already had an international reputation for her work with maize. As a graduate student, she had identified and labeled the plant's ten distinctive chromosomes, thus enabling researchers to make the careful comparisons of chromosomes over several generations that are necessary to genetic research. Shortly afterward, working with a graduate student, Harriet Creighton, McClintock proved that genes did indeed carry the hereditary information that determined a plant's characteristics— a crucial point that had previously been merely conjecture. Coming as it did before the elucidation of chromosomal composition and structure, McClintock's paper firmly established her in the top ranks of cytogeneticists—those in the pre–DNA era who studied genetics by examining not only the physical characteristics of hybrid plants but also their cellular material.

By 1941 McClintock had also done much of the enormous body of research that would lead her to conclude that gene expression could be controlled in maize by movable genetic elements. To put it simply, she discovered that a pair of genes along the ninth chromosome could, acting in concert, turn on and off the genes that code for kernel pigmentation. The activator, or Ac, gene, McClintock found, signaled to a dissociation, or Ds, gene to transpose itself, or "jump," along the length of the chromosome. When Ds genes jumped, they caused breaks in the chromosome; when they reinserted themselves further along the chromosomal arm, they inactivated neighboring genes. All this shuffling of genetic material showed up in the kernels as variegated pigmentation.

Excited by her findings, McClintock published a brief summary of her work in the *Proceedings of the National Academy of Sciences*. She waited to give a full presentation of the work, though, until the well known summer Symposia on Quantitative Biology at Cold Spring, probably the single most important biological meeting held each year. Writing in *Nature,* J. R. Fincham recalls, "She met with almost total incomprehension. Few understood what she was saying, and fewer still were prepared to accept it. Some, I am told, simply failed to see how one person could have done all the work necessary to establish the conclusions that she now presented in such concentrated form." George Beadle concurs: "Not many were convinced by her work, because it was so difficult to comprehend. It's clear now that her work is important, but it wasn't clear then." McClintock reacted by retreating. She had published research papers steadily, if sparingly, since she was a graduate student. Now she stopped publishing altogether.

Why was her work so poorly received? Most colleagues agree that the problem was two-sided. McClintock's papers are not models of lucidity; they are densely written and difficult to follow. Says Stephen Dellaporta, a young plant molecular biologist who is doing DNA studies of McClintock's transposable elements, "Behind every paragraph, there are piles of data. She may have done hundreds of experiments to back up a single statement." Furthermore, McClintock is reluctant to enter into discussions with uncomprehending colleagues. Her reticence is a result, an acquaintance believes, of "shyness mixed with very commanding intelligence—an intelligence like a bird of prey, like an eagle." Unwilling to explain herself to those who could not "hear" her, she simply continued her work in silence.

Those who know McClintock defend and respect her privacy. Although her friendships are carried on mainly at a distance or during brief intervals between experiments, she has many friends; some she has known for 60 years. Her small kindnesses are chronicled around Cold Spring Harbor: each year she presents a select few with cakes she has baked using the black walnuts she gathers in the fall. Especially to those who are interested in her work, she is giving of her time and energies.

Did she feel bitter about the reception she got? "No, no, no," she said at the Nobel announcement press conference. "I don't have any bitterness at all, not at all. I mean this seriously."

In fact, even at the time her work on transposable elements came out, McClintock was not the professional outsider that some make her out to have been. Cold Spring Harbor was frequented by the major biologists of the era— Luria and Delbrück, who are known for their work with bacteria viruses; Crick and Watson, who determined the structure of DNA— so McClintock was never far from the center of action.

Rumor has it that McClintock has been nominated many times for the Nobel. Why has recognition of her work on transposable elements been so long in coming? Owen Hannaway, a historian of science at Johns Hopkins, suggests that recombinant DNA techniques had to exist before McClintock's work could be verified in systems other than maize. "Here was a piece of work in conventional, very classical, early twentieth century genetics done at the time when there was a revolution in biology," he says. "It must have seemed utterly out of phase with the dramatic events that changed modern biology. In a curious way, the prize is an illustration of the wisdom of patience. Now, here we are with the technology that finds meaning in the earlier work."

Indeed, in the past ten years McClintock's studies have prompted scores of molecular biologists to begin studying maize. Her seed stocks have been propagated at labs around the world, and the knowledge she has gained is now being re-examined because of the insights it provides into the processes of gene regulation and mutations. She hopes that the trend will stimulate more young scientists to study whole organisms, as she did. "We need to have, now, a lot of naturalists," she has said, "people who know organisms. I think we have failed to make people know organisms."

Finally, is she pleased with the Nobel? In her formal statement, she said, "I was overwhelmed on receiving news of the Nobel committee's decision this morning; the prize is such an extraordinary honor. It might seem unfair, however, to reward a person for having so much pleasure, over the years, asking the maize plant to solve specific problems and then watching its responses." Privately, McClintock has a few waspish words for the politics of prizes and for the way that science gets done in general. But in the end, she has nothing but good to say about her prize and her institution: "The Carnegie Institution never once told me that I shouldn't be doing it. They never once said I should publish when I wasn't publishing. I gave up publishing in detail because I thought nobody was reading. And what's the use of publishing? I was having too good a time doing the work."

TEST QUESTION

In an essay of 3–4 pages (double-spaced), discuss those characteristics or qualities of the Nobel Prize winners, as well as any external circumstances, that contributed to their being chosen for the prize. Also discuss factors that may have prevented worthy candidates from winning.

You have 1 hour to plan your essay and then 45 minutes to write it.

You already have some of the information you need to answer this test question. The following six articles will give you additional information to do the essay.

Read these articles. Look for information relevant to your essay. Take notes in your own words.

In groups of three compare your answers. Try to find internal qualities and external circumstances that seem to be common among several of the laureates. Discuss the importance of the factors you selected.

From Heresy to Eternity

Nobel laureates in science seem to have one thing in common: they win prizes for ideas that their colleagues once thought were crazy. Take, for example, the British immunologist **Niels Jerne.** When Jerne explained to **James Watson,** co-discoverer of the structure of DNA, his theory about the way the immune system produces antibodies, the crusty Nobelist replied: "It stinks."

Watson was wrong. In October the Royal Swedish Academy of Sciences awarded Jerne, 72, a member emeritus of the Basel Institute for Immunology, in Switzerland, the Nobel Prize in medicine. He will share it with **Georges Köhler,** 38, also of the Basel Institute, and **Cesar Milstein,** 57, of the Medical Research Council Laboratory in Cambridge, England.

Jerne's so-called selection theory, the first of three seminal ideas about the immune system, explained the production of antibodies, proteins that recognize, attach to, and help eliminate viral and bacterial invaders called antigens. His second and third theories, developed in the 1970s, described how the immune system acts as a whole.

In 1974 Milstein and Köhler devised a way of culturing monoclonal antibodies, pure strains specific to single antigens. Monoclonal antibodies have become powerful tools for diagnosing and treating disease.

The technique involves creating a new type of cell, called a hybridoma, by fusing a tumor cell with an antibody-producing cell. The hybrid has the qualities of both parents—like most cancers, it can be cultured in vitro and can divide indefinitely, and it can also manufacture antibodies.

Köhler and Milstein made only one mistake: they did not patent their idea. Monoclonal antibodies are now a $500 million-a-year industry, and they are used in laboratories and hospitals around the world to investigate a wide range of ailments, including infectious diseases, autoimmune disorders, and cancer. "Scientists make terrible businessmen," comments a rueful Köhler. His share of the $190,000 prize should help ease the pain.

The winner of the Nobel Prize in chemistry, **R. Bruce Merrifield,** 63, of Rockefeller University in New York City, knows exactly what to do with his money. Says he, "I could use a new car." Certainly, he was surprised by the award: it was nearly a quarter-century ago that Merrifield invented a method of synthesizing proteins that has greatly stimulated progress in biochem-

istry, biology, and medicine.

Proteins are complex molecules made up of peptides—simpler chemicals composed, in turn, of strings of even simpler molecules called amino acids. In the early 1960s, synthesizing even the smallest peptide was a nearly impossible task, involving hundreds of steps. Merrifield's ingeniously simple solution: bind the first amino acid in the peptide chain to a solid plastic support, then attach subsequent amino acids one at a time, rinsing away excess raw materials after each addition. Merrifield's technique allowed him to develop a computer-controlled machine, now used in labs round the world, that automatically synthesizes peptides.

At physics symposia, his colleagues used to snicker when the Italian-born **Carlo Rubbia,** 50, first talked about building a particle accelerator that would create antiprotons and smash them into protons in order to create high-energy particles that have not been seen since the Big Bang, the fiery blast in which the universe was born some 20 billion years ago. This year Rubbia, now at CERN, the European Organization for Nuclear Research, in Geneva, had the last laugh. He and **Simon van der Meer,** 59, a Dutch engineer, were awarded the Nobel Prize in physics for

their work culminating last year in the dramatic discovery of the W and the Z, subatomic particles that transmit the so-called weak force, one of the four fundamental forces of the universe. For this work, Rubbia was honored as this publication's Scientist of the Year (DISCOVER, January).

In 1968, van der Meer designed a method that could be used for collecting and storing beams of protons and antiprotons. But he never published the idea, considering it "much too far-fetched." After the bosses of America's largest accelerator, Fermilab, near Chicago, turned down Rubbia's scheme to build a proton-antiproton collider there, the two men joined forces at CERN. Their efforts produced the three particles—a negative and a positive W, and the neutral Z. The discovery was an important step forward in the quest for a single theory that accounts for the natural forces in the universe.

Van der Meer was stunned. "It is completely crazy," he said. "Nobel prizes are for people like Einstein, Fermi, or Dirac." The jet-setting Rubbia, a physics professor at Harvard, said coolly, "I am going to consume a considerable amount of alcohol in the form of champagne, and then get back to work." Perhaps to go after another Nobel?

Debreu won Nobel Prize for economic equilibrium theory

Gerard Debreu, the 1983 Nobel Memorial Prize Winner for Economic Science, freely admits he's an "extremist," but he offers no apologies.

"I've gone a lot farther than most of my colleagues in striving for purity in my work," the 62-year old professor at the University of California Berkeley campus told *The Citizen* this week.

"In fact some think I've gone too far, but that is simply my approach to basic research."

Regarded as an economist's economist, the French-born Debreu won the $190,000-prize for his work in the highly-rarefied field of general equilibrium theory.

As Debreu describes it, "general equilibrium theory provides an intellectual framework to describe how the agents of an economic system make decisions; how they are compatible with each other; and together form an equilibrium for the system as a whole."

In other words, his densely mathematical theories strive to develop analytical tools that explain how complex economies function.

"His work is extraordinarily ambitious," says Queen's University economics professor Richard Lipsey. "He looks at everything as a whole and tries to show how it all interrelates while practical economists like me only look at bits and pieces and tend to ignore the integration."

To most laymen, and even many economists, Debreu's work is so esoteric that it defies comprehension.

"You never see his work on an economic policy document and for most economists he's so far away from policy that you couldn't talk to him," says Doug Peters, vice president and chief economist for the Toronto Dominion Bank on secondment with the Department of Finance.

Queen's Lipsey says that for this reason, applied economists tend to "sneer" at this line of inquiry.

"There aren't any immediate results and it won't be in my lifetime that the proponents of the theory sort it all out. But often things that start as esoteric and abstract turn out to be very fruitful."

Bent Hansen, chairman of Berkeley's economics department says that although Debreu's work is very abstract and very fundamental "everybody in the profession knows him and must demonstrate that they know his work."

Unlike the Nobel science prizes, which are usually awarded for specific breakthroughs such as the discovery of DNA, the economic prize has tended to be awarded for an economist's life work.

Debreu admits he is quite possibly the "least applied" economist to win the award in the 12 years an economy prize has been bestowed.

Debreu, who was born in Calais and came to the U.S. in 1950, first made his mark on the profession 24 years ago with his *Theory of Value: An Axiomatic Analysis of Economic Equilibrium*—a 114-page book of elaborate mathematical formulas, which was lauded at the time by the *American Economic Review* as possibly "one of the few classics of our period."

Because he was inspired by the work of nineteenth-century economist Leon Walras, Debreu has earned the title as the modern founder of the equilibrium theory.

Kenneth Arrow, a Stanford University economics professor, says Debreu has made great strides in recent years in developing mathematical techniques for discovering the prices at which supply meets demand in complex economies.

"His work includes a number of major innovations with practical applications."

Debreu is now trying to link "complexity theory," a new theory of algorithms, with the economic theory of information.

Debreu says the application of mathematics to economics for building problem-solving models has become more operational in the last ten to 15 years, especially with the use of computers.

"It's now possible to develop models for general equilibrium theory that can be applied to public finance and trade," he says.

Debreu shuns consulting offers from companies whose econometric models owe much to his work. And he steadfastly refuses to comment on current public policy issues, much to the frustration of interviewers and practical economists.

At a Berkeley news conference last week he reasserted his reputation as a pure researcher, saying he did not want to use the occasion to discuss his views of the Reagan administration's economic policies.

Debreu told *The Citizen* he wouldn't comment on such issues "because I don't do those sorts of short term applications. My concern is to make concise and rigorous studies in equilibrium theory. I make the economic system an object for scientific study."

At 80, Nobel winner still in love with science

Gerhard Herzberg has had a passionate affair with science for most of his life.

And as he approaches his 80th birthday, Canada's only living Nobel laureate has no intention of ending the romance.

"G.H.," as he is known to scientists around the world, continues to add to the more than 200 scientific papers he has published and remains an eloquent defender of so-called basic scientific research.

He works every day at the National Research Council on Sussex Drive and maintains his life-long resolve not to buy a television when there are more productive ways to use time.

In honor of Herzberg's 80th birthday Dec. 25, a series of public lectures is being presented by the NRC today and Friday at the Westin Hotel. Four Nobel winners are among the speakers and Gov. Gen. Jeanne Sauvé and Science Minister Tom Siddon are expected to attend a banquet in Herzberg's honor Friday.

The center of this attention is a compact, sprightly man with a concert-quality baritone voice, strong views about science and an enormous intellect.

Herzberg began his research into spectroscopy, the study of the absorption and emission of light waves and other radiation by molecules, nearly 60 years ago.

Scientists, once they can identify the characteristics of molecules, can match them with the light from stars, comets and other celestial objects to determine their temperature, density and chemical composition.

The 1971 Nobel Prize for chemistry was awarded to Herzberg for his work on the electronic structure and geometry of molecules.

His life has been devoted to defending and conducting basic research—the study of certain areas of science that have no immediate or obvious application.

Scientific discoveries that seem academic may prove useful in the future and lay the foundation for other advances, Herzberg said this week in an interview.

"And people who are involved in basic research are interested in increasing the fund of knowledge. Like music and art, it is one of the things that make men human."

Herzberg's stubborn pursuit of knowledge in the basement laboratories of the NRC has earned him dozens of honors.

He's a Companion of the Order of Canada; Carleton University named a science building after him; the Canadian Association of Physicists struck a medal in his honor; in 1975 the NRC created the Herzberg Institute of Astrophysics; and Kanata now has a Herzberg Road.

Herzberg was born in Hamburg, Germany and came to Canada with his first wife, Luise, in 1935.

When he joined the University of Saskatchewan at age 30, he was already one of the leading scientists in his field.

"He was the fifth professor in the physics department and I remember him as an enthusiastic lecturer," recalls Cec Costain, who attended Herzberg's undergraduate classes. Costain, who worked with Herzberg for more than 20 years at the NRC, says he influenced a generation of scientists.

After a decade in the Prairies, Herzberg taught for three years at the University of Chicago and in 1948 joined the NRC.

Once in Ottawa, he began assembling his spectroscopy laboratory, gathering a team of spectroscopists and the world's best post-graduate students who were attracted by Herzberg's reputation.

The Swedish academy, in awarding him the Nobel prize, said the laboratory "under Herzberg's academic leadership has attained a unique position as the foremost center for molecular spectroscopy in the world."

But winning the prize drastically altered his life.

"All sorts of people wanted to

147

hear lectures and for the first year or two I had two invitations a day. There was practically no science being done on my part,'' Herzberg said.

In recent years, Herzberg's influential voice as a Nobel laureate has been added to the appeal for world peace; a proposal for change to ward off starvation in under-developed countries; and to protests aimed at freeing Soviet dissident Andrei Sakharov.

''I don't think I have become more political, but if I see injustice and inhumanity, I feel I have to do something,'' he says.

He and Monika, the woman he married following Luise's death in 1971, still travel extensively.

Herzberg says he plans to concentrate in the future on an astrophysical problem related to a group of features in a spectrum of distant stars.

''I have an idea of what this might be and I am going to get involved with it,'' he said. ''There have already been some 100 different interpretations.

''Mine may be the 101st.''

2 Americans win Nobel medicine prize

Two Americans, Michael S. Brown and Joseph L. Goldstein, won the 1985 Nobel Prize in medicine yesterday for discoveries the Nobel committee in Stockholm said had ''revolutionized our knowledge'' of cholesterol metabolism and the treatment of cholesterol-related diseases.

The two, who are University of Texas scientists, found that cells of the human body have receptors on their surfaces that trap and absorb bloodstream particles that contain cholesterol. The Nobel committee termed this discovery ''a milestone in cholesterol research,'' leading to a new understanding of how excessive levels of fatty cholesterol accumulate to clog human arteries and cause strokes and heart attacks.

GENETIC FLAW UNCOVERED

The discovery, made in 1973, also revealed the underlying genetic flaw in those people who suffer from inherited high-cholesterol afflictions. Scientists said this suggested avenues of research toward developing effective drug treatments to reduce cholesterol levels.

In announcing the award, the Karolinska Institute in Stockholm said the research by Dr. Brown and Dr. Goldstein has ''drastically widened our understanding of the cholesterol metabolism and increased our possibilities to prevent and treat'' atherosclerosis, or hardening of the arteries, and heart attacks.

'SURPRISED AND HONORED'

Dr. Brown, who is 44 years old, and Dr. Goldstein, 45, are molecular geneticists at the University of Texas Health Science Center in Dallas. They will share a cash award of $225,000, the highest in the 84-year history of the Nobel prizes.

Their selection continued the American dominance in this category of the Nobel Prizes in recent years. American scientists have captured all the Nobel medicine prizes alone or jointly since 1975, except for 1982 and 1984. A total of 59 Americans have won or shared the prize since 1901.

Both Dr. Brown and Dr. Goldstein, who have collaborated in research for nearly two decades, were attending a scientific meeting at the Massachusetts Institute of Technology in Cambridge when they learned of the announcement.

''All I can say is I'm very surprised and very honored,'' said Dr. Brown. His colleague added, ''I'm still trying to believe it's true.''

Dr. David Baltimore, a molecular biologist who heads M.I.T.'s Whitehead Institute, hailed the two Texans' research as ''magnificent and fundamental.''

''When they discovered the receptors,'' Dr. Baltimore said, ''they changed a whole way of thinking about how cells and blood interact. The real problem turned out not to be in blood but in cells.''

Dr. Brown and Dr. Goldstein began their prize-winning research in an effort to understand the cause of familial hypercholesterolemia, or inherited high blood cholesterol.

About one in every 500 people has this condition, and in some rare cases it has caused heart attacks in young children.

Cholesterol is essential to life, being a primary ingredient of cell membranes, some hormones and bile salts. It originates from two main sources: within the body, primarily from processes in the liver, and from without the body through fat in food. Cholesterol is transported in the blood and lymphatic fluid in particles known as lipoproteins, a combination of fat and proteins. The most common carrier is low-density lipoproteins, or L.D.L.

DEFICIENCY IN RECEPTORS

Studying cultures of cells from healthy individuals and from those with inherited high cholesterol, Dr. Brown and Dr. Goldstein discovered what they soon learned was an important difference in the cells. The cells from people with inherited high cholesterol either lacked or were deficient in L.D.L. receptors.

Thus was revealed for the first time the mechanism by which a cell extracted cholesterol from the blood. The receptors are coated pits that envelop the L.D.L. particle and draw it inside the cell.

There, in tiny sacs called lysosomes, a kind of stomach for cells, the cholesterol is separated from other fatty material in the particle and digested by enzymes. Then it can be employed in manufacturing cell membrane or other products. In the liver, excess material is excreted into the intestinal tract. In other cells, it passes back into the bloodstream and must make its way to the liver, carried by high-density lipoproteins.

If there are not enough of these "good" lipoproteins, the excess material can build up in the arteries.

In a news conference at Cambridge, Dr. Goldstein said, "Our work has pointed to the importance of this receptor in control of blood cholesterol and how the receptor can be raised through drugs and a low-cholesterol, low-fat diet."

The Nobel committee's citation said, "Michael S. Brown and Joseph L. Goldstein have through their discoveries revolutionized our knowledge about the regulation of cholesterol metabolism and the treatment of diseases caused by abnormally elevated cholesterol levels in the blood."

On one level, by learning how cells process cholesterol-bearing particles, the scientists answered the long-standing question of why some people can eat more cholesterol-rich foods, such as eggs and red meat, and not have high blood cholesterol concentrations, while others on low-fat diets still have elevated cholesterol counts. The difference, it was discovered, was in the number and efficiency of the L.D.L. receptors. Some people are born with a greater or lesser capacity to develop receptors.

On a deeper level, Dr. Brown and Dr. Goldstein learned that the cell's capture of cholesterol out of the blood inhibits the manufacturing of new L.D.L. receptors on the cell surface. A reduced number of these receptors means that more of the cholesterol-bearing particles remain in the bloodstream, with the risk of accumulation in the arterial walls.

EXPERIMENTATION IN THERAPIES

Dr. John M. Dietschy, a colleague of the two scientists at the University of Texas, explained that this seemed to underlie the dietary link to cholesterol accumulation. If someone consumes food high in cholesterol, more of it flows through the bloodstream and is available to cells. If the cells can get their cholesterol from outside, they do, but it eventually leads to impaired ability to absorb blood cholesterol. Other environmental and hormonal factors may also turn off signals in the cells to produce the receptors.

In a telephone interview, Dr. Dietschy said experimentation in how diet and various drug therapies affect the cells' ability to extract cholesterol from the blood is "about to burst open."

"We can now tell a drug company how to design new medical treatments," he said. "In the next 10 years, we'll be able to develop and test medicines to improve the receptors and lower cholesterol levels in the bloodstream."

Dr. Brown has written, "More than half of all people in Western, industrialized countries, including the United States, have levels of circulating L.D.L. that are above the threshold at which atherosclerosis (the gradual clogging of arteries and other blood vessels with cholesterol) is accelerated."

Although people whose blood cholesterol level is 200 milligrams to 300 milligrams are considered "normal" by many doctors, Dr. Dietschy said such levels were "in fact, probably very high."

Stuttgart researcher wins '85 Nobel Prize in physics

Klaus von Klitzing, a 42-year-old physicist at the Max Planck Institute for Solid State Research in Stuttgart, West Germany, has won the 1985 Nobel Prize in Physics, the Royal Swedish Academy announced yesterday.

"It's fantastic! I can't conceive of it!" said Dr. von Klitzing, who was cited for his discovery in 1980 that electrical resistance occurs in extremely precise units. Because of its applicability to materials used in electronics, the discovery has become widely used in the industry and has spawned a host of follow-up experiments worldwide.

In announcing the award in Stockholm, the academy said the discovery "has opened up a new research field of great importance and relevance."

The effect discovered by Dr. von Klitzing makes it possible to probe the conductive properties of electronic components with extraordinary precision, making possible standardized specifications for highly diverse materials.

It has also made it possible to determine with much greater accuracy one of the most basic relationships in nature, the fine structure constant.

AMERICAN DOMINATION ENDS

That constant, whose effects are felt throughout physics, defines the ratio of roughly 1 to 137 of the motion of an electron in the innermost orbit around an atomic nucleus to the speed of light.

Dr. von Klitzing is the 16th German to win the Nobel Prize in physics, after a long period dominated by Americans. The last German, in 1963, was J. Hans D. Jensen, honored for his research on atomic structure.

Dr. Klitzing's achievement was to demonstrate with an effect discovered about a century ago by Edwin H. Hall, a physics professor at Harvard University, that, regardless of the material through which an electric current is flowing, the resistance of that material can, under special circumstances, be expressed in specific units.

This meant that the phenomenon can be governed by the same "quantum" behavior that affects virtually all known forms of energy exchange and particle behavior, forming a pillar of modern physics.

When an electric current flows through a metal strip that is exposed to a magnetic field perpendicular to that layer, the stream of electrons forming the current is deflected toward one edge of the strip. This creates an electric potential across the strip, known as the Hall voltage.

SHORT 'PLATEAUS' FORMED

What Dr. von Klitzing and, subsequently, other experimenters demonstrated was that, using extremely powerful magnetic fields and temperatures close to absolute zero, this Hall voltage varies in a step-wise fashion as the magnetic field, or the electronic current, is varied.

As the gate voltage in the current is increased, the Hall voltage decreases, but levels off periodically, to form short "plateaus." The gate voltage is that of the most energetic electrons in the circuit. Coincident with each Hall voltage plateau, resistance to the current vanishes and, with nothing to push against, its voltage drops to zero.

In the 1970's such step-wide behavior had been predicted, in general terms, by Tsuneya Ando and his colleagues at the University of Tokyo. It was assumed, however, that, if this were demonstrated, the results would depend on design of the experiment and the nature of impurities in the materials used.

"It therefore came as a great surprise," said yesterday's announcement in Stockholm, "when in the spring of 1980 von Klitzing showed experimentally that the Hall conductivity exhibits step-like plateaus which follow this rule with exceptionally high accuracy." No deviations from one-integer steps were observed as great as one part in a million.

RESEARCH IN GRENOBLE

The experiment was carried out while Dr. von Klitzing was working in a laboratory at Grenoble, France. At the time he was attached to the University of Würzburg, but it lacked a magnet powerful enough for his tests. He used a magnetic field roughly 300,000 times stronger than that of the earth's surface magnetism. The test was conducted in a metal oxide semiconductor field-effect transistor, or Mosfet.

Hall resistance as a universal unit of measure is defined as the Hall voltage (induced across the current flow) divided by the current in amperes. At its lowest energy level (creating maximum resistance) it can be expressed, in terms of physical constants, as the Planck constant divided by the square of the electron charge. This is roughly equivalent to 25,813 ohms.

The Planck constant is the ratio of the energy of a photon (such as a light wave) to its oscillation frequency.

That such a measure of resistance, and its multiples, should apply to all materials came as a complete surprise. According to a Reuters dispatch from Stuttgart, Dr. Klitzing had expected to find that the electrical characteristics of a semiconductor would depend on its crystal structure. Instead they proved to depend on a universal constant.

As noted by Dr. Klitzing's colleague, Hans Queisser, in a standard text on microchips, "We no longer need to learn how long, how thick, from what material a piece of wire has to be to create exactly one ohm (of resistivity). We can now define conditions which apply universally."

Last year a perplexing modification of the effect was noted by Dan Tsui, Horst Störmer and Art Gossard of A.T.&T. Bell Laboratories. The resistivities also occur in fractional increments as well as integers.

Speaking of the discoveries concerning the Hall effect, the Swedish academy said: "We are dealing here with a new phenomenon in quantum physics, and one whose characteristics are still only partially understood.

2 Americans share Nobel in chemistry

Two Americans, one from a small research center in Buffalo and the other from the Naval Research Laboratory in Washington, were awarded the Nobel Prize in chemistry yesterday for developing revolutionary techniques used to determine the structures of molecules vital to life.

The prize in physics went to a West German computer expert, Dr. Klaus von Klitzing, 42 years old, for developing an exact way of measuring electrical conductivity, which has become important to the computer and electronics industry.

The chemistry prize was awarded to Dr. Herbert A. Hauptman, 68, director of the Medical Foundation of Buffalo, and Dr. Jerome Karle of the Naval Research Laboratory. Together, they developed mathematical techniques through which X-ray crystallography can be used directly to deduce the three-dimensional structure of natural substances vital to the internal chemistry of the human body and of drugs that can be used to treat various human ailments.

YEARS OF COLLABORATION

Both scientists are natives of New York City, attended City College together in the class of 1937 and then collaborated for years at the Naval Laboratory.

In recent years artificial counterparts of steroid hormones useful in treating breast cancer have been developed with the aid of the techniques for determining three-dimensional structures. The same techniques have also been used in studying antibiotic drugs. Three-dimensional structure of brain chemicals such as the enkephalins have been determined in the same way. The enkephalins are thought to be natural pain-control substances produced by the human brain. Knowledge of the three-dimensional structure of the enkephalin molecule has been used in research toward the development of new pain-killing drugs.

Much current research is devoted to studies of the structures of hormones and many other biological molecules because structure often gives valuable clues to a substance's actions within the human body.

Thousands of such three-dimensional structures of small biological molecules have been worked out through use of the scientists' methods, producing a wealth of valuable new information for understanding the most detailed chemistry of life in health and disease.

The methods developed by the two Americans have been particularly useful in determining the structures of hormones, vitamins and antibiotics, but cannot yet be used alone to determine the structures of the molecules of large proteins. Many scientists, including the two Nobel Prize-winners, are now working to apply the techniques to solution of the three-dimensional structures of large molecules.

While both research institutions are recognized in the international community of science, the foundation in Buffalo is relatively little known in its own community. The foundation, with a total staff of about 50, specializes in the study of the human endocrine system.

The mathematical techniques developed by Dr. Hauptman and Dr. Karle were controversial for years, but are now used by scientists throughout the world. The two scientists will share the $225,000 award.

CHEERS ABOARD PLANE

When the announcement was made yesterday, Dr. Hauptman was in a swimming pool at the local Y.M.C.A. and Dr. Karle was on an airliner traveling to the United States from Europe. Dr. Karle learned that he was a Nobel Prize winner when the pilot of the Boeing 747 announced the award over the public address system late in the flight. The 280 passengers and crew members burst into applause and later toasted the scientist with champagne.

In announcing the chemistry prize award, the Royal Swedish Academy

of Sciences cited the two American scientists ''for their outstanding achievements in the development of direct methods for the determination of crystal structures.'' Scientists use X-ray studies of substances in crystal form to determine their three-dimensional structures.

In the past, other Nobel Prizes have been awarded for achievements in crystallography, but these have usually been for success in determining the structures of important individual substances. This year's prize is for the development of key methods that have helped the whole field to flower. One specialist said tens of thousands of structures had been determined in recent years using the techniques developed by Dr. Karle and Dr. Hauptman.

Twenty years ago, said Dr. William Duax, a colleague of Dr. Hauptman at the foundation in Buffalo, it took two years to work out the structure of a simple antibiotic molecule that had only 15 atoms. Today, he said, it is possible to determine the structure of a 50-atom molecule in two days.

X-ray crystallography has been used for many years to determine the three-dimensional structure of molecules that can be purified so completely that they form crystals. The X-rays reflected from these crystals form pictures that appear as arrays of thousands of spots of variable brightness. Until the work of Dr. Hauptman and Dr. Karle, the pic-

tures were used indirectly to guess at possible structures. Only through further research was it possible to prove whether a guess was correct.

The new methods for direct determination of three-dimensional structures were developed by the two scientists when they worked together in Washington in the 1950's and 1960's. They developed ways of calculating structure by analyzing the intensity of the points visible as dots in the X-ray pictures and calculating the ''phase'' of atoms in the structures. In this context, phase is an angular measurement that can vary from zero to 360 degrees. The advent of powerful modern computers has made it possible to use the two scientists' mathematical formulations on intensity and phase to determine quickly the three-dimensional structure of a molecule under study.

The seminal work done 30 years ago remained unaccepted and controversial for at least 15 years.

''In 1954, despite five years of work and 13 scientific papers on molecular structure determination, Herbert Hauptman had received virtually no support for his ideas from established X-ray crystallographers, some of whom were openly hostile,'' said a recent biological sketch of the scientist prepared by his foundation.

Today he and his colleague are considered the founders of a new era in research on molecular structure.

7

ARTIFICIAL INTELLIGENCE

CHAPTER CONTENTS:

This chapter looks at one new application of technology, expert systems. These are computer systems which attempt to learn and use what experts know about a topic. You will investigate the strengths and weaknesses of these systems.

This chapter and the next one give you the opportunity to practice the academic reading and writing skills you have learned in the earlier chapters. The reading for this chapter is very long, but if you remember that it is important to read only the information you need, you won't find it difficult to do.

The writing task in this chapter is a full essay. You must use information from two sources in order to provide all the information needed. This will again give you practice in choosing and organizing important information. You'll also be taught ways to help your reader understand your text by using definitions, examples, and restatements.

THINKING ABOUT THE TOPIC
Computers and You

This questionnaire is in two parts. Questions 1–5 ask for information about your experience with and attitudes toward computers. Questions 6–11 check how knowledgeable you are about computers. Don't worry if you find the questionnaire difficult. You'll expand your knowledge as you work through the unit.

Experience and Attitudes

1. Have you ever had a job where you had to work with computers?

_____ No   _____ Yes

If yes, describe the job.

2. Do you know how to operate a computer?

_____ No   _____ Yes

If yes, how did you learn?_____

_____

If yes, what kind(s) of computers can you use?_____

_____

3. List three ways that computers have affected your life.

_____

_____

_____

4. Everyone has been affected by the introduction and increased use of computers. Do you feel this increased use of computers will, on the whole, make life easier or more complicated for you?

_____ Easier   _____ No change

_____ Harder   _____ Unsure

5. Will computers affect your career in any way?

_____ No _____ Yes

If yes, how?_____

_____

Computer Knowledge

6. Microchips replaced _____.

    a. interface alignments   **c.** input commands

    b. punch cards   **d.** transistors

7. Printers, disk drives, and terminals are examples of _____.

    a. programs   **c.** hardware

    b. computers   **d.** operators

8. Which of the following is not a computer?

    a. a MacIntosh   **c.** a Vax

    b. a Peanut   **d.** a Winchester

9. What does VDU stand for?

10. You would find a CRT in a _____.

    a. printer   **c.** terminal

    b. tape drive   **d.** disk pack

11. Skinware is the term used to refer to _____.

    a. the covering around the CPU

    b. the people involved in computers

    c. the carrying case for a portable computer

    d. the covering around an Apple computer

12. Put the letter of the correct definition in front of the word in the first column. There are more definitions than words.

_____ Mainframe

_____ Modem

_____ Bit

_____ Floppy disk

_____ 256 K

_____ Byte

_____ SPSS

_____ ROM

a. A statistical software package
b. A single number used to encode data
c. Central processing unit of a computer
d. A memory chip which contains permanently stored information
e. A device which allows a terminal to interact with the main computer
f. The size of the memory of the largest commercially made microchip
g. An eight-number digit used to encode data
h. A device for the long-term storage of data
i. A small piece of data
j. The circuit system of a computer

"*THE PROBLEM SOLVER*"

Read the following article. Your purpose in doing so is twofold: first, to learn the highlights in the evolution of computers; second, to write a brief summary of this information. You will need to prove to your instructor that you understand and can select the important information. The following steps will lead you to the completion of these goals.

1. *(Individually):* Quickly *skim* the article to get a general idea of the kind of information presented here and how it is organized.

2. *(Individually):* Carefully read the article, underlining or highlighting the important information.

3. *(In groups of 3 or 4):* Discuss the following:
   a. The basic categories of information you should include in your notes
   b. How you might organize these so that you will be able to remember the information
   c. Criteria for good notes in this situation

4. *(Individually):* In your own words, make notes on the article, using the format you think best.

5. *(In small groups):* Compare your notes. Decide which are the best.

6. *(Individually):* Using only your notes and not the original text, write a summary of the highlights of the evolution of the computer. This should be no more than $1\frac{1}{2}$–2 pages in length (double-spaced). Hand it in to your teacher at the next class.

HISTORY OF COMPUTERS

The problem solver

WAS the computer invented 4,000 years ago? Some experts believe that Stonehenge was a computer for working out eclipses of the sun and moon. Others say that the abacus was the first computer; it was in use as a calculator in 600 B.C.

The fact is that the computer wasn't invented by any one person following a flash of genius; it evolved. It exists today because a lot of people worked on solving a lot of different problems.

Following the trail back almost demands the detective skills of a Sherlock Holmes. We'll trace one path that begins in Lyons, France in 1725.

The silk weavers of that fair city had a problem. Their fashion-conscious customers wanted new and complex patterns in the cloth they wove.

The system used to make these patterns had some built-in faults. Cords were tied to silk threads on the loom. When the cords were pulled, the threads were lifted so the cross-thread either went over or under them, giving the pattern. The job of pulling the cords was given to children. After long hours of work, the children often grew tired and pulled the wrong cords. The mistake could not be spotted until later, by which time the piece of cloth was ruined.

A fellow named Basile Bouchon found an answer. He borrowed a technique used by his father, an organ maker. He punched holes in a roll of paper, which was wound over a cylinder. The paper was pressed against the ends of a set of horizontal rods. Attached to the rods were the cords that pulled up the silk threads on the loom. The holes in the paper set the position of the rods. If there was a hole the rods didn't move; no hole, and the rods were pushed out by the paper, causing the cord to be pulled.

The history of the computer goes hand-in-hand with the search for solutions to problems.

The position of the holes in the paper was a code that was "read" by the rods to give the pattern. It was a simple "on" or "off" instruction. What Bouchon had hit upon was the binary code that is the basis of all computer operation.

In 1800 another Frenchman, Joseph Marie Jacquard, took Bouchon's idea a few steps further. He devised a system of cards with holes punched in them to replace the roll of paper. Jacquard got all the glory; his system is still in use today and is called the Jacquard loom.

Now, the trail crosses the English Channel to Cambridge, England. Here, we come across Charles Babbage. By all accounts he was exactly what you imagine a mad inventor ought to be like.

He had the idea of building a machine that could solve any mathematical problem thrown at it. The machine was a wonder of cogs, gears, sprockets, ratchets

and counters. Babbage called it the Analytical Engine. Unfortunately, it didn't work. But that wasn't Babbage's fault. He laboured over the thing for most of his life, until death brought an end to his toil in 1871. His design was sound, but the limited technology of his day just wasn't up to building the machine. Babbage had used an adapted version of Jacquard's card for programming his engine, as well as for its memory.

Another person to see the usefulness of the Jacquard card in solving mathematical problems was Herman Hollerith. He was working in the Buffalo office of the U.S. Bureau of Census. His bosses were up against a time problem. The Census was taken every ten years, but it was taking almost ten years to tabulate the results of the 1880 count. With massive numbers of immigrants swelling the numbers, they could see no way of finishing the 1890 Census before it was time for the 1900 count. They asked Hollerith to come up with a solution.

He took Jacquard's cards and punched holes in them to record details such as age, sex, size of family etc. Then, he built a machine which used electrified wires to count the data stored on the cards. The holes in the cards let the wires drop through to make an electrical contact. The signal produced moved a counter around one space.

The machine cut the counting time in half and made Hollerith a wealthy man. He went on to find commercial uses for his invention. Several mergers with Hollerith's firm produced a company called International Business Machines, which we know better by its initials.

For the next 50 years, Hollerith's design was improved, but all computers were still basically mechanical. Then, along came J. Presper Eckert and John W. Mauchly, two scientists at the University of Pennsylvania.

In 1943, the University and the U.S. Army were trying to find ways of improving the accuracy of artillery shells in hitting moving targets, such as aircraft. This involved a lot of calculations: speed of shell, speed and direction of target and wind, etc. All of these variables had to be worked out so that the gunner could see from tables where to aim his gun. The Army was using 100 people with mechanical calculators to work out these tables. However, this was too slow and inaccurate.

Eckert and Mauchly came up with the idea of using vacuum tubes instead of the cogs and gears of mechanical calculators. At about this time, other scientists came across Charles Babbage's work, which had lain unnoticed for 70 years. They found that Babbage had solved many of the theoretical problems that plagued the early electronic computer designers.

The advantage of the vacuum tube was speed—electrical signals travel at the speed of light; almost 300,000 km/second. The disadvantage was size.

The computer Eckert and Mauchly built in 1946 contained thousands of vacuum tubes, many kilometers of wire, and it consumed huge amounts of electricity. By today's standards, it was a museum piece. In fact, that's what it is today; it's on display at the Smithsonian Institute. It was almost out of date the day it was plugged in.

The trouble with vacuum tubes was they needed a lot of energy and had a habit of blowing. The solution was found in the transistor, which entered the scene in 1947.

The transistor does the same job as the vacuum tube; but it does it using much less energy, without wearing out, and it's only a fraction the size of its ancestor. The transistor revolutionized computers and set designers on the path they have followed since. The aim is to produce machines that are smaller, faster and cheaper.

The silicon chip, which first appeared in 1971, enabled computer designers to take a huge leap in the direction of small, fast and cheap. The chip is a wafer of silicon onto which thousands of miniature transistors are engraved, using a photographic technique. A chip smaller than your finger nail can contain some incredibly complex circuits. The chips can be mass produced, meaning they are very cheap.

When you need to describe the advances made in computers in the last 35 years, words like amazing, staggering or incredible aren't enough. Perhaps some examples will do the job.

Today's $5 silicon chip can do the same job as a vacuum tube ancestor costing $50 million.

If the car had been improved to the same extent as the computer, the $10,000 Cadillac of 1945 would now cost $5, travel at 1,930 km/hour and fuel consumption would be less than one litre per 100 kilometres.

If flying had developed as the computer has, a transatlantic trip would take just two minutes and the fare would be two cents.

In less than 35 years, computers have developed through four generations. Scientists are now working on the fifth generation of computers. These will be able to do even more astounding things than the machines available today can do. They'll respond to voice commands, talk back to users and even repair themselves.

One expert has taken the comparison with the 1945 Cadillac into the future. By 1990, that same car would cost 50 cents, travel at 80,500 km/hour and fuel consumption would be down to less than one litre per 1,000 kilometres.

We'll take a dozen please.

"MACHINES BUILT TO EMULATE HUMAN EXPERTS' REASONING"

The following news story from *The New York Times,* March 1984, discusses expert systems, a recent innovation in one branch of artificial intelligence. Read the article in order to answer the following questions:

1. What criticisms have been leveled at these "thinking machines"?

2. Construct a flow chart to illustrate the process by which an expert system is developed and used.

Machines built to emulate human experts' reasoning

MENLO PARK, CALIF.—Almost no college teaches it, but a new kind of engineering has burst on the American scene. Many people believe it may ultimately exert as profound an influence on the workplace as factory automation did decades ago.

It is called "knowledge engineering," and its task is to interview leading experts in science, medicine, business and other endeavors to find out how they make judgments that are the core of their expertise. The next step is to codify that knowledge so computers can make similar decisions by emulating human inferential reasoning.

The knowledge engineer does this by reducing the expert's wisdom to a series of interconnected generalized rules called the "knowledge base."

A separate computer program called an "inferential engine" is then used to search the knowledge base and draw judgments when confronted with evidence from a particular case, much the way an expert applies past knowledge to a new problem.

"In every organization there is usually one person who is really good, who everybody calls for advice," said Sheldon Breiner, chairman of Syntelligence in Menlo Park, which is attempting to build a system to make underwriting decisions for a major New York casualty insurance company that he would not name. "He is usually promoted, so that he does not use his expertise anymore. We are trying to protect that expertise if that person quits, dies or retires and to disseminate it to a lot of other people."

While knowledge engineering is still a primitive art, it has already been used with some success in prospecting for minerals, diagnosing disease, analyzing chemicals, selecting antibiotics and configuring computers. These programs are called "expert systems."

And such is their promise that hundreds of American companies have begun to look into the possibility of using expert systems to perform such diverse tasks as evaluating casualty insurance risks, making commercial credit decisions and controlling oil-well drilling, tasks that are extremely difficult and often done well only by a relatively small number of experts.

While industry has used computer scoring systems analytically to advise executives making decisions, designers of the new systems hope eventually to duplicate judgments by human experts.

For that reason, the potential commercial exploitation of expert systems has become one of the hot-

test new "games" here in California's region of silicon-based electronics concerns and in other centers of American high technology. Numerous small firms, like Syntelligence, have been set up in recent months by the engineer-entrepreneurs in this region, known as Silicon Valley, and the venture capitalists who back them.

Their knowledge engineers are now interviewing experts in insurance underwriting, military technology, investment banking, genetic engineering and other fields. In addition, some major companies, including Xerox and Lockheed have set up their own knowledge engineering groups.

The expert systems concept is a branch of "artificial intelligence," a broad term encompassing a variety of university research efforts in recent years to simulate human symbolic and subjective reasoning. Powerful computers have made it possible to solve problems not only algorithmically, or by numbers, but also by processing the words and symbols used in most specialized fields of expertise.

CRITICS EXPRESS FEARS

Some critics view knowledge engineering as a threat, as the vanguard of an Orwellian future in which thinking machines take control. But the knowledge engineers do not see it that way.

"We are trying to demystify it," Mr. Breiner said. "The systems are really not that exotic or powerful today. The expectations are too high about what they can do. These are advisory systems only." He added that the "domain expert" on whose expertise the knowledge base is built will always have more skill than the system and will still be needed to calibrate it.

Nonetheless, many say the possi-

bility of aggregating the knowledge and insights of several experts in the same field opens the prospect of computer-aided decisions based on more wisdom than any one person can contain.

Still, there are skeptics. Last April, at a conference on "Intelligent Systems" sponsored by the Woodrow Wilson International Center for Scholars, Roger C. Schank, director of the Artificial Intelligence Project at Yale, argued expert systems were flawed in that they could not perform a key function of the human brain: learning from experience.

All the intelligence in the system, he said, comes from the mind of the knowledge engineer. "We don't have programs that are truly creative, or truly inventive, or can understand the complexities of somebody's reasoning," he said.

A major limitation of expert systems thus far is that they work best in cases in which knowledge lends itself to classification of facts into neat categories, against which new evidence can be weighed and balanced. Medical diagnosis or chemical analysis are good examples of this. Much more difficult, the knowledge engineers say, is simulating the more creative, or "synthetic," kind of expertise that goes into designing a circuit, proving a mathematical theorem or writing a story.

ORIGIN OF SYSTEMS

The first expert systems were used for scientific and medical purposes. Among the pioneers was Dendral, a program developed by Joshua Lederberg and Edward Feigenbaum at Stanford University to identify organic molecules, which has proved faster and more accurate than human experts.

The new flurry of activity, however, is based on the growing perception that expert systems can be sold in the far more lucrative commercial markets. Among the new entrants are Applied Expert Systems of Cambridge, Mass., working on personal financial planning; Brattle Research of Boston, looking into investment portfolio management; Inference Corporation of Los Angeles, working on banking applications; Teknowledge of Palo Alto, Calif., doing various technical applications, and Intelligenetics of Menlo Park, involved in genetic engineering.

Syntelligence is as typical as any. Mr. Breiner, its 47-year-old chairman, was trained as a geophysicist at Stanford. He applied magnetometers to such diverse uses as uncovering hidden archeological sites, finding avalanche victims and discovering mineral deposits. He built a large fortune as founder of Geometrics in Sunnyvale, Calif., makers of instruments for oil and mineral exploration. Now he is off on knowledge engineering.

Syntelligence engineers are interviewing a dozen of the New York insurance company's top underwriters. They try to establish and refine rules and connections that underlie decisions. Typically, the engineers say, the experts bridle a bit, saying their knowledge cannot be so neatly encoded, that they go often by hunch and instinct.

"But if you press further, a lot of gut feeling is really very systematic, is not pure hunch," said Mr. Breiner.

The process usually involves reducing the expertise to several hundred rules stated in "if-then" terms. That is, if certain conditions exist, then certain conclusions are likely to be drawn. Thus, for example, a fire insurance underwriter evaluating a restaurant might say if the building construction is good, fire protection is nearby and there are no unusual hazards in the neighborhood, then the company will issue insurance.

This process goes on until a complex web of rules is spun. As a practical matter, the elements are not all equally important; so numerical weights are given to each statement. It is all knitted together into a set of "inference rules" characterizing the relationships between all the evidence available and the logical conclusions that can be derived from the information.

Human reasoning is then emulated by "chaining" forward and backward through the rules. That is, the computer either reasons forward from a set of facts toward a solution or backward by first setting up a hypothetical solution and then looking for the evidence to support it.

The "inference engine" is crucial to the system. It is designed to work on any knowledge base, to be detached and hooked in wherever needed, like a train locomotive. The engine asks the user the appropriate questions needed to answer the problem. It then sifts through the chains of rules set up in the knowledge base.

A major problem confronting the knowledge engineer is what to do when the experts being interviewed disagree. The choice is either to pick one and go with that expert or to do separate runs and let the user decide which to go with. Ultimately, in all cases, Mr. Hart said, "The human user retains responsibility for the decision."

Preparing to Write an Essay

You are taking a course called Business and Technology. You are required to write an essay which discusses some new technology that is being used by businesses. You decide to write your essay on expert systems. After reading something about expert systems you realize that there are a number of strengths and weaknesses in these systems. You decide to discuss these in your essay.

In addition to the information from the last article you read, you will need to read the following article, "Artifical Intelligence: An Assessment of the State-of-the-Art and Recommendation for Future Directions."

"ARTIFICIAL INTELLIGENCE: AN ASSESSMENT OF THE STATE-OF-THE-ART AND RECOMMENDATION FOR FUTURE DIRECTIONS"

This is a report written for people interested in artificial intelligence. You will need some of the information in this report in order to write the essay. Read the abstract on page 165.

1. Write a *one*-sentence summary of the abstract. Compare your summary to another student's and resolve any differences.

2. Read the paragraph which begins "Artificial Intelligence (AI) . . ." How is AI defined?

3. Scan the section entitled "Coverage of this Report." What two areas of AI are discussed in this report?

    a.

    b.

4. Look quickly through the report. The author has divided the report into *nine* main sections. List them next to the following letters (a–i):

    a.

    b.

    c.

    d.

    e.

f.

g.

h.

i.

5. What section will you need to read in order to write an essay discussing the strengths and weaknesses of expert systems?

Now read only the section you need for your essay. After you have finished reading, answer the following questions.

1. According to the article, what is expert systems research?

2. List the advantages of expert systems.

3. List the disadvantages.

Artificial Intel- ligence:

An assessment of the state-of-the-art and recommendation for future directions

ABSTRACT

This report covers two main AI areas: natural processing and expert systems. The discussion of each area includes an assessment of the state-of-the-art, an enumeration of problem areas and opportunities, recommendations for the next 5–10 years, and an assessment of the resources required to carry them out. A discussion of possible university-industry-government cooperative efforts is also included.

ARTIFICIAL INTELLIGENCE (AI) is the attempt to (1) understand the nature of intelligence and (2) produce new classes of intelligence machines through programming computers to perform tasks which require reasoning and perception. The goal of AI as a whole is to produce machines that act intelligently. By "act intelligently," we mean to cover a broad range of activities, only some of which are directly human-like; our machines may eventually be far better at certain intelligence tasks than people are (much as a calculator does long division better than people do), yet may lack other human char- acteristics (e.g. ambition, fear, general work knowledge, mobility). Important characteristics that such machines would have to have before AI could be said to have succeeded include common sense; the ability to learn from experience; the ability to accept, generate and act appropriately on natural language input; perception and general situation assessment; and so on.

Coverage of this Report

For the purposes of this report, we concentrate on natural language (NL) processing and expert systems.[1] Both of these areas have near term practical potential, and yet are sufficiently open-ended to remain interesting to researchers past the next ten years.

The biggest AI news of the recent past has been the commercial introduction and industrial use of the number of AI systems, especially NL and expert systems. This news is significant because (1) it has quieted critics who argued that AI would never produce useful results, and (2) the applications themselves have high intrinsic value. Some specific systems include:

INTELLECT (AI Corp., Waltham, MA) A natural language system that can be added to a customer's existing data base.

STRAIGHT TALK (Symantec for Dictaphone Corp.) A natural language data base system embedded in a word processor, intended for uses such as the storing of address, phone number, organization, and salary information.

R1 (Designed at Carnegie-Mellon University for Digital Equipment Corp.) An expert system that can check and correct the configuration of the 450 or so components that can go into a VAX computer.

PROSPECTOR (SRI International) An expert geologist system that can find commercially exploitable mineral deposits from assay data.

The Machine Intelligence Corp. Vision module (based on research done at SRI), a system that can be "taught" by a non-programmer to recognize and act

---

[1] Because we have researchers primarily from these two areas, in turn because these two areas were specifically selected for concentration by the workshop steering committee. However, there are many other important problems in AI that are not well-represented here. The areas of computer perception and pattern analysis are particularly unfortunate omissions. Other areas of major AI research are included to some degree, because they overlap other sections of this report (robotics, parallel and distributed hardware, software and programming environments, and information sciences). In each of these areas, however, AI has specific needs, often somewhat different from the rest of computer science, which deserve consideration. We hope that these important AI research areas will be considered in future assessment and planning meetings, especially because progress in natural language and expert systems ultimately depends critically on virtually all other AI areas.

upon a variety of parts on an assembly line, when used with a robot arm.

DENDRAL (Stanford) An expert system for discovering the molecular structure of organic compounds from mass spectrogram data.

MACSYMA (MIT) A general mathematical aids system, including the abilities to do symbolic integration, factoring, simplification, plotting, and much more.

MOLGEN (Stanford) An expert system for designing experiments in molecular biology.

In addition, there are a number of systems that, while not being marketed, have received fairly wide use, for instance:

MYCIN (Stanford) An expert system for medical diagnosis and treatment prescription.

EMYCIN (Stanford) MYCIN with specific medical knowledge removed, EMYCIN has been used by non-programmers to make expert systems in other areas such as tax advising and estate planning.

INDUCE/PLANT (University of Illinois) A system that has learned to generate its own rules for diagnosing soybean diseases from examples presented to it with better performance than most experts.

Dipmeter advisor (Schlumberger-Doll) A system for interpreting oil-well log data.

LISP machines (MIT; Symbolics, Inc; LMI, INC; Xerox; BBN) Computers specialized for the LISP language that pioneered the ideas of the personal workstation

and user-friendly programming environments.

There are in addition a number of companies that plan to introduce or use internally AI products in the near future, including NL systems from Texas Instruments, Cognitive Systems Inc., Symantec, and Hewlett-Packard, and expert systems from Teknowledge, Fairchild, Intelligenetics, Schlumberger and others.

Overview of this Report

In the sections that follow, we first discuss in some detail the nature of the most important current technical and scientific issues in natural language processing and in expert systems. We then discuss organizational problems, including difficulties involving manpower, equipment, funding, education, and cooperation between industry, government, and universities. This is followed by a list of recommendations that we believe can aid in keeping the U.S. lead in these important areas.

Natural Language Research

Endowing computers with an ability to communicate with humans in natural language (e.g., ordinary English) has been a major topic of research in AI for over 20 years. The ultimate goal of creating machines that can interact in a facile manner with

humans remains far off, awaiting breakthroughs in basic research, improved information processing algorithms, and perhaps alternative computer architectures. However, the significant progress experienced in the last decade demonstrates the feasibility of dealing with natural language in restricted contexts, employing today's computers.

Continuing research in this area seems likely to lead both to progressively more practical, cost-effective systems and to a deeper understanding of the natural phenomena of NL communication. Each of these goals has importance in isolation; pursuing them simultaneously enables progress on each to support progress towards the other.

Application areas

Natural language processing has a broad range of possible application areas.

Machine Translation [MT]. MT involves using machines to convert documents written in one natural language to corresponding documents written in another language, but with equivalent meaning. MT was proposed in 1946 and became a forerunner of today's work in AI. Creation of fluent translations remains an elusive goal.

Document Understanding. Document understanding involves reading documents by machine, and assimilating the information the documents contain into a larger framework of knowledge. After reading a document, a device of this sort might produce an abstract of it, alert people who are likely to be interested in it, or answer specific questions based on the information it contains. If such a device has read and assimilated many documents, it might act as a librarian, directing users to especially pertinent references.

Document Preparation Aids. These aids could perform the task of an experienced editor, detecting errors in spelling and grammar, and suggesting ways to rephrase passages of text to make them more understandable and to make them conform to the patterns of high quality language usage.

Document Generation. This task, related to document understanding, involves translating information stored in a formal language in a computer's memory into ordinary language. The documents produced might be single sentences or extensive texts. For example, information encoded in a formal language regarding the repair of an electro-mechanical device could be used as the basis for mechanically generating instruction manuals in a variety of natural languages. Moreover, from the same formal description, different manuals could be generated for different audiences such as end users, repair personnel, and engineers. Ultimately, documents could be tailored to the background of each particular individual, making each document more understandable and generating the correct level of detail.

Systems Control. This is the applications area with the greatest promise for near-term achievement. It involves the use of NL in the control of computer systems. By coupling a natural language interface with different types of devices, a range of possible systems may be produced, including systems that (1) provide answers to questions by accessing large data bases; (2) control such complex systems as industrial robots, power generators, or missile systems; (3) furnish expert advice about medical problems, mechanical repairs, mineral exploration, the design of genetic experiments, or investment analysis; (4) create graphical displays; (5) teach courses in a broad range of subjects, interacting with students in English.

Practical systems for (1) above are already commercially available, and rapid development of this area can be expected over the next several years. Little work has been done on area (2), but there appear to be no special technical obstacles to producing elementary systems in this area if programs are undertaken. Area (3) involves integrating work on natural language processing with work on expert systems; some limited demonstration programs using stylized input and canned output have been produced already, but much remains to be done. Areas (4) and (5) require considerable new work, but significant progress could be made if a concentrated effort were undertaken. (Note: Work in this area could help educate people in computer science in general and in AI in particular.)

In considering natural language as the command language for controlling computer systems, it is important to keep in mind that English is well-suited to some kinds of man-machine interaction and poorly suited for others (such as those involving extensive manipulation of numbers). English is often useful:

- when dealing with computer-naive users,
- for tasks which computer experts do infrequently,
- in situations where English is more concise than formal language, and
- for activities in which natural language is the subject of analysis, e.g. intelligence gathering.

Speech Understanding.
Speech understanding involves the coupling of natural language processing with acoustic and phonetic processing to achieve a device that can understand spoken as opposed to typed input. Advances in this area are currently inhibited primarily by the lack of satisfactory acoustic/phonetic devices for recognizing sequences of individual words in continuous speech. Special purpose parallel hardware for word recognition is being pursued by researchers outside AI.

Importance and economic impact

Perhaps the most important economic factor of the current age is that, as a society, we are moving away from an economy based on the manufacture and dissemination of goods to an economy based on the generation and dissemination of information and knowledge. Much of the information and knowledge is expressible in English and much of the task of gathering, manipulating, multiplying, and disseminating it can be greatly aided by computers. Thus research in NL understanding can have a two-fold positive impact in our shifting economy:

1. NL can enable computers to interact with users in ordinary language, and therefore it can make computer power available to segments of the population that are unable or unwilling to learn one of the formal languages usually required for interaction with computers.

2. NL can increase knowledge productivity in providing mechanical means for manipulating knowledge expressed as natural language text.

State-of-the-art in natural language processing

Currently, we understand how to do a reasonably good job of literal interpretation of English sentences in static contexts and limited, well-structured domains of application. This is not to say that there are no open problems in this area, but rather, compared with the other aspects of language to be discussed, there is a substantial body of known results and proven techniques.

A number of good application areas are now possible. Examples include NL data base front ends; NL interfaces for expert systems, operating systems, system HELP facilities, library search systems, and other software packages; textfilters, text summarizers; machine-aided translation; and grammar checkers and critics.

Parsing algorithms for syntactic analysis of sentences and techniques for semantic interpretation (to determine literal meaning) are well developed, making possible many practical applications.

It is now possible to think about a much wider range of types of NL processing because machines have become substantially larger and address spaces have become reasonable for NL systems. In the past, a great deal of effort was devoted to attempts to collapse code length so that space could be made available to expand the capabilities of NL programs. This is no longer such a problem, and we can trade off space for ease of programming.

However, extensive resources are required to develop a new NL application even in areas we understand quite well, because there is no such thing as a small natural language system. If a system is to accept *natural* language, that is, unrestricted text or what people naturally think of saying in the manner they think of saying it, it must have a large vocabulary, a wide range of linguistic constructions, and a wide range of meaning representations. A small system cannot be very natural.

Existing techniques begin to break down when we begin to scale up to more open-ended applications where inherent limitations of the domain are no longer adequate to resolve ambiguities in the language, or where sophisticated discussion of time or three-dimensional space is required, or where discussion and modelling of the beliefs, goals and rational behavior of intelligent agents is required.

Research areas in natural language

The most active current areas of research (and the most promising for new breakthroughs) lie in the area of recognizing the intent of speakers and the relationships between sentences in continuous discourse, taking into account the structure of the preceding discourse, the non-linguistic aspects of the situation of utterance, and models of the beliefs and goals of the communication agents.

Historically our understanding of the phenomena of language has moved gradually from the most visible and salient aspects such as phonology, lexicon, and syntax towards the more internal and intellectual elements of semantics, pragmatics, and reasoning. Like the stages of Piagetian development it has seemed that we must first gain a mastery of the earlier stages before proceeding to explore the later ones.

Natural Language Planning. A recent innovation, with enormous potential for increasing our understanding and capabilities in NL has been the evolution of a methodology in which communication is treated as a special case of a goal-oriented action in a common framework with nonlinguistic actions. This allows for planning and reasoning about goal-oriented activities which involve communication and acquisition of information as a part of the overall activity of a system. As a simple example, in order to get into a locked room occupied by a human, a robot might construct and execute a plan that would lead to its saying, "Please unlock the door so I can come in."

Speaker's Intent and Plan and Recognition. The planning approach to the problem of communication has put new flesh on the basic skeleton of the theory of speech acts advanced by philosophers Grice, Austin, and Searle and promises significant advances in linguistic fluency of communicating machines. It also provides a framework for nonlinguistic communication through actions such as pointing or displaying a picture. There are, however, substantial technical problems that must be addressed in order to realize the promise of this approach. These include development of reasoning systems capable of modelling and reasoning about the beliefs, goals, and actions of rational agents, the representation, organization and access of the knowledge necessary to support such reasoning, and the discovery of frameworks, methods and algorithms capable of combining syntactic, semantic, pragmatic and general world knowledge to perform the overall task of understanding an utterance in context.

Representation and Commonsense Reasoning. The emerging focus on problems of interpretation in context have suddenly put great stress on the problems of knowledge representation and commonsense reasoning. The solution of these problems requires extensive use of general world knowledge and knowledge about the rational behavior of intelligent, communicating agents. It is impossible to overemphasize the importance of representation and reasoning for this new (and final?) stage of learning about language.[2] To ex-

tend existing systems we must address many fundamental problems.

1. We must decide exactly what knowledge to include in an NL system. This type of knowledge is considered by people to be "commonsense," and is not codified anywhere.

2. We must commit ourselves to "primitive" elements, that is, items that can be used in definitions but that will not themselves be defined (except perhaps by reference to sensory systems).

3. We must devise appropriate notational systems.

4. Knowledge must be organized in memory to facilitate access. In particular, facts may need to be recalled upon demand, and facts relevant to the current context may need to be inferred automatically.

5. Knowledge and reasoning about the physical world is required for determining the referents of noun phrases, interpreting prepositional phrases, disambiguating word senses and generally understanding text that refers to some physical situations. This kind of knowledge is also critically important for judging whether NL is literally plausible, as opposed to metaphorical, humorous, sarcastic, or in error.

Generation. The areas described so far have treated language as an input modality only,

i.e., they have concentrated on language understanding. Current NL systems do not often use NL as an output modality, but this situation is expected to change quite radically in the future. Systems of the future will have to deal with situations where the system understands that a user doubts, is confused by, or does not understand the system's response. Such systems must be prepared to paraphrase or explain their responses. There is already a recognized need for all expert systems to be able to explain their reasoning and conclusions (see below).

There are three main aspects of generation: (1) deciding what to say, (2) deciding how to say it, and (3) finally saying it. Thus it should be clear that the previously mentioned research areas (especially planning, knowledge representation, and commonsense reasoning) are highly relevant to generation as well as to understanding.

Algorithms. The study of the formal properties of algorithms needed to manipulate the various types of NL representations mentioned above is itself an important research activity. We know something about parsing algorithms and algorithms for certain logic systems. We will need to know much more about algorithms, for example, those that allow us to combine syntactic, semantic, and pragmatic knowledge. One recent example is the discovery that grammatical representations that combine syntax and semantics (that is, provide grammatical representations that are convenient for semantic interpretation) have properties which make their parsing only slightly

---

[2] The research areas of knowledge representation and commonsense reasoning are areas likely to have considerable impact on expert systems work as well. Current expert systems are based on representations chosen specifically for an application, with little general scientific understanding of the power or limitations of those representations or the consequences which may emerge at later stages of development from representational decisions made at the outset.

more complex than the parsing of context-free grammars.

Scaling up—Learning. If a NLP (Natural Language Processing) system is to be useful, it must be able to handle a large vocabulary and have access to a knowledge base. This imposes two constraints upon the design of an NL system. First, it must operate efficiently when it is in possession of relatively large amounts of knowledge. Second, means must be found for building up large knowledge bases appropriate for NL understanding, and for progressively expanding a system.

Most working AI systems are of limited scope, and so there has been little experience with truly large scale AI systems. Therefore, it is an act of faith to assume that our current techniques will be effective in vastly larger systems. One possible avenue for research involves the further investigation of techniques from data base management, in which problems of scale are routine, but in which the data is much less complexly structured. Techniques specific to the management of large collections of complex knowledge need to be developed.

The desirability of a large and incrementally expandable system poses some quite general questions of system design. In addition, some problems arise that are singular to NLP. For example, it would be desirable to build a system that could learn both vocabulary and world knowledge by dialog in NL with a user or by reading text (e.g. dictionaries, encyclopedias, texts, stories, etc.). The simpler aspects of this problem are within our current

understanding. However, at the extreme end, one encounters problems of machine learning that require fundamental advances in our basic understanding.

Opportunities in natural language

Having reviewed the state-of-the-art and the major research problems for the next ten years, we would like in this section to briefly state some of the short term goals that could lead to significant improvements in NL technology. The highest priority should be given to the basic research issues enumerated in the section above, so there will be new application areas in ten years.

Although the research areas described above will require ten years or longer to arrive at [general] solutions, it is possible to make incremental contributions toward the limited handling of various discourse phenomena, such as ellipses (i.e. the omission of words that can be understood in context), recognizing a user's intent in restricted situations, discovering some of the user's beliefs from the presuppositions of the user's input, modelling aspects of commonsense, learning by reading text or engaging in dialogue, etc. It should be emphasized, however, that one should not expect progress in the basic research topics to be strictly incremental. There will have to be some major breakthroughs in order to obtain general and principled solutions for these topics.

Research and development of good NL tools should pay excellent dividends. We now have available a few parsers and knowledge representation systems, which should make it possible to build new systems more rapidly, by using off-the-shelf components for programs. We do need to have these systems well-documented, and we still need more experience in tailoring systems from these components, but there is the opportunity to begin building custom NL systems now, at least for limited task domains.

Because it is now possible to relatively easily produce special-purpose chips, the identification of potential parallelism in NL processing has gained importance. We can realistically consider algorithms for highly parallel word sense selection, truly concurrent syntactic, semantic and pragmatic evaluation of sentences, speech format extraction, etc. with the expectation that such work can lead to novel machine architectures more appropriate for NL processing.

Many good novel applications are possible within the next ten years, provided that we can solve some of the basic research problems enumerated above. Many of these arise in conjunction with "information utilities" (i.e., information services available via phone or cable connections). Possible public services include automatic directories of names, addresses, yellow pages, etc.; electronic mail; on-line catalogues and ordering facilities; banking and tax services; routing directions; access to books and periodicals, through titles, authors, topics, or contents; and undoubtedly many others. All of these services could also have on-line NL help facilities and manuals. There are parallel needs in business and in the military services, e.g., for command and control, inventory control, ordering and shipping, coordination of organization planning and plan execution, and so on.

Other good application bets concern the control of systems via NL. For example, we should, within ten years, be able to solve the problem of instructing robots in NL, much as one would instruct a human assistant. This can allow the robot to understand the goals of the instruction, rather than just the means for achieving the goals, as is the case now with teaching-by-leading-through-motions, or "teaching" by ordinary programming. Understanding goals would help a robot in dealing with a wider range of situations and in recovering from errors.

Research on speech understanding should have a high priority. Once continuous speech understanding is possible, the number of good NL application areas will grow dramatically. Provided that sufficient funds are made available, continuous speech systems seem close enough to reality that we should begin to think more seriously now about the realm of new application areas that speech systems will open up. It is critically important that we at the same time make substantial progress on the fundamental problems in NL understanding, so that we can move rapidly to produce useful systems. Speech recognition alone, without NL understanding and

action components, would be of little value.

Expert Systems

Expert systems research is concerned with the construction of high performance programs in complex domains. By "high performance" we mean functionality and efficiency comparable with or better than the best human experts. By "complex domains" we mean those application areas requiring substantial bodies of knowledge, often of an uncertain or judgmental nature. This potential for capturing judgmental knowledge expands the range of problems to which computers have been and potentially could be applied.

What differentiates the expert system methodology from traditional computer programming is an emphasis on the symbolic manipulation capabilities of computers, in particular the declarative representation of world knowledge, the explicit encoding of heuristics, and the exploration of non-numeric data structures for computer simulations.

State-of-the-art

As just mentioned, expert systems differ from more conventional computer programs (which, like econometric models, for example, may possess considerable "knowledge") by their ability to deal with uncertain and judgmental knowledge, represented in a symbolic (often declarative) form. Expert systems differ from other AI programs, such as natural language understanding programs, because of their concern for subjects that usually require

specialized training in a professional field, such as medicine, law, mathematics, or computer circuit design. It is perhaps one of the most surprising developments of the past ten years that a useful portion of the expert knowledge required for high-level performance in many of these fields can in fact be encoded in computer programs.

In addition to the high performance, most of these systems can explain their conclusions so that their users have a better understanding on which to base action and greater confidence in the quality of the systems' decisions. This feature can best be explained by considering two contrasting approaches that could be used in constructing a program for medical diagnosis. In a system based on statistical decision theory using joint frequency distributions over symptoms and diseases, for example, the physician user might be informed only that, given the symptoms, the most likely disease is diabetes. A physician would have to take the conclusions on faith, and even if it were highly accurate, a user would be reluctant to depend blindly on such a system. This use of unexplained conclusion is in sharp contrast to what most expert systems can provide. Current systems can describe the "chain of reasoning" employed by the system in reaching its conclusion. This chain refers to the judgments, assumptions, rules and intermediate conclusions used by the system. Physicians find these kinds of explanations absolutely essential when deciding whether to rely on the machine's diagnosis or not.

Despite their success, current expert systems suffer from a variety of limitations. Among those shortcomings that ought to yield to concentrated research efforts during the next ten years or so are the following: overly narrow domains of expertise; inadequate communication channels with the user (e.g. need for better natural language and graphics); inability to represent certain kinds of knowledge easily (e.g. knowledge about processes, time, three-dimensional space, beliefs of the user); and the great difficulty of building and modifying the expert knowledge bases on which these systems are based.

It is this last area, knowledge acquisition, where we can expect the most difficulty. Current systems are built by having computer scientists interview experts in the domain of application. The knowledge obtained from these experts, usually in the form of English sentences, must then be structured by the computer scientist (often called a "knowledge engineer") so that it can be unambiguously and economically represented in the computer. (Incidentally, this process of precisely structuring knowledge, for instance geological knowledge, for the computer can just as well be thought of as an advance in the science of geology as an exercise in system engineering.) Although it is reasonable to expect that we will be able to develop sophisticated computer aids for the knowledge acquisition process, it must be remembered that to completely automate the knowledge acquisition process will require rather dramatic advances in other areas of AI such as natural language understanding and generation, and machine learning.

Other problems that will require many years of work involve connecting expert systems to complex perceptual channels such as vision and speech. Although some work has already been done in this area, the general problems of interpreting visual images and connected speech are difficult long-term research areas.

Current research problem areas

Though we have reached a point where we can develop expert systems that can provide significant assistance within a narrow task domain, the systems which have been developed to date all suffer from several serious weaknesses. In general, there are (1) system development limitations, (2) competence limitations, and (3) use limitations.

System development limitations:

- Constructing an expert system requires several man-years of effort from a programmer with a background in artificial intelligence; since very few people have such a background, the number of expert systems currently being developed is small.
- The expert systems which have been developed to date are not at all general; each system is a "single customer," system.
- Since the knowledge which an expert system has is collected over time, often from several experts, it is not uncommon for some of the system's knowledge to be inconsistent; there are as

yet no good methods for identifying such inconsistencies, let alone repairing them.

Competence limitations:

- Since the knowledge expert systems have is relevant to a narrow domain that is somewhat arbitrarily delimited, the systems make myopic judgments.
- The systems do not have the ability to check their conclusions for plausibility; thus they sometimes make incredibly naive recommendations.
- Since the knowledge the systems have is almost exclusively "surface" (empirical) knowledge, they are unable to infer missing knowledge from general principles; thus their behavior degrades badly when knowledge is missing.

Use limitations:

- Almost no expert systems have natural language understanding systems as front ends; as a consequence, users may find expert systems unnatural to use.
- Though nearly all expert systems can provide explanations of how they arrive at their conclusions, these explanations are often not very convincing because thry are not tailored to individual users.
- Most expert systems take longer to perform a task than is required by human experts.

Research opportunities

While recent progress in expert systems has led to a number of practical programs, and to a strong interest by industry in this area, expert systems technology is still at a very early stage of development. Because we are at such an early stage of development, the single most important research investment in this area is probably to fund basic AI research. This section points out several specific research opportunities likely to lead to increased capabilities and a broadened impact for expert systems in the coming decade.

Knowledge Acquisition and Learning. Given the well-recognized knowledge-acquisition bottleneck, one major opportunity for increasing the power and decreasing development costs of expert systems is in developing new methods for knowledge acquisition and learning.

A small amount of research is currently going on in this area, ranging from development of interactive aids for validating, examining and debugging large rule bases, to more basic research on automated learning and discovery of heuristics. The former type of system (e.g. TEIRESIAS, Davis; SEEK, Politakis) has already been shown to be useful in development of expert systems. Systems of the latter type are still in the basic research stage, and further progress in this direction could have a major impact on expert systems technology.

Examples of interactive aids for debugging a rule base include:

TEIRESIAS—system aids user in isolating faulty rule in chain of inferences that leads to incorrect conclusion.

SEEK—system collects statistics on rule performance over a database of known correct patient diagnoses, to isolate incorrect rules, and suggest possible revisions.

Examples of systems that infer from provided data include:

Meta-**DENDRAL**—infers rules that characterize behavior of molecules in mass spectrogram, for use in DENDRAL system for chemical structure elucidation; infers these from given set of molecules and their known spectra.

INDUCE/PLANT—infers rules that characterize plant diseases, given data of symptoms and known correct diagnoses. These rules yield expert performances comparable to that attained using rules provided by human experts.

Examples of systems that learn heuristics (e.g., *control* knowledge, as opposed to factual domain knowledge) include:

LEX—learns heuristics for selecting among alternative applicable rules, in solving symbolic integration problems, analyzing the solutions, proposing heuristics, then generating new practical problems, etc.

EURISKO—discovers new circuit structures for "highrise" VLSI circuits, and discovers heuristics for guiding its search for new circuitry structures. This is an interactive system, and has been used in additional domains, such as elementary number theory, and naval fleet design.

While systems have demonstrated the feasibility and utility of computer aids for knowledge acquisition, further progress can have a major impact on development costs for expert systems, as well as on the level of complexity of systems which can be constructed. Specific problem areas for near-term research on knowledge acquisition and learning include research of methods for interactively and automatically analyzing and validating an existing knowledge base, and for isolating errors. Other promising directions in this area include:

1. Research on methods for inferring new inference rules from problem solving experience. For example, in an expert system for interactive problem solving, those problem solving steps provided by the user constitute inference steps that the system might assimilate and generalize into rules of its own for subsequent use.

2. Research on compiling "deep" knowledge into more efficient "shallow" inference rules. (This is in the context of expert systems that integrate multiple levels of knowledge of the problem domain.)

3. Longer term basic research on machine learning, essential to progress on developing shorter-term knowledge acquisition aids. Such basic research issues include developing methods for: (a) extending representational vocabulary; (b) learning by autonomously generating, solving and analyzing practice problems; and (c) learning domain knowledge by reading textbooks.

Representation. The representation of knowledge continues to be an area of fundamental significance to AI. By changing representations one can drastically affect the functionality, efficiency and understandability (and therefore modificability) of expert systems.

One key subtopic in this regard is the question of *representational adequacy,* i.e., the question of whether there is any way to encode certain facts within a language. In the past, research in this direction has led to results such as extensions to predicate calculus necessary to handle default knowledge. Representation facilities are another key topic. In the past such research has led to the development of convenient specialty "languages" based on frames and semantic nets. Perhaps most important is the actual representation of certain aspects of "naive physics" knowledge, representations of time, space, matter, and causality.

Inference Methods. Inference methods are crucial to the expert system methodology so that programs can apply facts in their knowledge bases to new situations. While substantial work has been done on inference, both by logicians and researchers in AI, certain forms of inference of particular significance require further study. Important topics here include reasoning by default, reasoning by analogy, synthetic reasoning (i.e., design), and especially planning and reasoning under uncertainty.

Meta-level Architecture. Meta-level architecture is a new area for research that has considerable potential significance. The goal is the construction of programs that can explicitly reason about and control their own problem solving activity.

The approach here is to view the problem of problem solving control as an application area in its own light, just like geology or medicine. Control recommendations can be expressed in a "declarative" fashion and a program can reason about these recommendations in deciding what to do. In this way one can build a system of multiple representation and inference methods, supply it with facts about its goals and methods, and allow it to decide which to use in a given situation. Many traditional knowledge representation techniques, such as defaults and procedural attachments, can easily be expressed as meta-level axioms. Key subproblems include the meta-level encoding of standard results from theoretical computer science, and the complication of programs built with meta-level architecture.

Research on User Interfaces. As expert system applications grow into increasingly complex problem solving areas, the importance of high-quality user interfaces will increase as well. Progress here involves issues typically associated with man-machine interfaces, such as the need for high-quality graphics, friendly interfaces, fast response time, etc. In addition, the nature of expert systems applications usually requires that a system be able to explain its problem solving behavior, how it reached its conclusions, what inference steps were involved, and whether the problem at hand is one for which it possesses appropriate expertise. For example, an expert system for medical diagnosis and therapy is much more acceptable if it can explain the reasoning behind its diagnosis and therapy recommendations. While current systems have capabilities for enumerating the inference steps involved in reaching conclusions, more sophisticated explanation facilities would greatly improve the acceptability and utility of these systems. One significant opportunity for improving user interfaces (especially for naive users) is to incorporate natural language interfaces into expert systems.

Organizational problems and needs

AI has a number of special difficulties because of the ambitious, open-ended nature of its enterprise, and because of the size of the research community compared to the size of the technical problems. In addition, AI suffers from many problems that are shared with the rest of science and engineering.

Even restricted NL and expert systems can be very large, and since the success of an approach cannot really be measured until a system embodying it is completed and evaluated, the design-test-redesign cycle tends to be long. The development of a full-scale system is also a problem. Let us suppose that we want a NL system with a 10,000 word vocabulary; while a portion of a lexicon for the NL system can be extracted from a dictionary, each definition also requires separate attention, since dictionaries do not contain all the information necessary (definitions tend to be circular). If a team approach to construction is used, the team must be small in order to avoid the types of problems encountered in the construction of operating systems—as a programming team gets larger, its members tend to spend more and more of their time talking to each other about standardization, inter-module communication, updates, etc., and produce fewer and fewer lines of code per person per day. On the other hand, if a programming team is very small, it will simply take a long time to produce the necessary code because of individual programming speed limitations. Similar problems arise with the building of knowledge bases for expert systems.

Progress is also slowed because Ph.D. candidates are expected to work independently; the design and building of any significant NL or expert system generally cannot be split very many ways while still allowing suitable academic credit to be assigned to all participants. Once a system has been shown to be feasible, there are further difficulties; universities are not in a good position to develop or support software, since the designer/builders generally leave after receiving a degree, and there are few academic points awarded for cleaning up someone else's system and making it robust.

Industries have special problems as well. The largeness of NL and expert systems, and the fledgling state of our current technology makes it difficult or dangerous to promise profitable products on any time scale short enough to be appealing to management. There is also a wide gap between many of the kinds of programs that are produced in academia and the kinds of programs that can become good marketable products. For exam-

ple, while story understanding programs are considered (rightly) an important current academic topic, such programs have no clear short term market potential.

The comments in this section so far have assumed that we will continue to do research in roughly similar ways to those that have been employed in the recent past, that is, that we will attempt to build AI programs that are "instant adults," systems which are the result of programming, not of learning. There has been a growing interest in learning over the last few years, although only a fraction of the learning research has been directed toward NL and expert systems. Certainly there are serious difficulties with the engineering of a system capable of learning NL or expert knowledge from experience (an "instant infant"). For NL, the most serious problem seems to be adequate perceptual apparatus for extracting "important" items from raw sensory data. Even if we could devise such a learning program, there is little reason to suppose that it could be programmed to learn language much more rapidly than a human can, which would mean that at least several years would have to pass before we could judge whether or not the system was adequate. And, of course, the chance of getting everything right the first time is close to nil. Nonetheless, this seems to be an important avenue to explore, to hedge our bets, to further cognitive science and perhaps to find a compromise position ("instant five-year-old"?) that would represent the optimal long-term route to fully general NL systems. Fur-

ther reasons for emphasizing learning include the observations that the only language users that we know are built through learning, and that we continue to use learning as adult language users, so that we probably need learning of some sort in our programs anyhow.

For expert systems, a key difficulty is that human experts are generally not very good at explaining the basis of the expertise. We are very far from knowing how to design programs that could build a suitable knowledge base and body of inference rules by simply watching problem situations and the expert's solutions for them. Again, such a system would have to have sophisticated ways of judging what items from its experience were important, and of inferring the nature of the knowledge of the expert from these items. This seems impossible without beginning with a highly structured system, about which we currently have very few concrete ideas.

Another practical problem is finding good application areas, that is, ones where NL or expert systems can be truly helpful, where the domain is well-circumscribed and well-understood, where the tools that we now have are capable of conquering the problem, and where typing is possible and acceptable as an input medium.

Finally, there is an acute shortage of qualified researchers. Since most actual application programs are likely to be the result of development by industry, it seems desirable to encourage more industrial effort. However, taking researchers away from universities reduces the number of faculty capable of supervising graduate students and carrying on much needed basic research.

Manpower

AI shares a severe manpower shortage with the rest of computer science and computer engineering. However, in AI the problem is compounded because a "critical mass" of researchers seems to be essential to carry out first-rate research. To be concrete let us list some of the requirements for doing NL or expert systems research.

Software support—Since AI uses language and systems software packages and often machines that are different from the rest of computer science, separate systems people are extremely important. At least one, and preferably two or more are needed. Implementation is essential: ideas cannot be tested without implementation, and many ideas result from the experience of implementation. The day of the single-researcher tour-de-force system has largely passed. Because implementation is a lengthy and costly process, it is important to argue before implementing. In arguing, the generation of new paradigms is important—a re-implementation of previous ideas is of little value.

Within NL, a modern system should have a user interface, a parser, a semantic interpreter, a knowledge representing and retrieving component, a discourse plan evaluator, a speaker modelling component, and a language generator. In addition, if it works on a data base or knowledge base of some kind, there is a further need for support. There are 6–7 different areas here, and even if each person is expert in three, there is a need for four or five people. The story is similar for expert systems: an expert system must have a large knowledge base, which generally requires at least one expert and one knowledge engineer. An expert system also requires a user interface, which involves both input understanding and output generating components. Again the minimum critical mass is four or five researchers. Using senior graduate students is possible, but turnover after graduation causes serious problems in keeping a system working. Using these criteria, only three or four U.S. universities have a critical mass in NL, and a similar number have critical mass in expert systems.

People who want to do AI research must also be cognizant of fields outside computer science/computer engineering: NL people ought to know linguistics and possibly psychology and philosophy of language; expert systems people must know about the knowledge area (medicine, geology, molecular biology) in which their systems is to be expert, vision people need to know about neuro-physiology and the psychology of perception, and so on. This means that effective critical masses may be even larger, and may only be possible in settings which can provide the right support outside of computer science/computer engineering.

Leaving the critical mass issue, there is a critical manpower shortage at universities, especially for research and for graduate research supervision. Few new Ph.D.s are being produced, and computer science suffers from a singularly high emigration to industry. Part of the problem is teaching loads. In a time of rapidly expanding demand for education in computer science/computer engineering, both for specialists and for those who want computer science electives, teaching loads are likely to be high. This is compounded by heavy graduate advising demands. Of the six faculty members in our group, one supervises twelve graduate students, two supervise ten each, one supervises six, and one supervises two. However, the one who supervises two also supervises eighteen full-time professional staff members and the one who supervises six has a relatively heavy teaching load. When the need to write proposals for the substantial equipment and research funding needed to support serious research are added, it is clear that faculty in AI may well have difficulty fitting in time for research. Graduate students have in some cases decided not to go into academia specifically because of what they have observed of their advisor's experience.

Industry too has problems, many not specific to AI. There is such a shortage of qualified personnel that nearly as many non-Computer Science (CS) majors as CS majors are hired for CS positions. CS education at universities also varies wildly in quality, especially at minor institutions, and there is no easy way (short of some form of profession certification) to judge the competence of prospective employees. No doubt, many of the problems in generating high quality software stem from poor education.

Equipment

AI research requires extensive computer facilities, with different types of computers than those used for large numerical tasks. There is a wide gap between the top few universities and research labs, and the rest of the universities doing AI research. The top several AI centers now have one powerful personal computer (usually LISP machines) for every three or four researchers (graduate students and faculty) as well as a number of larger time-shared machines, ARPANET connections, and other special-purpose equipment.

If reasonable AI research is to be done elsewhere, much more equipment must be made available. More equipment is also critically important to keep new Ph.D. graduates in academia: a number of industrial labs are at least as well equipped as the best universities. Graduate students are unlikely to want to go to a place that has computer facilities that are inferior to those they are accustomed to.

AI researchers at universities which do not have software support groups are now constrained to use a relatively narrow range of equipment types in order to be able to use shared software from other locations. The manufacturers of this preferred equipment (DEC, Xerox, Symbolics, LMI Inc., and a handful of others)

have not donated much equipment in recent years; the few exceptions have been universities that are already relatively well-equipped. The future looks a little brighter, since a fair body of AI software can now run under UNIX, and many manufacturers either offer, or plan to soon offer, machines (especially based on the Motorola 68000 chip) that can run UNIX. Maintenance funds are also critical; there have been cases where industrial gifts have been turned down by universities because maintenance was not included, and the universities had inadequate budgets to pay the maintenance costs.

An Assessment of Resources Required for AI Research

AI's main needs are manpower and equipment. Except for very limited special purpose applications, AI systems require relatively large program address space and relatively large numbers of machine cycles. When done on the time-shared machines in general use (e.g., Digital Equipment Corp VAXes and DEC-20s), research is clearly hampered by a shortage of machine power. LISP machines are much better, but some (e.g., Xerox 1108's at $32K each) have rather small address space, and the rest tend to be quite expensive (more than $75K) if dedicated to a single user. Very roughly about $25K–$35K in additional funds per researcher is needed to provide at least a sem-

blance of the best environment for AI research; anything less will mean that progress is slower than it could be. In this estimate, we have assumed that a number of researchers will get more expensive machines (Symbolics 3600, LMI Nu machine, or Xerox Dorado), and that shared facilities, terminals, modems, printers, mass storage, etc. must be purchased also. Including graduate students and research programmers, as well as faculty researchers, there are now probably 150 people doing work on NL and expert systems in universities. This brings the total expenditure needed to properly equip these researchers for maximum progress to about $5M. About $50K–$60K is required to properly equip each new faculty member.

Manpower needs cannot be solved quickly by simple infusion of dollars. Money that is spent on university equipment will probably do the most good, because it can help speed the research for graduate students, and it can also make universities relatively more attractive places to induce faculty members to remain and new graduates to choose in place of industry. This will in turn accelerate the production of new researchers. At the best, we are still likely to have a serious shortage of AI researchers for the foreseeable future: given that there are fewer than 25 faculty members who each graduate about 0.5 Ph.D. students per year, we can expect for the near future only 12 or so new NL Ph.D.s per year. In expert systems, the situation is a little better, with about 30 faculty nationwide, but there will probably still be no more than 15 new

Ph.D.s per year over the next ten years. Probably only about half of the new Ph.Ds. will go to universities, and it will be five years before the new faculty produce their first Ph.D. students. Thus the manpower situation for the next ten years is likely, in the absence of any massive intervention, to leave us with fewer than 100 NL faculty and about 100 expert system faculty members nationwide at the end of the ten year period.

As mentioned above, a possible way to increase our AI capability in the shorter term would be to encourage a crossover of faculty from areas such as linguistics or developmental psychology to AI NL research, and from various fields of expertise (e.g., medicine, geology, etc.) into expert systems research. There are already incentives for researchers with suitable backgrounds, since funding in many other areas (e.g., linguistics) has generally been cut along with social sciences. An infusion of researchers from these areas may have possible long-term benefits to AI NL research above and beyond providing more manpower; it is our belief that in order to truly succeed in producing general, robust NL systems, we must develop a far deeper science of human language understanding and language development, and it seems clear that expert systems research requires humans processing the specific expertise to be part of the effort.

It might also be helpful to provide graduate fellowships, though the most serious shortage seems to be supervisors of research, not interested students nor money to support the students.

Recommendations for the Next 5–10 Years in Natural Language

0. Don't expect too much; the number of researchers in the field is really quite small, and the size of the task of understanding is enormous.

1. Continue a broad range of basic research support; there is still a shortage of science on which to base NL system engineering.

2. Increase funding for equipment. Adequate equipment is essential if researchers are to produce working systems, rather than just theoretical advances. Such funding has many benefits: Increasing available computer power can dramatically cut the amounts of time and effort required to produce running systems, since easy-to-write though computationally expensive systems can then be considered. Squeezing a large program onto a small machine can be very time-consuming. If programs take too long to run, programmers start to work on speeding them up instead of working on increasing their range of competence. Making modern, powerful equipment available to universities will help them retain faculty. Despite the apparently high initial cost compared to salaries, money spent on hardware is likely to be a good investment.

3. Encourage resource-sharing, by funding specific research groups to develop, supply, and maintain a common body of research tools, for example AI programming languages, natural language parsers, knowledge representation systems, "empty" expert systems (i.e. reasoning and knowledge base access portions of expert systems with domain-specific knowledge removed), and programs for transforming programs from one language or operating system to another. To some degree, this recommendation is already being followed and has accelerated research progress.

4. Create and encourage development groups in industry and military labs, and encourage increased contact between such groups and university and industrial basic research laboratories. Universities are particularly ill-suited for developmental efforts, since there is a high turnover of key system builders, making it difficult to support application systems. In addition, we need all the effort on basic problems that can be mustered. Development could be handled by groups that have more traditional software backgrounds; once feasibility has been demonstrated, AI systems often look a lot like other programs. Possible incentives could include tax breaks and jointly funded university/industry research and development efforts, though the latter would have to be designed judiciously to avoid waste and mismatched expectations and capabilities.

5. Encourage industrial research laboratories to help by advising Ph.D. research whenever possible. Such cooperation can benefit the laboratories by providing relatively low-cost, high-quality staffing, and can help increase the size of the U.S. research community at a faster rate. This recommendation can work; SRI International and Bolt Beranek and Newman, Inc., among others, have successfully functioned as Ph.D. research supervising institutions for a number of years.

6. Maximize faculty research and research supervision time by providing partial academic year salaries as well as summer salaries.

7. Institute three- to four-year research initiation funding, including equipment funds, for promising new graduates who agree to stay at universities. Hewlett-Packard has already

undertaken such a program.

8. Encourage the design of novel supercomputer architectures that take AI needs into account; current supercomputers are number crunchers that are of little use or interest to AI, though AI badly needs computers with greater power. AI researchers have begun to design such machines at a few locations. AI people have had some success at computer design (e.g. LISP machines), but it would be desirable to have groups that specialize in computer design involved with such designs. Japan, in its 5th Generation Computer effort, has already undertaken such a goal, and it seems quite possible that even a partial success in their effort can cause serious erosion or loss of the U.S. high tech edge.

9. Encourage cooperation between AI NL research, and the traditional fields interested in language (linguistics and psychology). This can serve the purpose of aiding the building of a science of language and cognition, and can also provide a more rapid increase in manpower resources than is possible through the training of new researchers only. This recommendation may happen anyhow, since "social science" funding has been cut dramatically, putting pressure on many of the kinds of people that could help the AI NL effort. To make this work, a fair amount of re-education, especially in AI, computation and programming, will be needed along with some re-education of AI people in linguistics and psychology, to build a common knowledge base.

You've already found the advantages and disadvantages discussed in the third reading. In order to write your essay, you need to go back to Reading II, on page 160, to see if there are any advantages or disadvantages that were not included in the article on AI.

Look again at the article "Machines Built to Emulate Human Experts' Reasoning."

List any advantages or disadvantages of expert systems that were not mentioned in "Artificial Intelligence."

All writing involves choices. The author chooses to focus on particular ideas, to organize and develop them in a certain way, and to express them in a particular fashion. These choices are determined by the author's perceptions of his intended audience (their needs, desires, attitudes, level of expertise, etc.), as well as his purpose in relation to that audience.

Turn to pages 171–172 of "Artificial Intelligence: An Assessment of the State-of-the-Art and Recommendation for Future Directions." Look at the first seven paragraphs on "Expert Systems."

1. Skim this section of the article to find out which main ideas this writer has chosen to focus on.
2. **a.** Draw a tree diagram showing how he has organized these ideas.

   b. Why do you suppose he chose this particular sequence rather than any other?

3. The writer of this particular section has gone to great effort to ensure the reader's comprehension.

   a. In small groups, examine each paragraph carefully. For each one, observe the following:

   (i) which ideas or phrases the writer chose to clarify
   (ii) why the writer selected those particular ones
   (iii) the clarification technique in each case
   (iv) the effectiveness of each clarification technique

   Take point form notes.

   b. Compare your answers with those of another group.

Writing the Essay

The essay topic you have chosen for your "Business and Technology" course is a discussion of the strengths and weaknesses of expert systems. In an essay of this type, you are expected to summarize information, so it is important that you choose the necessary information and ignore extraneous details.

1. Complete the following steps using information from *both* the articles you read on expert systems.

   a. What are the advantages or strengths of expert systems? List the important ones first.

   b. What are the disadvantages or weaknesses of expert systems? List the important ones first.

   c. What focus statement will you need for your answer?

d. What conclusion will you need?

2. On a separate sheet of paper, make a rough plan of your answer. Ask your partner to evaluate it.
3. Write a first draft.

Clarifying for your Reader

The good writer makes every effort to ensure that the reader can understand the ideas. To promote this understanding, the writer tries to anticipate the reader's problems, particularly if the material is highly technical and requires a specialized vocabulary.

At times what may seem clear to the writer is, in fact, confusing to the reader, in which case, clarification of ideas and terms is necessary.

Concepts central to the topic are usually clarified early, while other, less germane ideas are generally dealt with as they appear in the text.

There are various ways to clarify—e.g., definition, explanation, exemplification, comparison, contrast, and restatement. The writer selects the one considered most effective for the purpose, depending on the nature of the audience and the information.

Let us consider this article from the point of view of clarity. We will look at the following aspects:

- the clarification techniques themselves
- the particular ones the writer chose
- their effectiveness as tools of clarification

Definitions

1. For each term to the left, find the definition and write it in the column on the right.

TERM	DEFINITION
a. Artificial intelligence (p. 165)	
b. MYCIN (p. 166)	
c. DENDRAL (p. 166)	

    d. PROSPECTOR (p. 165)

    e. INTELLECT (p. 165)

    f. Expert systems research (p. 171)

2. Frequently, the first noun in a definition states the general class of things the term belongs to. In all but one of the definitions above, circle this general noun.

3. Now look at the rest of the definitions, the part after the noun. What structure has been used to limit the generality of each of these nouns?

4. For each of the terms in question 1, note when they were defined and discuss why the writer chose to define them when he did.

Explanations

To ensure comprehension, the writer might decide to *explain* certain terms for the reader, particularly if the terms have a specialized meaning within the context.

1. In this context, what does it mean for a machine to "act intelligently"? (p. 165)

2. a. After the definition of "expert systems research," what terms did the author decide to clarify further? (p. 171)

    b. Why do you suppose he selected these particular terms?

Exemplification

1. a. In the paragraph on artificial intelligence (p. 165), what do "ambition," "fear," "general world knowledge," and "mobility" have in common?

b. Why did the author include them?

c. What structure did the author use to do so?

2. How does the author clarify the concept of "inferring new inference rules from problem solving experience"? (p. 173, col. 3)

3. a. What examples of human–machine interfaces has the author included? (p. 174, col. 2)

b. What structure has the author used in this case?

Comparison

1. Again in the first paragraph on expert systems, what comparison has the author used to demonstrate the superiority of machines over humans in performing particular intelligence tasks?

Contrast

Reread the first three paragraphs in the section on expert systems (page 171). The writer has used contrast twice in order to clarify the unique nature of these systems. In effect, this writer has anticipated two separate questions of the intended audience.

1. What are these two questions?

2. Why did the writer consider it necessary to make these distinctions before continuing the discussion?

Restatement

Restatement is an attempt to clarify through the rephrasing of a word, sentence, or passage.

1. Find the restatements for the following terms. Write them in column B.

–A–	–B–
a. "high performance" ("Expert Systems," para.1)	
b. "complex domains" ("Expert Systems," para. 1)	
c. "representational adequacy" ("Representation," para. 2)	

Now, go back over your first draft. Keeping your reader in mind, make any revisions and add information you now feel your reader needs in order to fully understand your ideas.

Follow the procedures for writing a final draft that are detailed in Chapters 1 and 5. Then give your essay to your teacher.

8
LUCY

CHAPTER CONTENTS:

Thinking About the Topic
Reading I: "Here's Lucy—Our Cousin"
Reading II: "The Leakeys—A Towering Reputation"
Answering an Exam Question
Preparing to Write an Essay

Reading III: "Facing Up to Man's Past"
Reading IV: "Were Lucy's Feet Made for Walking?"
Writing the Early Drafts
Writing the Final Draft

Anthropologists have long been concerned with discovering when and where humans first appeared. One difficulty has been to determine what differentiated humans from their earlier ancestors. Was it brain size and use of tools that distinguished humans from other animals or was it bipedality (the ability to walk upright)? In this chapter you'll read some new information about early humans and discover how scientists are interpreting this information.

The readings in this chapter are long. Again you must select and read only the relevant information. You'll get more practice in notetaking and summarizing.

There are two writing tasks in this chapter. You'll answer an exam question and write an essay. Both tasks will give you practice in the writing process. The exercises in this chapter will help you write clear and concise text.

Thinking About the Topic

A. Match the definition or description on the left with the term or person on the right. Put the correct letter in the blank.

1. _____ A hardened remnant or trace of animal or plant life from a past geological age, preserved in rock formations

2. _____ The science of ancient life that seeks to determine humankind's place in the course of natural events

3. _____ The head of a family of famous paleontologists

4. _____ The scientist who published a new theory of evolution in 1859

5. _____ A group of related species of animals or plants

6. _____ The science that seeks to reconstruct the context of early life and the course of human evolution

7. _____ The characteristic of walking on two feet

8. _____ Of or pertaining to land

9. _____ A primate who walks upright

10. _____ Any order of mammals, including humans, that has flexible hands and feet, with 5 digits on each hand and foot

11. _____ A basic category of plants or animals capable of interbreeding, comprising a subdivision of a genus

12. _____ Of or pertaining to trees

a. Louis Leakey
b. Charles Darwin
c. Genus
d. Species
e. Primate
f. Paleontology
g. Paleoanthropology
h. Fossil
i. Hominid
j. Bipedality
k. Arboreal
l. Terrestrial

B. In groups, compare and discuss your answers, resolving any differences.

C. Reread definitions 2, 6, 9, and 10 in part A. What common structure is evident in this group?

2. ⎫
6. ⎪
9. ⎬
10. ⎭

Now reread 1, 5, 7, and 11. What common structure is evident here?

1. ⎫
5. ⎪
7. ⎬
11. ⎭

Discuss these similarities with your teacher.

D. In the space below, keep a list of any other scientific terms you will need or want to remember. Beside each, write the definition.

TERM   DEFINITION

"HERE'S LUCY—OUR COUSIN"

In this chapter, we'll be reading about Lucy, a tiny skeleton whose significance has given rise to heated debates among anthropologists. On one side are Donald Johanson and Tim White; on the other, Richard Leakey and Jack Stern.

Below are the first six paragraphs of an article about the discovery of Lucy. The paragraphs, however, are not in the correct order. Read them carefully; then sequence them properly, putting the correct number in the blank. You have 20 minutes to complete this task. Then, check your answers in groups of three to four. Try to resolve any differences.

Here's Lucy— Our Cousin

THE THEME: The discovery and reconstruction of a tiny female skeleton about three million years old may change our ideas of how modern man had developed.

_____ Then, in January of this year, a new piece was added to the puzzle of human evolution. Dr. Donald Johanson, an anthropologist with the Cleveland Museum, announced a new find. The partial skeleton of a tiny female creature had been discovered in the Afar region of Ethiopia. The discovery was actually made in 1974, but it has taken this long to confirm and reconstruct the find.

_____ Before Charles Darwin it's safe to say there was no true science of anthropology. In 1859, Darwin gave us his theory of evolution which says briefly that all kinds of creatures evolve, or change, by adapting to their environment. The weaker specimens die, the fitter ones survive and grow stronger or smarter. Species which fail to adapt to their surroundings, like the dinosaurs, simply disappear.

_____ Darwin believed that man and the apes descended from the same ancestor, and the latest discoveries seem to support this theory. In 1973, Leakey described one of our African ancestors. His find was a man-like creature with a comparatively large brain. Leakey estimated its age at about two million years.

_____ Mankind is the supreme example of Darwin's theory of evolution— the only creature on the planet with the ability to reason. We are similar to the apes in many ways and, from the start, the big question has been whether the two species developed separately or whether they had a common ancestor. If the latter is true, when did the two species begin to branch off from this common ancestor?

_____ ANTHROPOLOGISTS have a larger bump of curiosity than most people. Their science is the study of humans and they will never rest until they find out just how we got to be the way we are today.

_____ Science has accepted Darwin's theory and anthropologists use it to explain where we came from and perhaps where we are headed. Richard E. Leakey, most famous of today's crop of anthropologists, puts it this way: "By searching our long-buried past for an understanding of what we are, we may discover some insight into our future."

Now read the following article, "Here's Lucy—Our Cousin". As you read highlight relevant information, and then write point form answers to the following questions.

1. According to the article, the discovery of Lucy has shed light on what two issues in anthropology?

2. What side of each issue does Lucy's skeleton appear to support?

3. What evidence is presented to support these two assertions?

4. What contradictory evidence is presented here?

Here's Lucy— Our Cousin

THE THEME: The discovery and reconstruction of a tiny female skeleton about three million years old may change our ideas of how modern man has developed.

ANTHROPOLOGISTS have a larger bump of curiosity than most people. Their science is the study of humans and they will never rest until they find out just how we got to be the way we are today.

Before Charles Darwin it's safe to say there was no true science of anthropology. In 1859, Darwin gave us his theory of evolution which says briefly that all kinds of creatures evolve, or change, by adapting to their environment. The weaker specimens die, the fitter ones survive and grow stronger or smarter. Species which fail to adapt to their surroundings, like the dinosaurs, simply disappear.

Science has accepted Darwin's theory and anthropologists use it to explain where we came from and perhaps where we are headed. Richard E. Leakey, most famous of today's crop of anthropologists, puts it this way: "By searching our long-buried past for an understanding of what we are, we may discover some insight into our future."

Mankind is the supreme example of Darwin's theory of evolution—the only creature on the planet with the ability to reason. We are similar to the apes in many ways and, from the start, the big question has been whether the two species developed separately or whether they had a common ancestor. If the latter is true, when did the two species begin to branch off from this common ancestor?

Darwin believed that man and the apes descended from the same ancestor, and the latest discoveries seem to support this theory. In 1973, Leakey described one of our African ancestors. His find was a man-like creature with a comparatively large brain. Leakey estimated its age at about two million years.

Then, in January of this year, a new piece was added to the puzzle of human evolution. Dr. Donald Johanson, an anthropologist with the Cleveland Museum, announced a new find. The partial skeleton of a tiny female creature had been discovered in the Afar region of Ethiopia. The discovery was actually made in 1974, but it has taken this long to confirm and reconstruct the find.

Lucy from Afar

The new species is known to science as *Australopithicus afarensis* (southern ape of Afar), but researchers have nicknamed the skeleton "Lucy." (A tape of the Beatles' song, "Lucy in the Sky with Diamonds" was playing while they were discussing their find). Lucy was probably 105 to 120 centimeters tall and about 20 years old. Her pelvis and knee joints show that she walked upright. Her skeleton, which is about 40 per cent complete, is about three million years old.

Apart from her age, which takes her back another million years before Leakey's find, the most interesting thing about Lucy is her head. Her skull is relatively small, leaving room for a brain of only 500 cubic centimeters as compared to 1500 for modern man and 700 to 800 for other early forms. Lucy's teeth, instead of curving as in a human jaw, lay in more of a straight line—like an ape's. Her canine teeth ("fangs") projected slightly less than an ape's. The overall tooth structure was halfway between human and ape.

The discovery goes a long way toward confirming Darwin's belief. "What we've found is a common ancestor for all later hominids (manlike creatures)," said Dr. Johanson's colleague, Dr. Timothy D. White. "It's just one more link in what we consider the chain of evolution."

Anthropologists have always argued over whether brain development came before walking upright or the other way around.

The discovery of Lucy seems to show that standing up came before everything else. "Now, for the first time, we've got a handle on the sequence," said Dr. Johanson. "Bipedalism (walking on two feet) preceded all the other characteristics we consider human."

The discovery of Lucy adds an important piece of the jigsaw puzzle of man's ancestry.

"THE LEAKEYS—A TOWERING REPUTATION"

Skim the *New York Times* article on the Leakey family, highlighting or underlining only information pertaining to the two topics listed below. Be careful. There is quite a lot of biographical information on the Leakeys that you may find personally interesting but which is irrelevant to the task at hand. Then reread the article, taking point form notes in the spaces provided.

1. The Order of Evolution: Bipedality Versus Brain Growth and Tool Use:

2. The Complete Bipedality of Lucy—Arguments For and Against:

The Leakeys: A towering reputation

Even bitter rivals find room to praise family's accomplishments.

ALONE among all the creatures, the species that styles itself wise, *Homo sapiens,* has an abiding interest in its distant origins, knows that its allotted time is short, worries about the future and wonders about the past.

This is the appeal of paleontology, the science of ancient life that seeks to determine mankind's place in the course of natural events. And it is the attraction of that extraordinary family of fossil hunters, the Leakeys of Kenya.

It is the Leakeys who, in a significant way, have given modern paleontology its place among the sciences. Admirers and critics alike have the family in mind even more prominently than usual these days following the recent announcement of a new find by one member of the clan and the publication of two new books about them.

The name Leakey is synonymous with the study of human origins. The family's excavations extend over much of East Africa and back several million years to the emergence of early man. They proved beyond doubt the African origins of man. They discovered and named

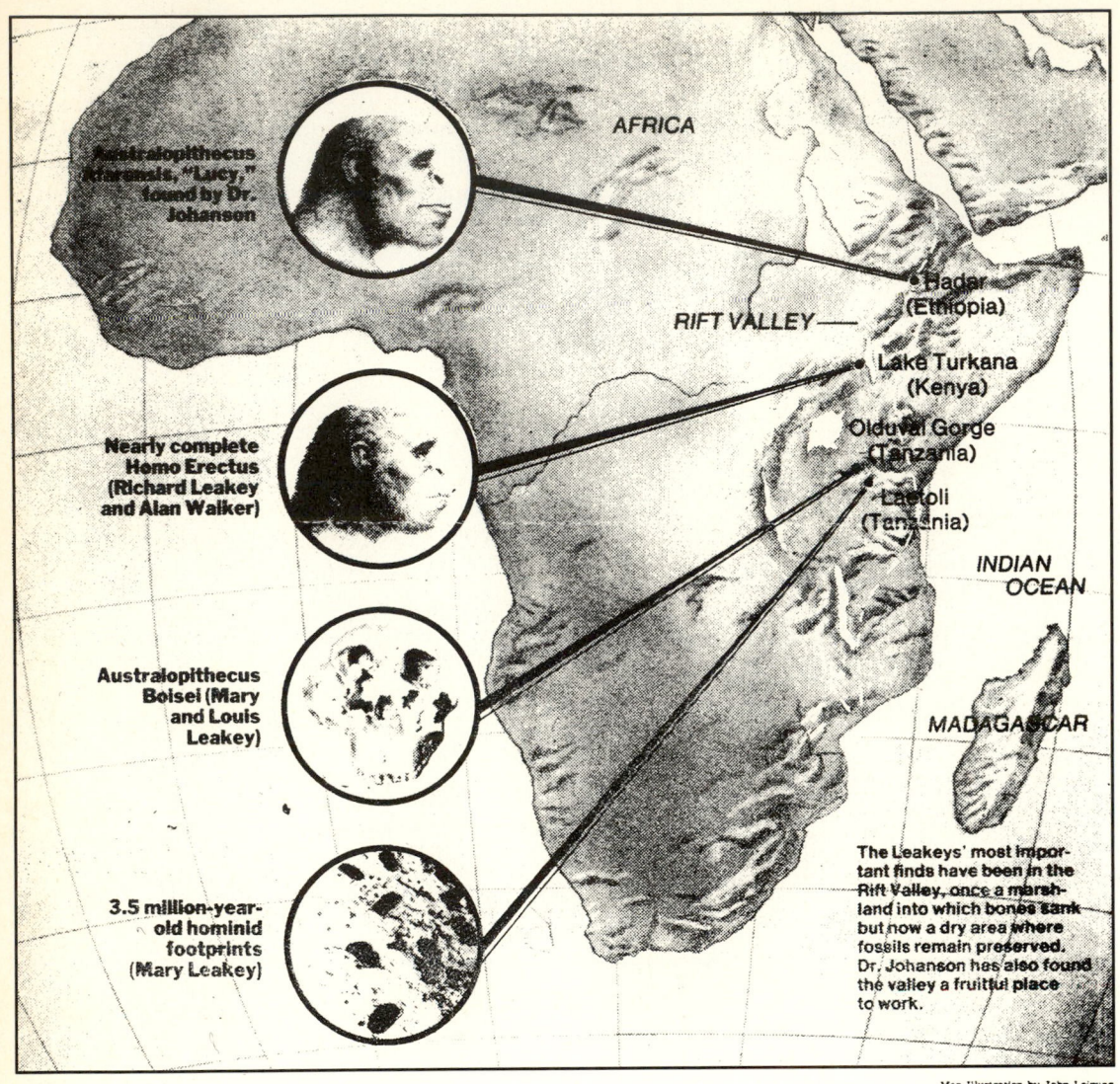

AFRICA

Australopithecus Afarensis, "Lucy," found by Dr. Johanson

RIFT VALLEY

Hadar (Ethiopia)

Lake Turkana (Kenya)

Olduvai Gorge (Tanzania)

Laetoli (Tanzania)

Nearly complete Homo Erectus (Richard Leakey and Alan Walker)

INDIAN OCEAN

Australopithecus Boisei (Mary and Louis Leakey)

MADAGASCAR

3.5 million-year-old hominid footprints (Mary Leakey)

The Leakeys' most important finds have been in the Rift Valley, once a marshland into which bones sank but now a dry area where fossils remain preserved. Dr. Johanson has also found the valley a fruitful place to work.

Map Illustration by John Leimung

the bones of the first human tool-makers, *Homo habilis,* and dug up the most complete skeleton of a more recent ancestor, *Homo erectus.* They found fossil footprints showing that human ancestors walked upright long before they made tools.

With their many expeditions and discoveries, the Leakeys have helped transform paleoanthropology in the last quarter of a century from the relatively simple pursuit of stones and bones to the more sophisticated science of reconstructing the context of early life and the fateful steps in human evolution.

As fossil hunters, the Leakeys are inspired, industrious, lucky and nearly always controversial. Some of the inferences they draw from discoveries have been proved wrong, as well as right. Their fame, which they cultivate to raise money

for further excavations, has caused some resentment among lesser-known scientists. But even their severest critics acknowledge the pioneering accomplishments of the Leakeys and say that the family's towering reputation is generally well-deserved.

The founder of the scientific dynasty was Louis S. F. Leakey, who died in 1972. He was born in Kenya to British missionaries, and when he returned there in the 1920's, after schooling in England, he began digging for bones. At the time, nearly all scientists assumed the birthplace of man was in Asia, not Africa. Mr. Leakey's early discoveries were decisive in overturning these assumptions and revealing the greater antiquity of early man.

Mr. Leakey's wife, Mary, learned paleontology from him and became an accomplished field collector in her own right. In fact, though her husband often received the credit, many of the most famous Leakey finds were made by Mary Leakey. She tells of the excitement and meaning of these discoveries in her autobiography, "Disclosing the Past," which was published this month.

Carrying on the family tradition is Richard Leakey, the second of their three sons, who is director of the National Museums of Kenya. He, too, has weighed in this month with an autobiography, "One Life." And two weeks ago, he and Alan Walker of the Johns Hopkins University School of Medicine announced the most recent in the long line of Leakey discoveries.

This was the skeleton of a robust 12-year-old male who lived 1.6 million years ago. It was identified as a rare specimen of *Homo erectus*, a direct ancestor of *Homo sapiens*, and described as the most complete skeleton of an early human ancestor ever found. The skull and bones were uncovered between layers of volcanic ash near Lake Turkana in northern Kenya.

ANALYSIS OF BONES

After a preliminary analysis, Mr. Leakey said the bones were impressive because they showed how humanlike our ancestors appeared that long ago and they indicated that

early man may have attained sizes comparable to modern man. (Early forms of *Homo sapiens* apparently evolved 400,000 years ago.) The boy was estimated to have stood five and a half feet tall. If he had lived to maturity, he might have reached a height of six feet.

For once, Donald C. Johanson, director of the Institute of Human Origins in Berkeley, Calif., was in agreement with the Leakeys. He called the skeleton a "quite extraordinary" find that should lead to a new understanding of *Homo erectus* anatomy.

But Dr. Johanson could not resist taking a swipe at Richard Leakey. "I'm a little surprised that everyone is so surprised that this was a large individual," he said, referring to the *Homo erectus* skeleton. "We've had pieces from China and Java that suggest that these individuals approached six feet in size. I don't think this aspect of the discovery is so astonishing."

These two rival superstars of paleontology, Dr. Johanson and Mr. Leakey, have battled openly for nearly a decade over the interpretation of Dr. Johanson's illustrious discovery, the bones of "Lucy" found at Hadar in the Afar region of Ethiopia. Dr. Johanson decided that Lucy represented a new species, *Australopithecus afarensis*, that was ancestral not only to the other australopithecine ape-men species (which came to an evolutionary dead end) but also to *Homo habilis*, a Leakey discovery, and hence the whole human line.

Despite their many differences, Dr. Johanson praised the Leakey family for drawing attention to the availability in East Africa of fossils for reconstructing human evolution and for "finding many specimens of great importance."

Similarly, Milford Wolpoff, a professor of paleoanthropology at the University of Michigan, who said he "probably disagreed with Richard as much as anyone," called the Leakeys "a centrally pivotal family" in the study of human origins. "They've turned out good ideas that stirred up controversy," Dr. Wolpoff said. "You had to make a good case to show they were wrong, when they were. This led to more thinking, more work. I call that progress."

It was a discovery by the Leakeys in 1959 that, according to F. Clark Howell of the University of California, marked "the beginnings of paleoanthropology in a modern sense." The pace of exploration quickened. The work became more scientific. Geologists and anatomists, not just bone hunters, joined the quest, a multidisciplinary approach that the Leakeys did much to promote.

One July day in 1959, while Louis lay ill in camp, Mary stumbled on some teeth and part of a jaw on a slope of Olduvai Gorge, one of their prime dig sites in Tanzania. Rushing back to her husband, she exclaimed, "I've found him— found our man!"

How the couple celebrated is not recorded. But in her autobiography, Mrs. Leakey writes that after an earlier major find they "cast aside care" and that was how their son Philip, "came to join our family."

The 1959 discovery turned out to be a 1.8-million-year-old fossil known as the "nutcracker man" because of its huge jaws and molar teeth. It was a member of the genus *Australopithecus*, more precisely, the boisei species. A few years later, at Olduvai and elsewhere, the Leakeys found the remains of *Homo habilis*, the earliest known ancestor in the direct *Homo* line and a contemporary of *Australopithecus*.

Like most of the sites being worked today, Olduvai lies in the Rift Valley, which runs through much of East Africa. Over the ages the valley has acted as a natural trap for sediments in which are preserved the fossils of early life.

3.5 MILLION-YEAR-OLD FOOTPRINTS

Mrs. Leakey believes her most important find was the footprints at Laetoli, a site near Olduvai. In 1976, while hurling dried elephant dung in a playful camp fight, a worker fell down and saw the first footprints. Some humanlike creatures 3.5 million years ago had walked through moist volcanic ash. They stood fully erect on their hind feet.

Darwin and most succeeding scientists had assumed that walking upright evolved after the development of larger brains and in the process of freeing the hands for making and using tools. But a few scientists had already postulated that bipedal locomotion preceded toolmaking by a long period. They suggested that bipedality evolved in association with the development of early human family life and male-female bonding. Walking upright freed the hands for carrying food back to share with the family.

In a lecture in New York recently, Mrs. Leakey said the Laetoli footprints were "proof positive" that bipedality came long before there is any evidence of toolmaking, which dates back little more than two million years.

Dr. Johanson's Lucy seemed to be telling much the same story. This skeleton and the bones of at least 13 other individuals were found at Hadar beginning in 1974. Dr. Jo-

hanson and his colleague, Tim White, announced in 1979 that Lucy's limbs were fully adapted to bipedality. These creatures were said to have lived between 3.5 million and 4 million years ago.

Some scientists, disputing this interpretation, note that Lucy's long, curved and heavily muscled hands and feet suggested grasping and that could mean that Lucy may have walked some but was still basically an arboreal creature. But the sparks really flew over Dr. Johanson's classification of Lucy as a new species that was the common ancestor for both the human and *Australopithecus* branches of evolution.

Opposition arose over whether the Hadar specimens represented a single species, or two, and if the species was essentially different from the long-established *A. africanus*. Phillip V. Tobias of the University of Witwatersrand in Johannesburg argues *A. afarensis* and *A. africanus* are one and the same. Dr. Tobias has built his career around *A. africanus,* which was first identified by his mentor, Raymond Dart, in 1924.

On the basis of new discoveries in South Africa, Dr. Tobias said last week "I do not believe that the differences that exist between Hadar and the Transvaal site are sufficient to justify Hadar as a different species."

There seems to be a tendency among some paleontologists to see new species every time they see a new specimen. "You see more variations in our own species on any street corner," says Dr. Wolpoff, "than you can see in some of these fossils."

The Leakeys were upset at Dr. Johanson for his decision to incorporate one of their Laetoli specimens into his newly designated species, *A. afarensis*. Their dig sites

were more than 1,000 miles apart and at first it seemed that Lucy was much older than the Laetoli fossils.

In her book, Mary Leakey argues that the revised dates for Lucy, making her possibly as recent as three million years, show that Dr. Johanson's fossils "are too young to occupy an ancestral position, even if they were otherwise appropriate."

Dr. Johanson responded in a telephone interview: "I think they feel a lot of what we've done has been a personal attack on their family. The most frustrating aspect of it is that neither one of them, Richard or Mary, will sit down and discuss their criticisms in a scientific journal. They have chosen to criticize us in the press."

The noise and rancor of this "public paleontology," as it is called by some disapproving scientists, has diverted attention from what some scientists believe are the more important issues and findings of early human studies.

As Dr. Wolpoff said: "What if Johanson was right and Tobias wrong? What if Leakey was right and Johanson was wrong? What difference would that make in the significant understanding of human evolution? You've got to say the answer is, none. It wouldn't change the pattern of evolution, just some of the details."

The pattern, according to Dr. Wolpoff, is that early man began to walk on his hind feet, then developed big brains and learned to fashion bone and stone tools. This seems "indisputable," he said, "whichever fossils gave rise to which later fossils."

But controversy in paleontology is perhaps inevitable, for scientists must of necessity work with such a few scraps of bone and somehow make the most of them. Dr. Walker, who is one of Mr. Leakey's colleagues, said; "When you get to the position in any science where with a piece of evidence sensible people disagree, then you haven't got enough evidence."

With this in mind, Dr. Johanson said that he would visit Ethiopia next month seeking permission to resume explorations at Hadar. Ethiopia has been closed to foreign scientists for several years because of civil war and disputes over licensing procedures for expeditions. Digging deeper into the fields where Lucy lay may settle some arguments over her place in prehistory—and probably, as often happens, raise new questions.

Mr. Leakey and Dr. Walker plan to return to the fossil-rich grounds near Lake Turkana next year. They hope to find the remaining bones to the *Homo erectus* skeleton they dug up this summer. They also want to explore sediments two million to three million years old, a period in time for which the fossil discoveries so far have been few and in which some fateful turning points in human evolution may be waiting disclosure by another Leakey expedition.

Answering an Exam Question

You are a student writing your final exam in Anthropology 100. One of the questions on the paper is the following:

The answer to the question of which appeared first, brain growth and tool use or bipedality, has changed since the time of Darwin. Outline the changes, summarizing the relevant evidence.

POINTS | 15 Content
5 Organization
5 Clarity and accuracy

Let's approach this problem using a series of steps.

1. Assemble the articles you've read so far, and your notes. Isolate the relevant sections, using boxes or highlighting.
2. Consider the following questions:

   • How many different theories are there?
   • What are they?
   • Which authorities believe which theories?

   Take point form notes on these questions, using key words to help you remember the important information.

3. Think about your organization.

   • What is the most logical way to organize your information?
   • Draw a quick sketch or diagram to show your organizational plan. Number the theories.

4. What will be your first sentence? How will you let your professor know when you switch to different theory?

5. Write your answer. You have 25 minutes.

Evaluating the Exam Answer

When evaluating the exam answer, keep in mind the following guidelines:

1. *Content:* With your teacher, decide what information should be included in a complete answer. There need not be 15 individual ideas.

2. *Organization:* In small groups, decide how the information should be sequenced. Consider the following questions:

- How many sections should your answer contain?
- Which one should come first?
- How should each section begin in order to help your reader follow the information?

3. *Clarity and Accuracy:* With your teacher, discuss what a professor probably expects in terms of clarity and accuracy.

Now, mark one another's papers by reading the answer 3 times:

Once for information—Assign points out of 15, based on relative completeness of the information provided.

Once for organization—Assign points out of 5.

Once for clarity—Assign points out of 5.

Give the papers back, discussing the evaluation with your partner.

Preparing to Write an Essay

You'll now begin work on the longer writing task.

In science, it is frequently the case that new information forces a re-evaluation of earlier beliefs. This was what happened to Darwin's belief that brain development and tool use preceded bipedality.

Similarly, the analysis of the skeleton of Lucy and other Hadar specimens has caused many scientists to rethink earlier claims about the presence of certain human characteristics in creatures of this era. The differing interpretations have brought about a major schism in the field, the experts aligning themselves in two main camps. It is this controversy that this next section will focus on.

Writing Task

The controversy surrounding Lucy centers on the extent of her bipedality and arboreality. Some scientists maintain that Lucy had a modern gait and was completely bipedal. Others claim that she still had a simian gait and was in transition between the two stages: partly arboreal and partly bipedal. Summarize the evidence supporting each of these two issues. Your essay should not exceed 4 pages in length. (*Note:* You are being asked merely to present arguments, not to evaluate.)

"FACING UP TO MAN'S PAST"

The next article contains information that will help you complete the writing task. Much of the paper, however, is *not* directly relevant. Before you read the article, then, you'll need to skim it, finding the useful sections.

Choose a partner. One of you will be A; the other, B. A will look for arguments that Lucy was *not* completely bipedal, but still partly arboreal. B will look for arguments *for* complete bipedality and against arboreality.

1. *(35 minutes):* As you read the relevant sections underline or highlight the important information (the arguments and their support). Then go back over the material, taking point form notes.
2. *(20 minutes):* Compare and discuss your notes with those of 2 other As or Bs. By the end of the discussion, you should have the following information in your own words in the appropriate space on the next page:

   a. Each *main argument* stated in one complete sentence
   b. Point form notes *explaining* or *clarifying* the argument
   c. Point form notes on the *support* for each argument

3. Using your notes, prepare a brief oral summary for your partner.
4. Give your presentation. Take notes on your partner's information. As you take notes, be sure to draw connecting lines between an argument and its counterargument.

Arguments for Incomplete Bipedality and Partial Arboreality	Arguments for Complete Bipedality and Against Arboreality

Facing Up to Man's Past

New studies suggest that man only recently diverged from the apes. The question is—how did it happen?

Like many eight-year-olds, Kenton is going through an "I hate girls" stage. He shuffles into the room, greeting the men with a hug or a pat on the back but ignoring the women. He tweaks a baby's toes and coos softly to it. The baby recoils in fear. Although Kenton stands only four feet tall and weighs just a hundred pounds, he does have a rather threatening mien.

On a tour of the laboratory, Kenton leads the way—hooting, clucking, and chattering in a non-stop bid for attention that most adults would not tolerate from a child. But Kenton is no child. He is a nearly full-grown chimpanzee, with powerful arms and sharp teeth that can bite through a human wrist. That is of little concern to the scientists working with him at the State University of New York at Stony Brook, because he is quite civilized. Says Randy Susman, an anatomist, "He's better toilet-trained than my three-year-old."

It seems appropriate that Kenton mixes so easily with the scientists. He is one of the stars of a Stony Brook research project that is adding to the growing body of evidence that man and ape are even more closely related than scientists had thought.

In the century since Darwin first suggested that man arose from ape-like ancestors, many scientific theories about how that ascension happened have proved to be wrong, often because scholars have refused to acknowledge the closeness of the man-ape kinship. Some biologists softened the blow to humanity's pride by placing human beings and apes in separate divisions of the animal kingdom, others by saying that man's ancestors were really more advanced than was generally believed.

Now, several lines of evidence are converging to upset these ego-salving views. Studies of apes like Kenton have convinced many scientists that man's forebears came down out of trees much more recently than was once thought. Newly found fossils from Asia have removed at least one ancient ancestor from the human line—a creature named *Ramapithecus.* And sophisticated techniques for comparing human and ape versions of the basic molecules of life have forced scientists to redraw the human family tree, putting people and chimps on the same branch.

The new evidence is still disputed by some scientists, but it has caused many others to revise their thinking as to when and how the human line originated. It has rekindled an old debate over when man's ancestors began to walk upright, and it was the focus of an acrimonious two-day conference in Berkeley, California, in April. It may help undermine the "species chauvinism" that still leads some people to deny man's close relationship to apes and other animals. Says anthropologist Vincent Sarich, (whose work has sparked much of the debate, "People go to the zoo and see their close anatomical kinship with chimpanzees, but they refuse to face up to the implications of that." David Pilbeam of Harvard, one of the country's foremost paleoanthropologists (scientists who use fossil evidence to study human evolution), puts the case more succinctly: "We should no longer say that we are descended from apes. We *are* apes."

Pilbeam himself turned up one of the key pieces of fossil evidence that has provoked the shift in anthropological thinking. In the 1960s, he and Elwyn Simons, then a professor at Yale, proposed that *Ramapithecus,* an ape-like creature that lived between 8 million and 14 million years ago, might have been a direct ancestor of man. *Ramapithecus* was known at the time mainly from its fossilized jaws and a handful of teeth. The jaws resembled those of a human being, and although the fanglike canine teeth were missing, Pilbeam and Simons concluded from the empty sockets that they must have been rather small. The size of the canine teeth suggest that *Ramapithecus* might have been a user of tools: apes use their outsized canines for defense, but human beings—who learned to defend themselves with weapons—evolved canines of very modest size. Also, the scientists concluded, if Ramapithecus did use tools, it might have walked at least partly upright in order to free its hands.

This vision of an erect, tool-using ancestor was fatally undermined in 1980, when Pilbeam and other scientists were scouring the barren Siwalik Hills of Pakistan looking for more fossil remains of *Ramapithecus*. A new member of the search team, scrambling down a gully that others had ignored, came across a fossil skull of *Sivapithecus*—already known to be a close relative of *Ramapithecus*—that remains the most complete specimen of either animal ever found.

Excavated, cleaned, and reassembled, the *Sivapithecus* skull—which included about two-thirds of the facial bones—looked anything but human. Rather, it had the close-set eyes, bulging brow, protruding jaw, and flaring cheekbones of a modern orangutan. Says Pilbeam, "It was clear that *Sivapithecus* was most likely on the orangutan line, and not a hominid [a term denoting man and his direct ancestors who walked upright]." The fossil skull, along with other bones found earlier from both *Ramapithecus* and *Sivapithecus,* also made it unlikely that *Ramapithecus* was a hominid. Pilbeam took the news in stride: "One of the advantages of adding new information is that, if you're sensible, you modify your ideas." But some paleontol-

ogists were sorely disappointed, because *Ramapithecus* had become a key piece of evidence in the decade-long debate over the age of the human line.

The debate had pitted the paleontologists, the traditional authority on such matters, against an unlikely group of challengers—the biochemists. Paleontologists, working from fossil evidence, were saying that human beings and apes had been evolving separately for at least 14 million, and possibly as long as 20 million to 30 million years. They based that conclusion partly on radioisotope dating methods that could reveal the age of many fossil-bearing rocks. Knowing *Ramapithecus's* age, and believing that he was an upright walker and a tool user and thus already well on the road to being human, they concluded that his ancestor must have split from the apes somewhat earlier. A family tree based on fossil knowledge from that era shows early divergence points for both man and apes and puts *Ramapithecus* squarely on the human line.

But by the 1970s that view had come under strong attack from biochemists, who dated evolution by using molecules and test tubes rather than fossils and radioisotopes. They believed that by measuring the degree of difference between the proteins (and, later, the DNA) of any two animals, they could estimate how long it had been since the animals last shared an ancestor. They drew up a new family tree, based on their "molecular clock." On this tree, the branching order of the animals and the relative length of each

branch were not dependent on fossil evidence, although the clock had to be "calibrated" with reference to some known fossil or geological event.

The molecular clock proved to be a major source of contention. It gave a more recent date than the fossils did for the divergence of man from apes. It showed that the split occurred only about 5 million years ago (give or take a few million), rather than 20 million to 30 million. Sarich went so far as to declare that "one no longer has the option of considering a fossil specimen older than about eight million years to be a hominid, *no matter what it looks like.*" At a time when *Ramapithecus* was still considered a hominid, that statement seemed arrogant, to say the least.

But now that *Ramapithecus* has been removed from the human line, many anthropologists find the molecular evidence more compelling. The consensus today, although still hotly contested by some, is that the man-ape split occurred about 5 million to 8 million years ago.

If the new date holds up, it will not be the first time scientists have had to readjust their thinking in order to place man closer to the apes. Charles Darwin and Thomas Henry Huxley started the process more than a century ago by declaring that the two shared a forebear. But as fossil discoveries accumulated, all-too-human scientists began to have trouble accepting what their all-too-ape-like ancestors looked like.

A classic example of this bias was the success of the 1912 Piltdown Man hoax. Someone concocted a fossil by combining a human skull with an orangutan jaw, and left it to be found at the site of an archaeological dig at Piltdown, England. The hoax was not exposed until 1953, largely because Piltdown Man satisfied the need of many scientists to see their ancestors as advanced creatures—particularly ones with large brains. Meanwhile, genuine but less brainy ancestors, such as Peking Man and the ape-man known as the Taung Baby, from South Africa, won only slow and grudging acceptance.

One reason for the concern over braininess was that it seemed such a fundamental human trait. Historically, scientists had believed that the features that seemed chiefly to distinguish man from the apes—small canines, large brains, the use of tools, and upright walking—were so interrelated that they must have evolved together. Thus, a tool-wielding animal would need to walk upright in order to free its hands. The use of tools would require further development of the brain, and weapons would obviate the need for weaponlike teeth. Scientists envisioned these four characteristics as driving one another in a big feedback loop. The record of man's ancestors, they believed, would portray a gradual increase in brain size coupled with an increasingly upright posture, the shrinking of canines, and the slow acquisition of technology.

Since 1970, a virtual explosion of new fossil evidence from East Africa has shaken that premise. The oldest known fossils of large-brained hominids are specimens from Kenya of *Homo habilis,* the earliest member of the *Homo* genus, which originated around 2 million years ago.

That is also roughly the age of the oldest known stone tools. But fossil discoveries in Ethiopia have established that human ancestors with brains not much larger than those of chimpanzees were walking erect twice as long ago. Even more dramatic, scientists working in Tanzania with Mary Leakey, widow of the grand old man of paleoanthropology, Louis Leakey, have found rock bearing clear footprints left by two upright hominids trudging through volcanic ash 3.6 million years ago.

Anthropologists now agree that bipedality, or upright walking, long preceded larger brains. In fact, many think bipedality was the crucial difference that dictated the evolutionary paths followed by human beings and apes—the erect posture freeing the hands and setting the stage for the use of tools and for the enlargement of the brain, which proceeded gradually over 2 million years.

This perception has focused new attention on a diminutive female known as Lucy, the nickname given to a skeleton more than 3 million years old discovered by a French-American team in Ethiopia in 1974. Lucy is important because it includes about 40 percent of the bones of a single skeleton—a remarkable portion for so ancient a specimen. From the lengths and sizes of various bones, the scientists could determine how Lucy moved about. Anatomist Owen Lovejoy of Kent State University, who worked with its discoverer, Donald Johanson, then of the Cleveland Museum of Natural History, has reconstructed the Lucy pelvis

and found it remarkably similar to that of a modern woman. Lovejoy found that the top of the thighbone is constructed to bear the animal's full weight, the thighbones slope inward to center the weight in mid-stride, and the knee and foot swing freely for the return step—traits he calls "indicative of full-blown bipedality."

But claims that Lucy was so upright a creature came under sharp attack in April at a conference on the evolution of human locomotion held at Johanson's Institute for Human Origins, in Berkeley. Spearheading the challenge were three of the scientists from Stony Brook who work with Kenton the chimp. According to them, Lucy's hip, knee, and foot bones had primitive features showing that she was, as Stony Brook's Jack Stern put it, "no more than halfway to bipedality." His colleague Bill Jungers pointed out that Lucy's toes are long enough and her legs short enough that she must have had to lift her feet high off the ground with each step she took. Rather than striding gracefully through the savannah, Jungers says, she may have walked something like a human toddler (babies' feet are big compared with their legs).

With such an ungainly motion, Lucy would have been easy prey for lions or hyenas if she had not had somewhere to escape to. And the Stony Brook group thinks that the place may well have been where Lucy's ancestors lived—in the trees. Her shoulder, hand, and foot bones, as well as the relative proportion of her limbs, show features of an adept climber—at least compared to human beings. Says Randy Susman, "The idea is that we were scrawny, vulnerable little things, living half in the trees, with small brains and no stone tools. We were a much more apelike creature in this early part of our existence."

To back up their position, the Stony Brook scientists cite their innovative studies of the way animals use their muscles when they move about. Using a technique called radio telemetered electromyography, the scientists poke tiny electrodes into the leg and hip muscles of human volunteers and apes—including Kenton—and wire them to Walkman-sized radio transmitters that make it possible to measure the muscle firings as the subjects move freely about. One study shows that people use their lower leg muscles for walking in much the same way chimps use theirs to clamber up tree trunks. This discovery suggested a novel answer to the question of how human beings came to be upright walkers. Says Stern, "It's easy to get from climbing to erect walking."

The question is, why did man's ancestors make the change? After all, says Lovejoy, "bipedality is a terrible form of locomotion." It requires a difficult balancing act, cuts in half the amount of muscle power that can be applied to running, and leaves the biped vulnerable to predators if just one leg is damaged. The

explanation, Lovejoy proposes, may be that the transition to upright walking enabled these early creatures to produce more offspring. As he sees it, the males and females of Lucy's progenitors abandoned the polygamous behavior of other apes and paired off. That way, the males could be sure of the paternity of their offspring and would be willing to help the females rear them. The need to bring home provisions encouraged an upright posture that would free the hands for gathering. The young could remain dependent on their parents for longer periods of time, which eventually permitted the handing down of culture and the expansion of the brain.

Many anthropologists find that picture far too speculative. Others, such as the Stony Brook scientists, do not concern themselves with *why* man's ancestors stood upright but with when and how. Most agree that the question will never be answered until they find the fossils of Lucy's immediate forebear. This animal, if the molecular date of divergence is correct, could be the longsought "missing link," the last common ancestor of apes and men.

The search is all the more important because, while there is a fairly good fossil record of man's ancestors for 4 million years back, a "fossil gap" exists

beyond the 4 million-year mark all the way to about 10 million years ago. Paleontologists around the world are trying to fill this gap. In Africa, for example, scientists working at the national Museums of Kenya with Richard Leakey—Louis and Mary's son—have targeted their fossil search on beds older than 4 million years. Other scientists are re-interpreting the few fossils already known from that time period—including a 5.5 million-year-old jawbone from Kenya that may belong to the same species as Lucy.

But still other scientists doubt whether the "missing link" that connected Lucy with her ape progenitors will ever be found. They think that the first human ancestor may have arisen so rapidly that the fossil record—which provides only a spotty glimpse of the past—may never show the transition.

An even more fundamental question: Will scientists be able to recognize the missing link if they stumble onto it? In a recent article in the *American Journal of Physical Anthropology,* Susman and Stern predict that Lucy's forebear will not show her combination of tree-climbing and bipedal traits at all, but will look like just another ape. "The challenge," they write, "may lie in our ability to identify this ancestor as a hominid."

Sharing Your Knowledge

After you have finished your presentations, do this activity with your partner.

For each of the following arguments, select the name of the scientist(s) proposing it. Then place both the name(s) and the arguments in the appropriate spaces in the following table.

Arguments

1. The primitive features in Lucy's hip, knee, and foot bones show that she was only halfway to complete bipedality.
2. The reconstructed pelvis shows that Lucy was completely bipedal.
3. Lucy's long toes and short legs indicate that she would have had to lift her feet high off the ground to run.
4. The thigh bone was constructed for full weight bearing. It slopes inward to center the weight in the middle of the stride.
5. The knee and foot swing freely, as in humans.
6. Measurements of muscle firings in the legs and hips of chimps and humans show that humans use their lower legs for walking in the same way that chimps do for climbing.

Scientists

Stern and Jungers

Owen Lovejoy

Susman

Partial Bipedality/Arboreality		Complete Bipedality	
Proponent	Argument	Proponent	Argument

"*WERE LUCY'S FEET MADE FOR WALKING?*"

Read paragraphs 1–7 of the article; then answer the questions in Part A.

Part A: The Scientists and Their Views

1. On what key issue do all the scientists totally concur?

The next two questions focus on the two issues of the debate.

2. a. Which scientists believe that Lucy's *style of locomotion* was totally modern?

b. Which ones hold that her gait was more simian in style, with a bent hip and a bent knee?

3. Which group of scientists would argue that *arboreality* was no longer important in the lifestyle of Lucy and her contemporaries?

The rest of the text is long and rather complex. For that reason you will share the workload with a partner. One partner will do Part B that follows; the other will do Part C.

Part B: Arguments for a Modern Gait and Against Arboreality

Read these instructions carefully. As you read the rest of the article, you'll be looking for arguments and evidence that Lucy's gait or style of locomotion was essentially modern, that she was no longer arboreal. Look for the arguments themselves and any evidence or research that supports the arguments. Include the names of the scientists.

1. Highlight this information as you find it. Then, take notes on the information, using your own words as much as possible. Use quotation marks where you use the exact words of the text. Leave plenty of space between chunks of information, and write on only one side of the page.
2. With 2 other B's, compare your notes. Make sure you understand the information.
3. Together, go through your notes. Label "MG" any evidence that supports a modern gait, and label "AA" any evidence that is against arboreality.
4. Then cut your evidence into strips, putting "MG" information on one page and "AA" information on another. Group together evidence that comes to the same conclusion.
5. Prepare a 10-minute oral summary of your information for your partner. Make sure to state your arguments clearly, one at a time, and to present the evidence for those arguments. Include the names of the scientists responsible for the support. Your partner will want to be able to take clear notes on your information. Your partner will ask questions if necessary.

Part C: Arguments for a Simian Gait and Arboreality

Read your instructions very carefully. As you read the rest of the article, you'll be looking for arguments and evidence that Lucy's gait or style of locomotion was essentially simian, of the bent-hip, bent-knee variety, and that she was still partially arboreal. Look for the arguments themselves, any evidence or research that supports this position, and the names of the scientists involved.

1. Highlight this information as you find it. Then, take notes on the information, using your own words as much as possible. Use quotation marks where you use the exact words of the text. Leave plenty of space between chunks of information, and write on only one side of the page.
2. With 2 other C's, compare your notes. Make sure you understand the information.
3. Together, go through your notes. Label "SG" any evidence that supports a simian gait, and label "FA" any evidence that is for arboreality.
4. Then cut your evidence into strips, putting "SG" information on one page and "FA" information on another. Group evidence that comes to the same conclusion.
5. Prepare a 10-minute summary of your information for your partner. Make sure to state your arguments clearly, one at a time, and to present the evidence for that argument. Include the names of the scientists responsible for the support. Your partner will want to be able to take clear notes on your information. Your partner will ask questions if necessary.

Were Lucy's Feet Made for Walking?

Paleoanthropologists debate the style of locomotion of the earliest known human ancestor, *Australopithecus afarensis*

(1) How did human ancestors between 3 and 4 million years ago move around in their daily lives? Did they stride bipedally, in the manner of modern humans, and thus spend most of their time on the ground? Or did they retain a substantial element of their ape-like heritage and were thus anatomically adapted for climbing trees?

(2) These questions formed the focus of the first scientific meeting held by the Institute of Human Origins in Berkeley.* On view were casts of the relative abundance of hominid fossils from the Hadar region of Ethiopia, which are dated at something between 3.0 and 3.6 million years, and the smaller collection of fossils and the famous footprints from Laetoli in Tanzania, which are in excess of 3.5 million years old. With a rich paleontological display of this sort, soundly argued answers could be confidently anticipated.

(3) No one, however, expected a consensus. Rival positions had already been clearly delineated between several research groups and each was certain to mount a spirited attack on the others. This meeting was not to be a perfunctory presentation of warmed-over papers but a real opportunity to challenge and respond. The high tension atmosphere of mixed apprehension and expectation was subdued only slightly by the unfortunate absence of the French contingent, Yves Coppens, Brigitte Senut, and Christine Tardieu, from the Musée de

l'Homme and the University of Paris. A potential three-cornered fight thus reduced in the event to a tussle between two teams, one based at the State University of New York at Stony Brook and the other scattered between Berkeley, Kent State University, and the Cleveland Museum of Natural History.

(4) With the 40 percent complete famous "Lucy" skeleton to argue over, plus a host of other postcranial bones from many

other individuals, it was somewhat ironic that the conference's lively discussion session should concentrate on the form and function of Lucy's fingers and toes. Why, with the pertinence of the lower back, pelvis, and lower limb to the mode of bipedality, did the discussion turn to fingers and toes? With an uncanny resemblance to the outcome of a political scrap, both sides interpret this development as a victory for their camp and a climb-down by the opposition.

(5) "I went to the meeting expecting to eat some crow," says Randall Susman of Stony Brook, "but our fundamental thesis went unchallenged." By contrast, Tim White of Berkeley suggests that "The reason the discussion went the way it did was because they didn't want to confront Owen Lovejoy on the important parts of the skeleton. Owen's arguments were devastating to their case."

(6) Spectators to the contest were impressed by turns with the high quality of research presented first by one side and then by the other, and there was much sagacious head-nodding at how very difficult is the business of interpretation. There was also a wide discussion of the importance of sociopolitical influences in both sides' defense of their positions. Protagonists in the Berkeley–Cleveland camp have for years promulgated the idea of an essentially modern gait in these earliest hominids and, it is said, they are reluctant to admit of anything that smacks too much of being ape-like. The Stony Brook team, some of whom are primatologists, champion the

---

* "The Evolution of Human Locomotion," 22–23 April 1983, Institute of Human Origins, Berkeley, California.

expression of simian behaviors in early hominids, not least, it is said, because such a position allows them to describe Lucy and her fellows by the emotive and newsworthy sobriquet of "missing link."

(7) Lest the friendly, and sometimes not so friendly, rivalry displayed at the Berkeley meeting should be taken by observers to indicate a state of chaos in paleoanthropological thinking about early hominid locomotion, both sides in the debate were careful to emphasize that there is complete agreement on the central point. The fossils and the footprints indicate that by 3.5 million years ago our ancestors walked on two legs rather than on four. At issue, however, are two questions. First is the style of this bipedality: was it essentially modern or did these creatures walk with a bent-hip, bent-knee stance as chimpanzees occasionally do? Second is arboreality: was the early hominids' use of trees so important a part of their lives that climbing is reflected in their anatomy?

(8) The shift from being a tree-climbing primate to walking bipedally on the ground requires, as Lovejoy has frequently stressed, a fundamental reorganization of skeletal and muscular structures in the lower body. A chimpanzee waddles when it walks on two legs because it has a long rather than a squat pelvis, the angles at the hip and knee joints don't allow the weight to be placed directly under the center of gravity, and the muscles between the thigh bone and the pelvis function in climbing and not in balancing the pelvis during the swing phase of bipedal gait.

(9) The lower back, pelvis, and lower limb of *Australopithecus afarensis,* which is the taxonomic name given to the Hadar and Laetoli hominids, are without question derived in the human direction. And the great toe is no longer opposable, as in apes, but is locked in line with the lateral toes, as in humans. No one describes the *A. afarensis* anatomy as completely modern, but rather as "a mosaic of human-like and ape-like features." Although the hands and feet are like those of modern humans in many ways, the digits in both are ape-like in being curved, a feature that betrays the frequent application of considerable stress on the bones.

(10) The relative completeness of the Lucy skeleton has allowed William Jungers of Stony Brook to examine the limb proportions in these early hominids. Lucy, it turns out, had forelimbs of comparable length to those of modern humans but her hindlimbs were relatively short. "This arrangement means that *Australopithecus afarensis* would have had a short stride length," concludes Jungers, "which is what we see in the Laetoli footprints. It also means that *afarensis* would have been less energetically efficient than a longer-limbed hominid."

(11) Jungers also estimates that the relative length of Lucy's foot was greater than in modern humans, being 35 percent of the hindlimb length as compared with 26 percent. At least part of the difference is due to the longer toes. "This foot/hindlimb ratio would demand a greater clearance in the swing phase, which would affect not only energetics but style of gait."

(12) At the very least, then, Lucy's bipedal gait would have been slightly different from that of a modern human: not quite as bad as trying to walk on dry land wearing swimming flippers, but in the same direction. According to Susman and Jack Stern, colleagues of Jungers at Stony Brook, the effect of the higher foot/hindlimb ratio would be only a small component in the difference in gait between *Australopithecus afarensis* and *Homo sapiens.*

(13) Stern and Susman have examined the anatomy of the lower back, pelvis, lower limb, and foot and have conducted electrical studies on muscle action in humans and chimpanzees. Their conclusions, published recently in a massive paper in the *American Journal of Physical Anthropology,* are several. *Australopithecus afarensis* was indeed "well down the road toward full-time bipedality," but its gait was a bent-hip, bent-knee posture reminiscent of bipedal chimpanzees. In addition, this early hominid, "retained many features that enabled it to use the trees efficiently for feeding, resting, sleeping, or escape."

(14) The Hadar fossils reveal a great range of adult body size, a feature that has been interpreted as sexual dimorphism: the big individuals were males and the smaller ones females. Stern and Susman detect morphological differences between the large and small individuals and interpret this to mean a greater penchant for arboreality in the putative females than in the putative males.

(15) This assertion by the Stony Brook group skirts close to a sen-

sitive issue that hangs over the Hadar hominids. Although the suggestion that the fossils represent a single species, *A. afarensis,* has met with wide approval, acceptance is by no means universal. Among the dissenters are Coppens and his colleagues, which is one reason why their absence from the Berkeley conference was regretted. The French team base their conclusions on morphological differences they see in the knee and elbow joints of the small and large specimens.

(16) Donald Johanson, director of the Institute of Human Origins and, with White, co-namer of the species *A. afarensis,* suggested that the French arguments are weak. "We have heard what Brigitte Senut and Christine Tardieu have said . . . but they have not presented their evidence in a constructive way. They don't respond to calls." Coppens' colleagues visited Berkeley and Kent State during the past year to discuss their ideas. "We sat down with Brigitte Senut and went through every point she made, and they all fell away. Owen did the same with Christine Tardieu. There is, I'm afraid to say, still a lot of sloppy science. The science needs and respects a degree of rigor." Johanson's remarks were described privately as "totally inappropriate" and "a cheap shot at the French."

(17) Rigor was certainly evident in Lovejoy's presentation, in which he showed that the architecture of the head of the *A. afarensis* thigh bone is built to withstand vertical forces exerted during bipedalism and not the forces encountered during climbing. He began his talk, however,

by stating that he had now restored—not just reconstructed—Lucy's pelvis and that "Susman and Stern's conclusions drawn from the unrestored pelvis are not valid." Lovejoy followed this with a list of items in which, he said, the Stony Brook team had been misled or had gone astray. He also argued that the pelvis now showed that *A. afarensis* walked with an essentially modern bipedal gait.

(18) Stern and Susman say that even if they do accept Lovejoy's restoration, which they are not inclined to, the half-human, half-ape architecture "is still compatible with a lack of full extension of the lower limb." The shape of the pelvis is in fact crucial to the Stony Brook argument about the bent-hip, bent-knee gait, as they noted in their recent *AJPA* paper. Russell Tuttle, of the University of Chicago, notes that Stern and Susman have worked only with a cast of the pelvis while Lovejoy has had access to the original. "In a case of this sort you have to go with the person who has studied the original," says Tuttle.

(19) For Tuttle the decision on style of bipedality goes with the Berkeley-Cleveland group, but on the question of arboreality he sides with Stern and Susman, partly because he has argued a similar case for some years. The principal issue of the lengthy discussion session was, why are Lucy's fingers and toes curved? What was she grasping so powerfully?

(20) Alan Bernstein, of the Hospital for Special Surgery, New York, said that "All you can say is that grasping is consistent with arboreal behavior, but it doesn't rule out other behaviors." By way of

analogy he said that although all flying birds have feathers, not all feathered birds fly. White, Lovejoy, and their colleagues liked this argument. Tuttle, Stern, Susman, and Jungers did not. Variously they pointed out that every primate with curved fingers and toes is arboreal and those that are terrestrial have straight toe and finger bones. "If you can show us a primate with curved phalanges that is not arboreal then we will accept your argument that we must think of alternative behaviors," challenged Stern. "Ours is the parsimonious position."

(21) Bruce Latimer, of Kent State University, rejected tree climbing as a major adaptation because of the disappearance of the opposable great toe. He also suggested that curved lateral toes might be the result of stresses involved in toe-off in a bipedal gait that uses all digits and not just the first, as in humans. Lovejoy discounted climbing because, he said, with the anatomical sacrifices made toward bipedality in the lower limbs you would expect to see an enhancement of arboreal characters in the upper limb. "You don't," he asserted. "In fact there is a reduction of such characters."

(22) Asked to describe how he thought *A. afarensis* moved, Lovejoy said it had "a unique mode of locomotion," a phrase that delighted the Stony Brook contingent. "This was a major concession," says Jungers. "He's always said it was completely modern before." Beyond saying the locomotion was unique, however, Lovejoy declined to be specific, a reluctance that Stern and his colleagues took to indicate an absence of

ideas. "We shouldn't impose our ideas on the fossils," retorted Lovejoy. "We should let the fossils speak for themselves." Tuttle considered this statement to be not very helpful and said it was incumbent upon Lovejoy and his colleagues to present reasonable alternatives.

(23) And so it went on, sometimes rather boisterously. Meanwhile, in his usual quiet demeanor, Henry McHenry, of the University of California at Davis, had pointed out that the postcranial morphology of *A. afarensis* at the Hadar was very similar to that of *Australopithecus africanus,* a presumed descendant. One so-far-undescribed finger bone of *A. africanus* from South Africa is said to be curved in the manner of Lucy's, but not to the degree. By contrast with the similarities in the postcranial skeleton, the head and teeth of these two species differ considerably. Whatever locomotor behavior is implied by the skeletal architecture of *A. afarensis* and *A. africanus* is, says McHenry, "a relatively stable adaptation." This stability might be taken to imply that the arboreal features retained are there not simply as evolutionary baggage but as important functional structures.

(24) White contends that, as humans we are overimpressed by the features in the postcranial skeleton that are ape-like, which, he suggests, are relatively few. A chimpanzee would recognize how very human-like Lucy's skeleton is, he says.

(25) Although the presentations revealed strong polarities among the main protagonists, it emerged that many observers would feel comfortable with a compromise position, an argument promulgated by Tuttle. He sees *A. afarensis* as having had an essentially modern bipedal gait while retaining significant anatomical adaptations to arboreality.

(26) Tuttle was, however, pretty much alone on another issue, that of whether the feet of *A. afarensis* as seen in the Hadar foot bones could have made the footprints at Laetoli. White, who was involved in excavating the prints, thinks they could, because, he says, the feet and the prints are essentially modern in form. Stern and Susman also think they could, but in this case it is because they see the feet and the prints as those of a climbing animal. Tuttle, who has studied the prints in detail, says the feet and the prints don't match, principally because he would expect the curved toes to have left a distinct impression. There is no such impression.

(27) White and a graduate student Gen Suwa have reconstructed a Lucy-sized foot, based on inferences from bones at Hadar and Olduvai Gorge, and demonstrated that the diminutive foot would indeed fit within the diminutive prints at Laetoli. Nevertheless, the absence of deep impressions from the lateral toes still left Tuttle unimpressed. "The Laetoli prints are much more human-like than can be inferred from the Hadar foot bones," he says. "If someone were to find curved toes at Laetoli I would change my mind, but not until then."

(28) Lucy's fingers and toes really did cause some problems.

Argument/Counterargument

Work with your partner to do this activity. Have your previous notes and readings close at hand.

1. Reread the writing task on page 199. What readings will you need to consult to do the task?
2. From your notes, choose one argument from the article you just read. Then try to find the counterargument from your partner's notes. Put it beside the first argument. Proceed this way until all arguments are accounted for, either in pairs or as separate arguments. You should now have a complete set of notes from "Were Lucy's Feet Made for Walking?".

3. Make sure each partner has a complete set of notes.
4. With your partner, go back over the chart you completed on page 201. Add any other arguments or evidence, fitting it appropriately into your notes.
5. Working with another pair of students, fill in any gaps in your information.
6. Individually, draw a sketch showing how you will sequence the sections of your essay. Use a separate page.
7. What is the thesis of your essay? Write your focus statement.

Writing the Early Drafts

1. Write draft 1 of your essay for next day. Double space your writing so that you will have room to make changes.
2. You can't do everything at once, so first concentrate on information and organization. When you finish the first draft, you can go back over your text, putting in transition sentences that guide your reader from one section to the next. Leave room to do this.
3. Don't worry about accuracy and emphasis. You will work on these as you revise your first draft and do the final version.
4. When you have finished draft 1, consider this question: How will you introduce the topic and lead your reader to your focus statement? Write the inform section of your essay.

As you wrote your first draft, you concentrated both on including all necessary information and on organizing it for your reader. Now let's consider the language you used to convey this information.

The next two exercises will help you achieve clarity and emphasis, two important qualities of good writing. The first quality, clarity, is essential if your reader is to understand the ideas in your text. The second, emphasis, enables your reader to isolate and remember the important information.

Achieving Clarity and Emphasis

Using Relative Clauses

Read the following pair of sentences:

- Paleontology is a science of ancient life.
- This science of ancient life seeks to determine humans' place in the course of natural events.

Now read the following sentence, in which the author avoided repetition by combining the two earlier sentences into one more economical, mature sentence, using the relative *that.*

"Paleontology is the science of ancient life *that* seeks to determine humans' place in the course of natural events."

Which, that, who, whom, and *whose* are called *relatives.* Each refers to a noun that has occurred earlier in the sentence. The construction begun by each of these words is called a *relative clause.*

Relative clauses allow you to show clearly the relationships among ideas, to add ideas that clarify or expand the main idea, and to avoid needless repetition. Here's an example:

"The lower back, pelvis, and lower limbs of *Australopithecus afarensis,* which is the taxonomic name given to the Hadar and Laetoli hominids, are without question derived in the human direction."

1. Refer to the preceding sentence and answer the questions that follow.
   a. Which is the independent clause?

   b. Which is the relative clause?

   c. Which idea is more important?

2. How does the writer show this relative importance
   a. in the choice of clauses?

   b. in the sequencing of these clauses?

3. Why do you think the writer chose to put that information in the relative clause instead of in the independent one?

Using one of the relatives, combine each of the following pairs of sentences into one clearer, more economical sentence. Write this sentence on the lines provided.

1. a. This assertion by the Stony Brook group skirts close to a sensitive issue.

   b. This issue hangs over the Hadar hominids.

_____

_____

2. a. Anatomist Owen Lovejoy of Kent State University worked with Lucy's discoverer, Donald Johanson.

   b. Owen Lovejoy has reconstructed the Lucy pelvis.

_____

_____

_____

3. a. Tuttle has studied the prints in detail.

   b. Tuttle says the feet and the prints don't match.

_____

_____

_____

4. a. The second issue is less tangible and relates to a point in time.

   b. At this point in time, humans and great apes last shared a common ancestor.

_____

_____

_____

5. a. Still other scientists doubt whether the missing link will ever be found.

   b. The missing link connected Lucy with her ape progenitors.

_____

_____

_____

As a class, discuss your sentences with your teacher.

Using Appositives

When you cite an authority, it is important to establish the credentials of that person, so that you gain credibility in the eyes of your reader. You also need to show your reader how this new information is connected to the old. You can do this with a relative clause:

> Dr. Donald Johanson, who is an anthropologist with the Cleveland Museum, announced a new find.

Usually, however, this additional information appears in the form of a reduced relative clause, in this case, an appositive. In the text, the writer chose to write the following sentence:

> Dr. Johanson, an anthropologist with the Cleveland Museum, announced a new find.

Note that the second, more economical version, places somewhat less emphasis on this additional information.

Combine each of the following pairs of sentences, placing the secondary information in a *reduced* relative clause.

1. a. Dr. Timothy White claims that Lucy is a common ancestor for all later hominids.

b. Dr. White is Dr. Johanson's colleague.

_____

_____

_____

2. a. One of Johanson's opponents is Richard Leakey.

b. Richard Leakey is an eminent researcher on the history of humans.

_____

_____

_____

Discuss your sentences with your teacher.

Using Participles

Another way of adding information economically is to use participles. Read the sentence below containing a full relative clause.

White and a graduate student . . . have constructed a Lucy-sized foot which is based on inferences from the bones at Hadar and Olduvai Gorge.

Now read the sentence using a reduced relative clause.

White and a graduate student . . . have constructed a Lucy-sized foot based on inferences from the bones at Hadar and Olduvai Gorge.

Note that the revised version has dropped both the relative and the "be" auxiliary. The result is a more economical, somewhat less formal construction.

———————————————

Decide on the main idea of each of the following pairs or groups of sentences. Then, using at least one reduced clause, combine them into one sentence.

1. **a.** A fossil is a hardened remnant or trace of life from a past geological age.

   b. A fossil has been preserved in rock formation.

   _____

   _____

   _____

2. **a.** *The Origin of Species* was published in 1859.

   b. It contained a new theory of evolution.

   _____

   _____

   _____

3. **a.** Susman and Stern's conclusions were drawn from the unrestored pelvis.

   b. Susman and Stern's conclusions are not valid.

   _____

   _____

   _____

4. **a.** These differences of opinion extend the arguments.

   b. The arguments were debated at the Institute of Human Origins symposium on hominid locomotion.

   c. The symposium was held earlier this year at Berkeley.

   d. These differences of opinion have arisen through differences in interpretation of material.

   e. Lucy's limbs were compared with this material.

   _____

   _____

   _____

   _____

5. **a.** This perception has focused new attention on a diminutive female.

   b. The diminutive female is known as Lucy.

   c. Lucy is a nickname.

   d. The nickname was given to a skeleton more than 3 million years old.

   e. The skeleton was discovered by a French-American team in Ethiopia in 1974.

   _____

   _____

   _____

   _____

Discuss your sentences with your teacher.

Varying Word Order

The basic word order in English is S–V–C (subject, verb, complement). By rearranging the word order slightly, however, you can make your writing not only clearer but also more emphatic. The two most important positions in an English sentence are the beginning, which usually contains the topic of the sentence, and the end, which usually contains the new information about the topic. The end is the most emphatic position.

INTRODUCTORY "IT"   One way to achieve emphasis in your writing is to use "It" to introduce your topic. Read the two sentences which follow. Which one is more emphatic?

1. The Leakeys have given modern paleontology its place among the sciences.
2. It is the Leakeys who have given modern paleontology its place among the sciences.

Using the "It" construction, followed by a relative clause beginning with "who" or "that," focuses the reader on the Leakeys and their contributions.

You can also use this method to heighten a contrast between the new information and the idea in the previous sentence. For example:

> Many anthropologists have contributed to our body of knowledge about ancient life, but it has been the Leakeys who have given modern paleontology its place among the sciences.

Rewrite each of the following sentences, using the introductory "It" to emphasize the underlined word or phrase.

1. Darwin first suggested that humans arose from apelike ancestors.

   _____

   _____

2. The discovery of Lucy caused a major schism in the field of anthropology.

   _____

   _____

INTRODUCTORY "WHAT"   The introductory "What" can be used in much the same way as the introductory "It," to increase emphasis and to heighten a contrast. For example:

1. Many anthropologists agree with Johanson that bipedality preceded brain development. But they cannot accept the idea that Lucy was completely upright.
2. Many anthropologists agree with Johanson that bipedality preceded brain development. What they cannot accept is the idea that Lucy was completely upright.

As with "It," "What" increases the contrast forcing the key idea to the most emphatic position in the sentence—the end.

Use the introductory "What," to revise the following sentences, making them more emphatic.

1. The scientists have observed the same fossils. Their interpretations are different.

_____

_____

2. Arguing over current specimens will not solve any disputes. Digging deeper into the fields of Hadar may provide the answers.

_____

_____

Writing the Final Draft

1. Reread your first draft. See if there is any information you want to emphasize, using the introductory "It/What" constructions. Revise as you wish.
2. Read your entire essay aloud (quietly). Listen carefully to the language in the text, making sure that the ideas in each sentence are stated clearly. Trust your ears. The fact that you are working with two senses gives you an advantage.
3. Revise as necessary.
4. Write the final draft of your essay, checking for spelling and punctuation.